TUSCANY FOR THE SHAMELESS HEDONIST

ARIELA BANKIER

2018

Front Cover Photo: IKunl/Shutterstock.com

Back Cover Photo: StevanZZ/Shutterstock.com

Series Manager: Ariela Bankier

Editor: Emma Tracey

Technical Editor: Lorna Simons

Fact checking: Irene Loiudice

General note: Travel information tends to change quickly. In addition, the recent economic crisis has influenced many businesses and attractions, including restaurants and hotels. Shops may close without notice, and some sites may change, or reduce, their opening hours unexpectedly. For this reason, we recommend confirming the details in this guide before your departure, just to be on the safe side.

Disclaimer: Although the author of this guide has made every effort to provide readers with the most accurate and up-to-date information (as of the date of publication), she accepts no responsibility for any damages, loss, injury, or inconvenience sustained by readers of this guide. The author makes no warranties or representations of any kind regarding the accuracy of the information (text or maps) listed in this guide, including the completeness, suitability or availability of the products and services listed, and does not endorse, operate, or control any of the products or services listed in this guide. The author is in no event liable for any sort of direct or indirect or consequential damages that arise from the information found in this guide. If you have come across any errors in this guide, please let us know so we can correct our future editions. If you have any comments or concerns, please write to this address: info@travel-italy-guru.com

Thank you!

Contents

Foreword to the Third Edition–2018

Today, the abundance of online information about Florence and Tuscany seems to make a traditional guidebook almost superfluous. But in reality, nothing could be farther from the truth. These days, travelers are bombarded with "Top 10" lists and all sorts of endorsed reviews; every restaurant is described as "the best meal I had in Italy," and every sight and attraction is said to be "incredible." Because of this overabundance of data, it is essential to find a reliable source of information—a guide that will help you sift through this plethora of recommendations and zoom in on what is truly worth your time and money. That way, your trip to Tuscany will actually be as spectacular as you hope and deserve. Luckily, we're here to help!

For over a decade we have been touring Florence and Tuscany —tasting, exploring and immersing ourselves in the local culture. The guide before you is the result of our travels: A personal book of recommendations, in which we share with our readers the region's secrets, and list our favorite sights and attractions.

Our 2018 edition of *Tuscany for the Shameless Hedonist* includes a number of new features that will help you plan the trip of a lifetime. We've added new tips about organic and biodynamic wineries, craft breweries throughout Tuscany, award winning pizzerias in Florence, and pecorino cheese workshops. We've also explored additional off-the-beaten-path towns and attractions, especially in southern and eastern Tuscany. These new tips will allow readers to expand their itineraries, and discover parts of the region that usually remain blissfully hidden.

Enjoy!

Also by Ariela Bankier:

Florence & Tuscany with Kids

Venice & Verona for the Shameless Hedonist

There is a difference between a good trip and an incredible one.

And while planning a reasonably enjoyable vacation in Tuscany isn't too much of a challenge, designing a unique and memorable journey is an entirely different story.

Tuscany for the Shameless Hedonist 2018 was written for travelers who, much like the author of this guide, want more. For those who aren't interested in settling for the usual round of restaurants and touristy shops and sites that are listed in most guides. Rather, it was written for fellow travelers who seek to discover and experience the very best that Tuscany has to offer— from dinner in a real, operating prison to tiny delicious restaurants only the locals know about, from fantastic wine tours and beautiful night spas to boutique hotels and thousand-year-old castles, from exciting vespa rides in San Gimignano to moonlit horseback treks across the Chianti hills.

This guide is the result of over a decade of research, and includes suggestions and ideas that will speak to different travelers. It was composed with passion and, naturally, reflects our taste. But we have taken into account the opinions of many others. We have trusted the experiences of friends, family, and local connoisseurs, too, in the hope of offering a comprehensive and balanced list. For this reason, we recommend using this guide as **a reference book, alongside your standard guidebook.** Read through it, pick the suggestions and itineraries that interest you most, and incorporate them into your trip. Even if you use no more than five to ten of our recommendations, we are confident those will be some of the most memorable moments of your vacation.

There is something for everyone in the guide. **Foodies and wine lovers** will discover dozens of recommendations to help them navigate Tuscany's myriad restaurants, wine cellars, best pizzerias and top artisanal shops. We make suggestions on where to buy sumptuous olive oils, moist *ricciarelli* cookies, flawless focaccias, flavorful pecorino, and glorious truffles. Naturally, we also list the best restaurants where you can enjoy fresh, perfectly prepared seafood, tender steaks, incredible pasta, quality cold cuts, and delicious *antipasti*.

We lead you to the best *gelato* in Florence, the most delectable chocolates in Lucca, secret trattorias in Siena, and to the finest Michelin-starred restaurants. And, of course, we explain the regional wine tradition: where to buy the best bottles of Chianti, Brunello, and the Super-Tuscans; which monasteries prepare the most delicious tonics; how to traverse the *enoteche* of Montepulciano, Montalcino and San Gimignano; and which wine tours and tastings should not be missed.

Shopping enthusiasts and those looking to get up close and personal with the best of Italian fashion will enjoy our tips. For bargain-hunters, we know all about discounts on Dolce & Gabbana, Prada, and Roberto Cavalli from Tuscany's leading outlet stores. We also explore old-world antique and décor shops in Lucca, family-run studios stocking handmade leather goods in Florence, and some of the best-value boutiques in the region. Those looking for unique souvenirs will enjoy our tips on where to find traditional artisanal alabaster artifacts, as well as fashionable handmade Italian jewelry, shoes and gorgeous bags.

Nature buffs and adventure-seekers will appreciate our tips about guided hikes and excursions, including incredible jeep-led tours of the marble quarries in Carrara and hikes across the stunning Orcia Valley. We also offer lists of the best panoramic spots in Tuscany, hidden corners for a memorable picnic, and secret little areas of natural beauty that will take your breath away. **History and art lovers** will revel in our suggestions about colorful medieval parades and jousting matches, little-known museums and Renaissance-era villas that once belonged to the Medici family, and tours of historical gardens that are still owned by noble families.

We make a point of recommending activities that are suitable for **various budgets**. And while we do propose a number of high-end resorts and pricey award-winning restaurants, we also believe that a shameless hedonist doesn't necessarily have to be a big spender; in fact, many of the most delicious and unique discoveries we've made in this region are surprisingly affordable. We have added to the current edition of this guide several more budget-friendly tips and suggestions, which will allow our readers to enjoy the marvels of Tuscany without breaking the bank. We've also added several new tips exploring unique and off-the-beaten-path attractions.

Lastly, we do our best to make our readers' traveling experience as easy and hassle-free as possible, leaving them time and energy to focus on authentic Tuscany at its best. For this reason, we have included valuable information in our detailed introduction that will help you bypass the most common tourist pitfalls. We have also included a detailed index at the end of the book, listing the featured attractions and recommendations by category. To read more of our reviews and updates, visit us at: www.travel-italy-guru.com

We hope you have a wonderful Tuscan adventure and discover the charms of this region, just as we have been doing for the past decade.

Buon Viaggio!

Ariela Bankier

Map of Tuscany

How Long Will It Take to Get There?

Florence to Pisa, 1 hour

Florence to Radda in Chianti, 1 hour

Florence to Montepulciano, 1.2 hours

Florence to Lucca, 1 hour

Florence to Siena, 1 hour

Florence to Arezzo, 1 hour

Siena to Pienza and Montalcino, 1 hour

Siena to San Gimignano, 40 minutes

Siena to Porto Ercole, 1.5 hours

San Gimignano to Volterra, 40 minutes

Lucca to Carrara, 45 minutes

Lucca to Forte dei Marmi, 30 minutes

Pisa to Bolgheri, 1 hour

Montepulciano to Cortona, 40 minutes

Planning Your Trip

Choosing When to Travel

Tuscany changes from season to season, and each season has its advantages and disadvantages. Most tourists visit the region during the summer months, with July being the busiest time in Florence. There are pros and cons to summer travel in Tuscany. On the one hand, most of the cultural events and festivities take place in the summer and the days are longer, which means you can get more done. The fine weather permits you to explore the countryside, and to hike or laze on the beach, and hours of operation for attractions are longer, as they are adapted for the influx of tourists. On the other hand, everything is crowded and there are long lines for every major attraction. Italians are on vacation, too, so the beaches and major tourist attractions are absolutely packed. Hotel prices are also higher, and a well-located apartment, room, or villa can cost 35% to 40% more during high season.

The loveliest time of the year to visit Tuscany, in our opinion, is in September and October, just before the *vendemmia* (the vintage, or fall grape harvest), when the air cools down but the days are still long and the majority of places are still open. After November, rain tends to spoil most of the fun, and a lot of places—including restaurants, museums, and attractions—close down or drastically reduce their hours until the season begins again in April. Spring is also very pleasant, and in May and June you will enjoy great weather, although some rain is still possible.

Documents You'll Need before Leaving

If you are an EU citizen, you will just need your ID card. We also recommend bringing your national health certificate with you; it allows you to receive free emergency medical treatment if needed. If you are from outside the EU, you will need to bring a passport. Passports must be valid for at least six months after the date of your entry into Italy. We also recommend making photocopies and virtual copies of all your important documents in case anything gets lost or stolen. Scan the documents and email them to yourself, or save them onto a USB, or both.

If you plan on renting a car, you will need a driver's license and a credit card. Most companies require at least two years of driving experience, and the credit card must be under the same name as the driver's license. You may also want to print out driving directions to your hotels, or at least the hotel where you'll be staying your first night.

If you've booked your ticket or rented your car online, print out the confirmation letter and the e-tickets. Some companies require just the code you were sent; others require the actual printed ticket or voucher, especially if there is a barcode on it. If you're flying with low-cost companies like Ryanair and EasyJet, carefully read about their check-in process and luggage limitations, which can be very strict.

Local Money

Like the rest of the EU, prices in Italy are in euro. As of January 2018, €1 was worth about US$1.07 or £0.71, but you should check the exchange rates yourself before traveling. You can change money in the airport and in most city centers, though it is much easier to find a place to change money in Florence than in Pisa, Lucca, or Siena, let alone the smaller hill towns. When changing money in Italy or in your home country, ask for bills no bigger than €50. €100 bills are hard to break and €500 bills, which are very rare, will arouse suspicion.

If you have an international credit card (a very useful item; contact your bank for more information), you can also simply withdraw money in the local currency from ATMs across Italy. Though these cards do save a great deal of hassle, they are also notorious for the high commissions charged by the banks for both withdrawals and conversion from dollars/pounds to euros, so do check in advance what those might be. We also recommend notifying your bank before you leave the country that you will be using your card abroad. Some travelers forget to do so, and their card gets blocked, because it is assumed that their card was stolen and is being used fraudulently. Lastly, note that American credit cards and European credit cards have different security systems. While the new standard in Europe is cards with microchips (and PIN codes), many cards in the US still rely on magnetic strips. Though most machines in Italy can read both types of cards, some machines, especially automatic machines (such as ticketing machines in train stations, gas machines in gas stations, etc.), might not be able to read your card. If that happens, use cash instead of your card, or go to the ticket office, where they usually have more sophisticated machines that should be able to read whichever card you have.

Fraud

Two of the most common types of fraud involve counterfeit bills or coins and identity theft. The probability that you will be given a counterfeit €20, or even €100, bill is extremely low. This trick is mostly used in stores when trying to scam the owners. Counterfeit coins, however, are a popular trick in markets; check the €2 coin you're given as change to make sure it really is a €2 coin and not an old 500-lire coin. The two look very similar, but the lire coin is obviously now worth nothing. Identity theft is more common, and happens when thieves attach a small camera to ATMs to steal PINs. Simply cover your hand with your other hand, wallet, or scarf while entering the PIN to avoid any problems.

Crime

Tuscany is a very calm area, and even though there is, naturally, some criminal activity, as there is in any other country, it is rare for tourists to feel unsafe. The biggest hassle is pickpockets, especially in Florence. The city's main train station, Santa Maria Novella, is particularly notorious, as are the bus stops, especially the Number 7 bus stop to Fiesole. A little common sense will go a long way toward avoiding unpleasant events. Don't carry all of your money in one purse so that, even if you do get targeted, you won't lose $600. Carry the barest minimum of money in the purse or wallet on your body, and, if possible, place your credit cards in a safety sleeve or in money belt, and make sure to tuck it inside. If your hotel has a reliable safe, leave some of your money there. Don't put your wallet in your pocket or in the outer or side pockets of your backpack or purse, where it can be pulled out without you even noticing. We promise you that the pickpockets in Florence could teach Fagin, Oliver Twist and the rest of the crew a trick or two.

Don't put your documents and cash in the same purse or wallet; that way, if your wallet does happen to be stolen, you will still have your passports and tickets, and your vacation won't be ruined. Keep a piece of paper with the emergency number of your credit card company so you can call immediately if your credit card is stolen, and always take extra care when in touristy, crowded spaces or on crowded transportation. If you do get robbed, you will need to file a complaint at the police station, so they can help you get new documents and for insurance purposes. Try do this as quickly as possible, as some banks and insurance companies insist that you lodge a complaint within the first 24 hours of the robbery.

Insurance

Consider taking out some sort of travel and luggage insurance. There are several options available, and a quick search online will yield affordable results. If you plan on partaking in any physical activities while on vacation, from horseback riding to Vespa tours, good travel insurance becomes an even better idea.

Emergency Numbers and Medical Emergencies

Call 113 or 112 from any phone to reach the police. Call 118 for an ambulance.

If you need a pharmacy or hospital, or any other shop or service, call 1254. This number will put you in touch with a sort of information service, where an operator will help you find whatever you are looking for. Alternatively, use the Italian yellow pages website: www.paginegialle.it

Doctors in Florence

A standard visit to the doctor costs around €60-€100; a higher fee may be charged if you show up without an appointment. If it is an emergency, go directly to the hospital. You won't be turned away, even if you don't have insurance, and it may very well cost less than a private doctor.

Dr. Stephen Kerr is a general practitioner and family physician trained in Britain. Office hours: Monday to Friday, 9:00 a.m. to 3:00 p.m. (by appointment) & 3:00 p.m. to 5:00 p.m. (without appointments). His clinic is at Piazza Mercato Nuovo 1, Florence. Tel: 055.288055, Cell: 335.8361682, www.dr-kerr.com.

Medical Service Firenze offers a team of English speaking practitioners. Their office is located on Via Roma 4, Florence. Specialist visits can be organized when necessary, and they make house calls 24 hours a day. The office is open (for appointments and walk-ins) Monday to Friday, 11:00 a.m.– 12:00 p.m. & 1:00 p.m.–3:00 p.m. & 5:00 p.m.–6:00 p.m.; Saturday, 11:00 a.m.– 12:00 p.m. & 1:00 p.m.–3:00 p.m. Find out more here: www.medicalservice.firenze.it, or call: 055.475411.

Dr. Giovanni Fazi is a dentist trained in the US. Office hours: Monday– Friday, 9:30 a.m.–1:00 p.m. & 2:30 p.m.–7:30 p.m. His office is at Via A. La Marmora 22, Florence. Tel: 055.583258.

To find a full list of doctors in Tuscany, consult the American or British embassy websites—both offer an updated list of English-speaking physicians. Regardless, we highly recommend bringing some basic medicine with you, especially if you suffer from any medical conditions. Bring ear and eye drops, pain-killers, antacids, vitamins, and, of course, whatever prescription drugs you require. (Bring extra, just in case.) There are numerous pharmacies in Tuscany, but they don't necessarily carry the specific medicines you are used to, and trying to translate the name or find out the local equivalent of the medicine you need when you are ill can be quite a hassle.

Calling Home and Using the Internet While in Italy

Aside from the well-known apps and programs you can use on your computer or smartphone to call home, such as Skype and WhatsApp, you can also buy a local SIM card to use during your travels. This is a good idea if you plan on staying for a week or more in Italy. Keep the SIM after you go back home and use it on your next trip. It should remain functional for two to five years.

A local SIM card will work with your phone as long as you have a GSM-compatible, unlocked phone—which means it will work in Europe—and your phone allows the use of SIM cards other than the original one. If you don't have such a phone, you can get one in Italy for as little as €50 for a basic phone and slightly more for a phone with Internet. An Italian SIM card costs €5 to €10 and is already charged with that amount. You can add more money and activate an internet service that will allow you to use your phone and the Internet for a very low fee during your entire time in Italy. You will need ID or a passport to buy a SIM card, as the shop must make a photocopy for legal reasons. Normally, your phone will be activated within 24 hours or less. You can buy a SIM card at any of the main cell phone providers. Shops can be found on the main streets of the larger towns, and at the larger train stations; we personally recommend TIM and Vodafone. Ask for *ricaricabile*, which means pay as you go, and ask the shop to activate the cheapest Internet offer they have, which usually works out at around €9 per month. Be sure to remember to deactivate the service when you leave Italy. If you are using your own phone, make sure you deactivate international data roaming, which can be very costly.

Getting Into Italian Mode

Hours of operation

As time goes by, more shops and museums are adopting what is known as *orario continuato*, which means they are open all day long, but this is not yet the norm for Italian businesses. Many places, especially in smaller towns, still operate according to traditional business hours.

Shops: Monday–Saturday: 9:30/10:00 a.m.–1:00 p.m. and 3:30/4:00/5:00 p.m.–7:00/7:30 p.m. Sunday: Most shops are closed or open only during the morning hours. Many shops are also closed on Monday mornings. In smaller towns, it is common to find that all shops are closed for no apparent reason on a specific weekday, which changes from town to town (though it is usually Monday, Tuesday, or Wednesday).

Banks: Monday–Friday: 8:30 a.m.–12:30/1:00/1:30 p.m. and 2:00/2:30 p.m.–3:30/4:00/4:30 p.m.

Trains: There are very few trains after 10:00 p.m. and virtually no trains between midnight and 5:00 a.m., except for a few night trains, which cross the region and make a number of stops.

Museums: It depends on the specific museum, but some museums are closed on Mondays. The museums in Florence are particularly known for their tricky opening days and hours. Luckily, you can pick up a printed sheet with the updated opening times of all the Florentine museums from the local tourist office, which is located in front of the Santa Maria Novella train station.

National Holidays

Everything—including museums, attractions, and most shops and restaurants—will be closed on:

January 1—New Year's Day; **January 6**—Epiphany; **Monday after Easter** (Easter Mon-day); **April 25**—Liberation Day; **May 1**—International Workers' Day; **June 2**—Republic Day; **August 15**—Assumption Day; **November 1**—All Saints' Day; **December 8**—Immaculate Conception Day; **December 25**—Christmas; **December 26**—St. Stephen's Day.

Traveling Off-Season and in August

August, though part of the high season, is a time when many Italians go on vacation. Although they often don't bother to make any mention of it on their websites, many restaurants and shops close for a week or two for what is known as *ferie*, or holiday. This is most common during the second and third weeks of August. If you are traveling during that period, it is a good idea to double-check if a place is open before driving specifically to visit it. You should also know that many markets are closed, too, and since the Italians themselves are on vacation, it might be more difficult to find an available room in popular resorts, especially on the beach. For these reasons, July is a better month to travel in Tuscany.

When traveling off-season, from November to April, you run the risk of finding quite a few places, such as various attractions, restaurants, shops, and even some museums, closed or with reduced hours of operation. While most restaurants in the main cities, such as Florence, Siena and Lucca, do remain open, many restaurants in the countryside and in small towns shut down completely during the winter, especially if their clientele usually consists of tourists rather than local patrons. In addition, many restaurants, including those in the main cities, shut down for the winter break, which lasts from the third week of December until January 7. Some tourist attractions also close down in January and February and reopen in March. Double-check everything to be on the safe side. This is yet another advantage of having a local SIM; you can always call before driving somewhere, avoiding the disappointment of finding closed doors.

Understanding Italian Addresses and Phone Numbers

Home and office telephone numbers have an area code, followed by the number. Rome's area code, for example, is 06. Milan's is 02. Most towns in Tuscany have an area code that begins with 05. Florence's code, for example, is 055. Pisa's is 050. Whether you call a number from within Italy or from abroad, you will have to dial the full area code, including the zero at the beginning (unlike area codes in other countries, where you remove the zero when calling from abroad). **Cell phone numbers** in Italy begin with 3. For example: 338.2222222 or 329.4444444, etc. Calling a cell phone costs more than calling a land-line.

Addresses in Italy will always include the name of the street and the house number. In **Florence** a slightly different system is used, and there are actually two types of house numbers: Red numbers (marked with the letter R), which are used for businesses and shops, and black numbers, which don't have a specific marking, and are used for home addresses. It is not uncommon to find on the same street both black and red numbers. For example: Via Dante 4, and farther down the street, Via Dante 4R.

Throughout Tuscany, addresses will always specify not only the name of the city in which a certain hotel or shop is located, but also the name of the province. For example: Via Dante 4, Altopascio (Lucca). In this case, Lucca is the province (not the town). There are 10 provinces in Tuscany, named after the 10 largest towns in the region, and each province includes, in addition to the main town itself, dozens of smaller towns and villages. The 10 provinces are: Florence, Pisa, Lucca, Siena, Arezzo, Grosseto, Livorno, Lucca, Massa-Carrara, Pistoia, and Prato. It's worth noting that most Tuscan provinces are quite large; before booking a hotel or restaurant, always check on Google Maps where exactly these venues are located. This will help you avoid unpleasant surprises, and having to drive for hours on narrow countryside roads to reach remote hotels.

Note that in some cases, especially when looking for hotels, *agriturismi*, and restaurants that are located in the countryside, you will encounter this type of address: Agriturismo Buongiorno, Via Puccini 14, Loc. San Giuliano Terme, Pisa. Loc. stands for *località*, and it simply means a suburb, or a small village, that technically is part of the town but is physically located outside the town itself. If you don't have a car, you will have a very difficult time reaching these places. Another type of address you may encounter is: Agriturismo Ciao Bella, Pod. Marche, Volterra (PI). Pod. stands for *podere*, which means a horse ranch or farm. In this example, the ranch is located near Volterra (but not actually in Volterra), and the town of Volterra is within the province of Pisa (PI). A *podere* will always be in the countryside. If you book an *agriturismo* or dinner in such a place, see if they can give you their GPS coordinates, which will make navigation much easier.

Transportation

Coming to Tuscany by Plane

The main airport in Tuscany isn't the one in Florence, as many would expect, but the Galileo Galilei Airport in Pisa. Thanks to several low-cost companies that have diverted their flights to Pisa in recent years, the airport has grown significantly and improved. It is small but modern and efficient, very close to town, and close to the highway. All of the major car rental companies have offices on the premises. If you are arriving from Europe, you will find the best deals with low-cost companies like Ryanair and EasyJet, which both fly to Pisa. If you are flying from the US, there are daily direct Delta flights from New York to Pisa. Alitalia and several other companies also offer direct flights to Pisa, as well as connecting flights to various Italian cities. Find out more here: www.pisa-airport.com.

That said, the Florence airport has grown in recent years, and today it is home to a number of low-cost companies, too, including Air-Berlin, Vueling, and others. Find out more here: www.aeroporto.firenze.it.

Wherever you land, we recommend renting your car at the airport (and not in Florence's city center), for two reasons. First, both airports offer more convenient offices, with all the leading companies gathered in one place, instead of scattered around town. Second, and more importantly, many rental companies in Florence are located inside the city center, near the limited traffic zone (commonly known as "ZTL"; see the explanation below about what ZTLs are and why they should be avoided.) This means that, once you get your car, while trying to drive out of the city center and get on the highway, you might find yourself accidentally entering a ZTL, which can lead to some very hefty fines. The rental car offices in the airports, on the other hand, are just a few meters from the highway.

Moving Around in Tuscany

A common dilemma for many visitors to Tuscany is whether they should rent a car. The short answer to that question is yes, you should rent a car. Without a car, it is very difficult to visit anything off the beaten path, including hill towns, wineries and vineyards, and special little restaurants and resorts. You won't be able to book a stay in a charming little *agriturismo* or B&B either, as those are not serviced by public transportation. Without a car, you stand to waste a great deal of your time by having to depend on the sometimes erratic bus schedules, which are especially difficult on Sundays and holidays.

The only case in which you don't need to rent a car is when traveling in Florence, Pisa, Lucca, and Siena. If you plan on visiting only these four destinations, and nothing in the countryside, then you can do very well using only public transportation. In fact, if your visit is limited to these four places, then driving a car is not only unnecessary, it's actually a bad idea. These are all towns whose historical centers, or *centro storico*, are marked as ZTL (*zona traffico limitato*, or limited traffic zone). This means they are closed to non-residential traffic. If you drive into a ZTL without a permit , notice of a hefty fine of around €100 will arrive by mail. Since all four major towns are easily accessible by train, and their historical centers are small enough to be visited on foot, a car really isn't necessary.

Driving, Parking, and Renting a Car in Italy

Driving in Italy

If you are an EU citizen, your driver's license is valid in Italy, and you need no other documentation. If you are traveling from outside the EU, you need to obtain an International Driving Permit before leaving for Italy. Driving in Italy is just like driving in any other country. Don't be intimidated by stories of horrifying and insane Italian drivers; for the most part, they are not true.

There are two kinds of highways in Italy: free and toll. Those with a toll are called *autostrada*, and they are marked with green road signs. The free roads have different names, but are always marked with blue road signs. The advantages of the toll *autostrada* are that it takes less time to reach your destination and the maximum speed limit is higher; it can be as high as 130 kph (kilometers per hour).

The maximum amount of alcohol permitted in your blood while driving is 0.5 mg/ml. This is especially relevant if you plan on doing any wine tasting in the many delightful little vineyards scattered throughout Tuscany during your trip.

The **ZTLs** are an issue that many tourists aren't aware of. They should be, however, as it is the main reason tourists get fined when traveling in Italy. Most towns in Italy protect their historical centers, which is where most of the attractions are, by defining them as ZTLs (limited traffic areas) where only residents can drive and/or park. There are security cameras at the entrances to ZTLs; they register your vehicle number and send you, or your rental company, a fine. Together with handling fees charged by the rental company, it is about €100.

Stories about tourists getting confused and entering the same ZTL three times in less than 10 minutes and being fined each time are more common than you'd think. Our best advice is to simply avoid driving in the city, especially in Florence. Most town centers in Tuscany are so small you don't really need a car anyway. If arriving with a car, park in a car park outside the *centro storico* and walk or take a bus or tram to the center. You will usually be able to find very accessible car parks, especially in touristy towns.

What does a ZTL sign look like? It's a white circle surrounded by a red ring; next to it is another sign saying ZTL (*zona traffico limitato*).

Parking in Italy

Parking spaces marked with white lines, or no lines at all, mean parking is free. That is, of course, unless there is a sign prohibiting parking in that area. Blue lines mean you have to pay for parking: Look for the parking meters around the lot, decide how long you will stay, and put the appropriate amount of change in the machine. Take the receipt the machine prints out, and put it, facing out, on the dashboard of your car, near the steering wheel. Yellow parking lines mean you can't park there; such spaces are reserved for those with a permit.

Renting a Car in Italy

The major rental companies in Italy are Avis, Europcar, Sixt, and Hertz. We suggest looking into all four before booking a car. You can rent a car in Italy if you are over 21 and have had a license for more than two years. Some companies require only one year of driving experience. When renting a car, you have to present a personal identification document, a passport (ID card for EU citizens), and a credit card (not a debit card). Both must belong to the person who is renting the car. For example, you can't rent a car with John Smith's license and pay with Jane Smith's credit card. There are a number of insurance options, but we recommend taking the most comprehensive. Regardless of the type of insurance you have, mark every scratch and bump on the car. Some insurance deals declare themselves as all-inclusive, but the small print can reveal that damage to mirrors, for example, or the underside of the car, or the wheels, is not covered.

Be aware that most cars in Italy have a manual transmission, or stick. If you don't feel comfortable driving such a car, make sure you specifically order a model you are comfortable with. Cars that run on diesel (instead of gasoline) will save you money.

In Italy, gas is called **Benzina** (the word 'gas' has a different meaning in Italian, and refers to Methane gas, not fuel/gasoline). Always fill up the gas tank when returning the car; you will be charged extra if the company has to fill it up for you. You may also be charged extra for returning the car very dirty. You don't have to take it to the car wash; just make sure it's acceptably clean. Charges can also be incurred for returning the car at a different office from the one where you picked it up, for handling any fines or tickets you received, and for renting accessories such as a GPS, snow chains, baby seats, etc.

GPS units are very useful and we highly recommend using them with this guide for a number of reasons. First, they are far more convenient than maps (phone apps like Waze are excellent, but consume your battery very quickly, leaving you lost with a lifeless phone). Second, signs in Italy are often hard to understand or follow. It is not unusual to find a tiny sign indicating the exit to the town you need just a few meters before the exit itself. Often signs on regular country roads (i.e., not *autostrada*) are quite small and can't be easily seen from afar. Rural roads are very poorly illuminated, and it is highly unlikely that you will see any of the signs at all if driving after dark. A GPS will save you the hassle of having to play detective, and indicate when and where to turn. If you plan on renting a car with a GPS for a week or more, it's probably cheaper to buy your own GPS, as long as it has recently updated European maps on it. You can walk into any of the three largest chain stores for electronics in Italy, Mediaworld, Euronics or Unieuro, and buy a GPS for less than €100, including all world maps, and then take it back home with you.

Snow chains are obligatory by law if traveling between mid-November and mid-April in Tuscany. Rental companies never seem to mention this, but if you are stopped by the police and don't have either snow chains or winter tires, it is you who will have to pay a hefty fine, not the rental company.

One last thing, try not to fill your car with gas on Sunday. There is usually no one manning gas stations on Sunday, so you will have to use the automatic machine; it isn't complicated at all, but may be a problem if you don't have the exact change.

Moving Around in Tuscany on Public Transport

Trains

Trains are a great way to move around and reach the main towns (Florence, Siena, Pisa, Lucca, Grosseto, Livorno, etc.). The central stations are often called *Stazione Centrale* (pronounced "statsione chentrale") and marked like this: FS. Alternatively, it may simply be based on the city's name: Pisa Centrale, Siena Centrale, Lucca Centrale, etc. There are a few exceptions—Florence's main train station, for example, is called Firenze SMN (Firenze Santa Maria Novella).

The main train company in Tuscany is **Trenitalia**, which is also the largest company in the country. While other companies (such as **Italo**) only offer connections between the major cities in Italy (Rome, Venice, Milan etc.), Trenitalia covers every nook and cranny. Train ticket prices have gone significantly up in recent years, but you may very well find interesting offers and save a great deal of money if you book in advance. Find out more here: www.trenitalia.com. www.italotreno.it

Buying a Ticket

There are two kinds of Trenitalia trains: regular trains, known as *Regionale* trains, and high-speed trains, known as *Freccia* trains. When traveling inside Tuscany, you will mostly be using the *Regionale* (regional) trains. The high-speed *freccia* trains connect major cities—like Rome and Milan or Florence and Venice—but not small towns like the ones in Tuscany. *Freccia* tickets are more expensive and they book for a specific time and place. Regional trains, on the other hand, have no specific booking restrictions.

To buy a ticket in the train station, go to the ticket office (*Biglietteria* in Italian) or use the self-service machines; they are easy to use, and you can select a menu in English, too. But before you start, take a look at the illustrations above the machine; some only show a credit card, which means they don't accept cash. Note that when purchasing a ticket from the self-service machine you will be given the option to purchase either first-class tickets, or second class tickets. And while the first-class on the *Freccia* trains is more comfortable than second-class, on regional trains there is no difference whatsoever between the cabins. So, on regional trains, it makes sense to choose the second-class option and save the money!

Always validate your ticket before getting on the train on one of the little white and green machines near the tracks. A ticket is valid for six hours from the moment it is validated. A non-validated ticket can lead to a hefty fine.

Finding Your Way in the Train Station

With the exception of Florence, most train stations in Tuscany are rather small. Tracks are called *binari* (singular: *binario*). In every station you will find screens or electronic boards listing the departing trains (*partenze* in Italian). When you look for your train on the departures board, it may list a different destination than what is on your ticket. Let's say, for example, that you've just bought a ticket to go to Pisa from the Florence train station. Your ticket says "Pisa" and you were told at the ticket office that the train would leave at 4:00 p.m. Yet, when you check the departures (*partenze*) board to find out which track (*binario*) your train is leaving from, you don't see a train leaving for Pisa at 4:00, only a train to Livorno. Don't be alarmed. The station that appears on the departures board is the final destination, and most regional trains (and some high-speed trains) make several stops along the way. It is very likely that your stop isn't the final destination of the train, which is why it doesn't appear on the board. Simply walk to the track and check the more detailed board on the platform itself. It will list all the stops along the route. If you are still unsure, simply ask one of the staff at the station.

Urban Buses

Every town and city has its own bus system. This means that a bus ticket you bought in Florence won't be valid in Siena, and the bus ticket you bought in Pisa is useless in Lucca. Small towns in the same area, on the other hand, are usually serviced by the same bus company.

The easiest way to buy a bus ticket is at a newspaper stand, or at the *tabaccaio* (cigarette shop). There is always a newspaper stand in mid-sized and large train stations. Ask for a bus ticket, "*Un biglietto per l'autobus per favore*," (pronounced, "oon bilieto per l'aootobus, per favore"). If there is no place to buy a ticket, try buying one on board, though it will be more expensive and the driver will ask for the exact amount. It is unlikely he will be able to break any bills.

Like the train, you must validate your bus ticket once you get on the bus. While the validating machines for trains are outside the train, on the platform, the validating machines for buses are inside the bus itself. These are usually little machines at the front and back of the bus. Depending on the city, bus tickets are usually valid for about an hour from the moment you validate them.

Extra-Urban Buses

Most towns can be reached by train or bus. However, several towns, specifically hill towns (such as San Gimignano, Volterra, Cortona, Monteriggioni, Radda in Chianti and many others), can only be reached by bus, as the trains can't climb that high. These buses are called extra-urban buses, and they usually leave from the train station or a block or two away. Extra-urban buses from Florence leave from an area located just two minutes away from the station. With your back to Santa Maria Novella, turn right, and walk along the street until you see the buses.

Eating and Drinking in Tuscany

Food is one of the greatest perks Italy has to offer, and this guide goes to great lengths to introduce visitors in Tuscany to the many gastronomic delights available in the region.

Italian food served outside Italy can be quite different from the original version. Italian restaurants in the US, for example, tend to prepare heavier, creamier versions of traditional Italian food, so it might take a few tries to get used to the new flavors.

The tips in this guide are, as a rule of thumb, dedicated to the the most authentic venues in the region. Among the recommendations listed you will find, side by side, high-class bistros and street food vendors, Michelin-starred restaurants and tiny *trattorie* serving the freshest pasta, chic *osterie* run by promising chefs and award-winning olive oil mills, recommendations for luxurious hotel bars and farms in the valley selling pecorino cheeses and truffles. We feel that the mix of high and low is an important part of the uniqueness of Tuscany; you can find subtle brilliance in the most unexpected places, and those who choose to focus solely on the well-known spots are surely missing out.

The Origins of Tuscan Cuisine

The Tuscan kitchen is often called *la cucina povera*, or "the poor man's kitchen," and indeed, many dishes were originally born of necessity. To understand the way these dishes came about and the basics of Tuscan cuisine, it is important to remember the peasant tradition from which modern Tuscan cuisine grew. While vast parts of Tuscany now seem like places of luxury, not that long ago, this was a relatively poor land. Locals used everything they had to survive, and nothing was ever thrown away. Three- and four-day old bread was transformed into a tasty and nourishing soup with beans, black cabbage, and other winter vegetables—the famous *ribollita*. In the summer, it could be mixed with creamy tomato sauce to make the mushy but delicious *pappa al pomodoro*. Alternatively, the most basic ingredients—vinegar, some vegetables from the family vegetable garden and olive oil—were tossed together with day-old bread to make the tart and fresh *panzanella*. Bread wasn't the only ingredient that was never thrown away. To this day, there is a saying in Tuscany—*"del maiale non si butta niente"* meaning "you don't throw away any part of the pig." Indeed, it isn't rare to see older men and women buying traditional sausages made with certain parts of the pig that would make most tourists shudder.

Nowadays, Tuscan cuisine is varied, and each area of the region prides itself on its own typical specialties, in addition to the well-known pasta and meat dishes that you can find all over Tuscany. In Siena, you will find the *pici* pasta, a handmade, chubby macaroni. In Livorno, the restaurants compete over who makes the best *cacciucco*, a typical fish and seafood stew. Lucca is famous for its tortelloni, filled with ricotta cheese and spinach (or meat and prosciutto) and served with a meaty sauce that is similar to ragu. In Florence, they are proud not only of their steaks (the famous *bistecca alla fiorentina*, naturally), but also of their *lampredotto*, a dish made of the cow's fourth stomach served on a bun, which today is a popular street food. The Maremma region in Southern Tuscany is famous for its meat, while the hilly towns in the Garfagnana in Northern Tuscany, are known for chestnut flour-based dishes, as well as rich stews, farro, and their potato focaccia.

Eating Like a True Italian

The three main meals are *colazione, pranzo, and cena. Colazione* (breakfast) is usually eaten at a bar; in Italy, that isn't a place that serves alcohol, but a place that serves coffee and snacks in the morning. Italian breakfast is very limited, which can be a big surprise for guests expecting a large affair involving eggs and bacon at their B&B. Instead, it usually consists of nothing more than a cappuccino, brioche, and some marmalade or Nutella to spread over a piece of toast. *Pranzo* (lunch) is usually served between 12:30 and 2:30. You will find very few, if any, restaurants that serve lunch later than 2:30 or 3:00. *Cena* (dinner) is served between 7:30 and 9:30. With the exception of pizzerias, most places won't seat you at a table after 9:30 or 10:00.

Unless you buy a sandwich to go or sit down for a light lunch in a bar, you will usually eat in a *ristorante, trattoria,* or *osteria*. A ristorante is the more high-end, serious dining option, stylish and reserved, with prices to match. Osterias and trattorias are more homey places; they cost less and have a

more casual atmosphere, but they can also be huge discoveries, as they often offer excellent, authentic Tuscan food. Trattoria Mario, in Florence, is a perfect example. Here you'll find no-frills service, tiny tables, and waiters who yell the order right into your ears, but the food is delicious and as Florentine as you can get, and the prices are modest. Il Campano in Pisa and Taverna San Giuseppe in Siena are other examples of excellent places that combine an easygoing rustic feel with reasonable prices and, more importantly, quality dining. To discover the best that Tuscany has to offer, we suggest mixing and matching, trying out both homestyle trattorie and upscale, sophisticated restaurants.

Whichever restaurant you choose—a neighborhood diner or a 5-star extravaganza—remember that most restaurants in Italy are closed one day a week (usually Monday or Tuesday), even in high season. Whenever possible we have inserted the relevant info in the guide, but for places not mentioned, check the restaurant website or call to see when they are closed.

What Should We Order?

Breakfast

If you ask for *un caffè*, you'll get an espresso. Alternatively, ask for a cappuccino, or for a *caffè al latte*, which is closer to the Starbucks version of coffee, with a lot of milk. Note that if you ask for a latte (the popular American term), you will simply get a glass of milk and a perplexed look. You can also try a macchiato, which is an espresso with a touch of milk foam. Our personal recommendation for the hot summer months is to ask for a *shakerato*. This is a cold coffee, shaken with ice cubes. If you want it sweetened, make sure you ask for it *con zucchero*. Accompany that with a brioche or croissant; there are plenty to choose from, and they will all be on display, together with a small selection of savory sandwiches. If you eat standing at the bar, as most Italians do, you will be charged less than if you sit down at a table and order. If it's been a long day of sightseeing, and you need an afternoon pick-me-up, you can always ask for *un caffè corretto*, which is an espresso "corrected" with a shot of grappa, sambuca or some other liqueur.

Lunch/Dinnertime

Traditionally, a meal starts with an *antipasto*, which is a selection of meats, cheeses, *crostini* (bruschette) and other little bites that will awaken your appetite. The *primo*, or first dish, usually follows and is most typically pasta or soup, or risotto. Next is the *secondo*, or main dish, which usually consists of meat or fish. The *secondo* can be served with a *contorno*, or side dish—usually vegetables, roasted potatoes or French fries—and is followed by a *dolce*, or dessert and a coffee (*espresso* or *macchiato*; an Italian will never order a cappuccino after a meal). At dinnertime, this is occasionally followed by an *ammazzacaffè*, also known as a *digestivo*. This is a liqueur, like limoncello, (or, often, some local concoction made by the owner's grandmother) to help you digest. Of course, the entire meal is accompanied by wine, whether that is the house wine or your choice of bottle, and water.

Clearly, you won't be able to order this much food every time you sit down to eat. What most Italians do is choose either a *primo* or a *secondo* and add to that something small that can be shared, like an *antipasto*, a *contorno*, or even just a dessert. Whatever you order, bread and water will be brought to the table. Bread is free, included in the price of the coperto (see below), while water is charged separately. You can ask for spring (still) water, called *naturale*, or fizzy water, called *frizzante*. We have yet to see an Italian restaurant that serves tap water. Your bread basket will usually contain a few slices of Tuscan bread (which is unsalted), regular salted bread, and sometimes focaccia and *grissini* (though not always).

Naturally, when eating in a trattoria or osteria, you will be asked if you want the house wine to go with your food. Though the house wine is often perfectly tasty, in recent years we've started ordering a bottle from the menu. The reason is simple: If you are planning to drink more than a glass each, it is worth it to pay a little extra and get a bottle of something better to complement your meal, rather than settling for whatever the restaurant has on hand at the moment.

Antipasto

For the antipasto, you will often be served a plate of *salumi* (also known as *affettati*). *Salumi*, not to be confused with salami, is a general name for cold cuts, salami, and cured meats. This will typically include some of the Tuscan highlights such as *prosciutto* (usually prosciutto *crudo*, not *cotto*), *salame* and *finocchiona*, which is a salami seasoned with fennel seeds. Other, more specific *salumi* may also be included, such as *lardo di Colonnata* (a seasoned, aged lard from northern Tuscany, see tip 124); *prosciutto or salame di cinghiale*, meaning a prosciutto or a salami made with wild boar meat; *prosciutto di cinta senese*, which is a prosciutto from an indigenous breed of Tuscan pig, called Cinta Senese; *bresaola*, or cured beef; *mortadella; pancetta*, and more. Another popular option is *crostoni*, which are slices of toasted bread, each with something different served on top. The most traditional is the *crostone toscano*, which is served spread with liver paté, but you will usually also find a crostone with *lardo di Colonnata*, with black cabbage, mushrooms, tomatoes, or fresh olive oil (the famous *fettunta*). A cheese plate, which will typically include different kinds of pecorino cheese, can also be served as an *antipasto*, but it will more commonly be either a *secondo* (main dish) or a dessert.

Primo

On the menu for the *primo* you will usually find either a soup or stew, like *ribollita*, or perhaps a bread salad, such as *panzanella*. However, the real stars of the *primo* section of the menu are, naturally, the pasta dishes, and the occasional risotto plate (risotto isn't typical of Tuscany, but rather of northern Italy).

The *primo* is often the best dish in a Tuscan restaurant—*pasta cacio e pepe* (pasta with cacio cheese and black pepper), *tagliatelle con ragù di cinghiale* (tagliatelle with wild boar ragu), *ravioli con ricotta e spinaci* (ravioli filled with ricotta and spinach, usually served with a butter and sage sauce), *gnudi* (nude ravioli, made of the filling without the actual pasta, served with a light buttery sauce), *pappardelle alla lepre* (flat, wide pasta served with rabbit ragu), *tortelli di patate* (potato-filled tortelli, served with ragu or other sauces), and *pici all'aglione con briciole* (*pici* served with garlic and fried bread crumbs) are just a few of the typical *primo* dishes you will find.

Secondo

For the *secondo*, you will normally be given a choice of fish- or meat-based dishes, depending on the restaurant; though, in truth, most offer a selection of both. Tuscans love meat and meat dishes are treated with great importance. The *tagliata* (sliced steak served with different toppings: anything from porcini mushrooms to arugula and shavings of *parmigiano reggiano*, parmesan cheese) is very popular, as is the famous *bistecca alla fiorentina* (Florentine-style T-bone steak). This *bistecca* is a huge affair, priced by weight and served seared on the outside and bloody on the inside. If you like your meat well-done, or if you simply don't have much of an appetite, then steer well clear of this dish. Also popular are *il peposo* (a beef stew), *arista* (pork roast), *bollito misto* (boiled beef), *cacciucco* (the famous fish and seafood stew from Livorno), and the *baccalà* (salted cod), which is served with different sauces.

Contorno

For the *contorno*, you will often find *patate al forno* (oven-baked potatoes), *patatine fritte* (French fries), *fagioli* (white beans), *spinaci* (spinach), *ceci* (chickpeas), *verdure alle brace/alla griglia* (roasted vegetables), *insalata mista/ insalata verde* (a simple salad, though you should know that the Italian definition of a salad is very limited, usually involving little more than lettuce, a few other green leaves, and a couple of lonesome cherry tomatoes).

Cheese Plate

Personally, we can't get enough of the Tuscan cheeses. There are many recommendations in this guide for little *caseifici* (cheesemakers) who produce the very best of the best, places any foodie will appreciate. Even if you don't plan on driving across the countryside and doing some cheese tasting, you can still enjoy many of the best products in shops and restaurants. A Tuscan cheese platter will usually include a selection of the local pecorino cheeses served with marmalade and/or honey. The sweetness of the marmalade really brings out the deep flavors of the cheese, allowing you to more clearly appreciate the top-quality products of this region.

Pizza

Pizza, of course, is a hugely popular choice for many Italians. A meal in a pizzeria is much cheaper than a dinner in a trattoria. We recommend choosing a pizzeria that advertises itself with the magic words *forno a legna* (real wood-burning stove). Gusta Pizza in Florence (Via Maggio 46R), Funiculà in Pisa (Lungarno Mediceo 43), Pizzeria da Felice in Lucca (Via Buia 12), and Consorzio Agrario in Siena (Via Pianigiani 5, just off Via Banchi di Sopra) are all very good.

Vegetarians

There are a few precautions you should take when visiting restaurants in Italy as a vegetarian. First, you should know that most (but not all) soups are made with a meat or chicken stock. If you are unsure about the contents of a dish, just ask: *"Sono vegetariano, c'è carne o pesce?"* (Pronounced, "Sono vegetariano, che carne o peshe?"). The Italian idea of vegetarian can be difficult, however. They have no trouble telling you if there's meat in the dish, but they often don't think it's a problem if there's chicken broth, lard, gelatin, or any other animal by-product.

More than once we have asked whether a certain dish was vegetarian, and were told that it was. On further investigation we found small pieces of salami in the sauce, or a distinct meaty flavor of the broth. When we inquired whether there was indeed any salami in the sauce we were told, "Yes, but just a little bit—for the taste!" by a rather offended cook. Luckily, new regulations require that food shops and restaurants provide precise information regarding a dish's contents, in case any of the diners are allergic to certain ingredients; this should help vegetarians, too.

You should also know that most hard cheeses are prepared with *caglio*: rennet produced from cows. Some cheesemakers offer cheeses made with *caglio vegetale*, suitable for vegetarians. Vegetarians should also avoid anything containing *strutto* and *lardo*, both of which mean lard. It might seem strange, but *strutto* is sometimes found in breads, focaccias, and pastries.

Dessert

Italians have a talent for salty baked goods—their focaccias and schiacciatas are famous worldwide. Italian desserts, on the other hand, can sometimes be a little disappointing; they tend to suffer from lack of imagination and are often rather heavy. With the exception of a real *ristorante*, desserts will typically be weak and not homemade. If they do make their desserts in-house, the owners will usually make a point of explicitly stating *dolci fatti in casa* (homemade dessert) on the menu. Look around and check out the desserts served to others in the restaurant. If they look disappointing, skip them and head for *gelato* instead. Strolling through quiet streets enjoying good ice cream is often so much more pleasant than a heavy dessert in a trattoria.

If you are interested in trying the local desserts, here are a few options you will almost always find: *panna cotta* (cooked cream), *torta della nonna* (cooked

custard pie with pine nuts on top), *semifreddo* (a frozen dessert made with ice cream), and *torta del bischero*, also known as *torta co' bischeri*, which is a pie filled with chocolate, grapes, raisins, canned fruit, and pine nuts. The simplest dessert you will encounter is *cantuccini* (known abroad as biscotti), which are typically served with a sweet local wine, the *vin santo*.

Tipping and the Coperto

To request the bill at the end of your meal simply ask the waiter for "*il conto per favore*," pronounced as it is written. Once this is done, the issue of tipping arises. Restaurants in Italy charge what is called a *coperto*, which means a fixed fee for "opening the table." Contrary to what many tourists believe, it has nothing to do with how much bread you eat or whether you ask for water or not.

It is rare for a restaurant to charge more than a €2 *coperto* for each person at the table, though be warned that if a restaurant is located in a very tourist-focused area, or if it is a 5-star or Michelin-starred restaurant, the *coperto* will easily be doubled. Water (still or fizzy) is charged separately; no restaurant will serve you tap water. Should you wish to leave a 10% tip at the end of a dinner in addition to the *coperto*, you may of course do so, but only do this if you were especially pleased with the service, as it is not obligatory and Italians very rarely tip. Some restaurants, again mainly in the more popular touristy areas, have begun to add an automatic 10% service charge to the bill. This is added alongside the *coperto*, but it is not yet the norm. Tipping in taxis, hotels, etc. is totally up to you. It will be appreciated, but it isn't considered a major faux pas if you don't do it. The one case in which tipping may be a good idea is when someone goes out of their way to help you, in which case a tip is the best way to show your appreciation.

Italian Wine

There are many books written just on the complex and fascinating subject of Italian wines, so any introduction we give here is only meant to be used as a very general primer. If you are interested in a detailed account, we recommend writings by Kerin O'Keefe, Jancis Robinson, and Robert Parker, all of whom are extremely knowledgeable, interesting writers who have covered the subject in great depth. However, seeing as there are several recommendations in this guide for various wine tastings and tours, it would be foolish not to provide a general summary of the Italian wine industry.

The most famous wines in Tuscany are Chianti, Brunello di Montalcino, Nobile di Montepulciano, Morellino di Scansano, Carmignano, Vernaccia di San Gimignano, and Bolgheri (one of the leading Super-Tuscans).

Chianti

Tuscany's pride and joy is divided according to the areas that make it. Chianti made in the area around Siena, for example, is called Chianti Colli Senesi. The most famous Chianti, and the one most worth your attention, is the Chianti Classico, which comes from the traditional growing area in the heart of the Chianti region, from towns such as Gaiole in Chianti and Castellina in Chianti. Chianti is made with 75%–100% Sangiovese grapes, and the rest of the wine is made up of other local Tuscan grape varieties, such as the Malvasia and Canaiolo grapes.

Brunello di Montalcino

Often referred to simply as 'Brunello', this is one of Italy's best known wines, and is especially beloved by the American market. Brunello has a more austere and complex taste, but a good bottle of Brunello also enjoys power and complexity few other wines can compete with. Brunello is produced in the area around Montalcino, a small town in the Val d'Orcia, and is always made with 100% Sangiovese grapes.

Nobile di Montepulciano

Unsurprisingly, this wine is made in the area around Montepulciano and consists of a mix of Sangiovese and Prugnolo Gentile grapes. It is smoother and more delicate, fruity, very elegant and a deliciously drinkable wine.

Bolgheri DOC

Bolgheri DOC is a relatively new category of wines, and refers to Super-Tuscans made in the area around Bolgheri on the Tuscan coast, with varieties of grapes that aren't originally Tuscan, such as Cabernet Sauvignon. The current official formula for Bolgheri specifies that these wines must be made with no more than 70% Sangiovese grapes, no more than 70% Merlot grapes, and no more than 80% Cabernet Sauvignon grapes.

Super-Tuscans

Super-Tuscan wines were born when prominent growers (mainly from the noble Antinori family) began experimenting and making wines with grapes that were not indigenous to Tuscany, such as Cabernet Sauvignon and Merlot. Officially, these wines did not fit into any of the common classifications (Chianti, Brunello, etc.), and were thus classified as *vino da tavola* (table wine), the lowest quality of wine. However, as time went by, and several American wine connoisseurs began expressing an interest in these wines, the Super-Tuscans' reputation changed and they were even re-categorized (as IGT, see explanation below). Today they are some of Tuscany's most famous (and expensive) wines. Tignanello (by Antinori), Sassicaia, and the Masseto (by Tenuta Ornellaia) are a few of the most famous Super-Tuscans.

Wine Classification

All Italian wines adhere to a classification system set by the government. This system protects local production, so that wine from the North of Italy, for example, won't be able to advertise itself as Chianti, while also ensuring that certain quality standards are adhered to. This system defines four major categories:

Vino da tavola (table wine) is the simplest wine available. Don't bother to waste your time with it.

IGT (*indicazione geografica tipica*) defines wine that comes from a specific geographic location. Though not the highest classification, there are some very good wines in this category. Most IGT wines are quite simple, but it is important to remember that many of the best and most expensive Super-Tuscans are also classified as IGT, since they don't belong to any other category.

DOC (*denominazione d'origine controllata*) means you are guaranteed a product of a certain quality, from a specific area.

DOCG (*denominazione d'origine controllata e garantita*) marks the highest-quality wines.

The best way to learn more about Italian wines is, quite simply, to drink them. In Italy, wine isn't considered a snooty hobby reserved for the rich, but rather a way of life and a popular, traditional passion. Most Italians grow up with wine on their family dinner tables and develop a palate from a young age. Many, and not necessarily foodies, are well-informed about good products.

Wine is such an important part of the Tuscan way of life that we have included several tips on wine tours, estates, tastings and similar activities. These can be the beginning of a more serious learning endeavor, or just a fun, light, tasty experience. The choice, of course, is yours. Personally, we adhere to the idea that wine should be an enjoyable and open activity. And while relying on the advice of experts, we also feel it should not be followed blindly. Wine is, after all, a matter of taste, and sometimes the wines that receive attention and the highest marks from authorities in the field aren't necessarily the ones you might enjoy most.

Prices, too, can be misleading, and while they can offer guidance, they are not an automatic guarantee of the quality and taste of the wine. While we do very much enjoy an €70 bottle of Brunello, or a €150 bottle of Sassicaia, the time we've spent in Tuscany has taught us that there is an incredible variety of excellent wines for €25 or less. (Try the entry-level Chianti from Castello di Ama, Montepulciano Nobile from Salcheto, Brunello from Tenute Silvio Nardi, Bolgheri Rosso from Le Macchiole or Ser Lapo from Mazzei, all reasonably priced at €20–€25, and you will understand what we mean). You can even find very good wines for less than €20, which are, at the end of the day, what most Italians drink. Wine can be bought at an *enoteca* (wine shop) or at a supermarket. The larger supermarkets, which are located at the outskirts of the city (you'll need a car to reach them, naturally) have a respectable selection of local Chianti and Brunello bottles, as this is where most Italians go to do their shopping for their party or family dinner.

Booking in Advance

If there is a specific restaurant you want to try out, we highly recommend booking in advance. During the summer months, restaurants in towns like Florence, Siena and San Gimignano are always packed, so go ahead and call a few days in advance, to make sure you find an opening. The same goes for booking an *aperitivo* in a sought-after location, or room in a popular B&B, villa, or *agriturismo*. Booking can, in some cases, be done by e-mail, but in our experience, a phone call is usually better.

Italian Manners

Italians take manners very seriously. They pride themselves on their *buona educazione*, proper education, and appreciate it when others play by the same rules. It's considered rude, for instance, to ask for something without first saying *scusi* (meaning excuse me, pronounced "skuzi"). Starting a conversation with scusi and ending it with *grazie tante* (thank you very much—note that the word is pronounced graziE, not graziA, as many tourists mistakenly say) will make a good impression and help you get better service in hotels, restaurants, and attractions. The polite way to say goodbye is *arrivederci*, while the polite way to say hello when arriving somewhere is *buongiorno* or *buonasera*, depending on the time of day. Of course, like anywhere else, a smile can go a long way.

That said, we have to admit that no matter how polite a tourist may be, service in Italy can be lacking at times. Though the majority of Italians we have met have been very welcoming, be prepared for the occasional annoyed waiter. If it makes any difference, know that it's usually not personal; salesmen and waiters are often just as short with locals as foreigners (to many of the local businesses, a foreigner is anyone that didn't grow up on the same street and go to the same school as they did). Sometimes you may get the feeling that Italians get better service, and occasionally you'll be right. Often however, it's not because you are being discriminated against, it's simply due to the language barrier. Most Italians don't speak English very well and keep their sentences as short as possible to avoid embarrassment.

Lastly, it is worth mentioning that Italians are very fashion-conscious and concerned about style, and usually prefer to dress up rather than down. Take a look around any centrally located piazza in Italy on a Saturday night at the Italian women in skimpy dresses, 6-inch heels and perfectly done hair, and the Italian men in chic jackets and pricey shoes, and you'll immediately understand what we are talking about. Though not as stuck-up as starred restaurants in Paris, the high-end restaurants in Tuscany do welcome more elegant attire. You will probably feel more welcome (and get better service) if you dress the part.

Lodging in Tuscany

One of the most difficult tasks for a tourist is choosing a place to stay. There are thousands of hotels, B&Bs, *agriturismi* (B&Bs with active farms, usually producing olive oil or wine) and resorts in Tuscany. Most of the recommendations in this book are written with the idea of hedonism and decadence in mind, so you will find a number of suggestions for impeccable hotels, fairy-tale resorts, historic residences, and chic little country retreats. However, we intentionally did not limit our recommendations to modern hotels, nor did we favor the 5-star Disneyland-type resorts that have been built in recent years in Tuscany. On the contrary, charm and individuality were key factors. To us, much like restaurants, some of the best lodgings are the smaller, intimate, and perhaps even rustic places that offer a glimpse into the romance of daily Tuscan life.

The main advantage of the high-end places, other than the question of style, is that the service they offer is often better, as well as the amenities: air conditioning, decent-sized bathrooms and bedrooms, comfortable beds, elevators and sometimes, though not always, a stronger guarantee of attentive, professional staff. The main advantage of the *agriturismi* and B&Bs is that are that they feel more personal, authentic, and intimate.

Renting a villa or an apartment for a week or two in the Tuscan countryside, or in Florence, is a very popular choice, too. We would recommend consulting websites such as homeaway.com, homeinitaly.com, discovertuscany.com, tuscany-villas.it, and luxuryretreats.com.com to find a wide array of homes, villas, and apartments for rent. We also highly recommend checking the reviews of other travelers on websites such as TripAdvisor and booking.com before you book.

If renting an apartment, be sure to ask what's included in the price to avoid unpleasant surprises. Is there a minimum number of nights? Are all cleaning charges included? Will you be charged separately for electricity, gas, or heating, and if so—how much? Does the price include a weekly change of linen and use of the laundry room and Wi-Fi? Does the price include parking? Is the apartment properly furnished and adequate for daily cooking and living? This last question is especially important if you plan on shopping in local markets and cooking for yourself most nights.

Whether you rent a villa, a room in a B&B or *agriturismo*, or book a hotel, location is always important. Some places are located deep in the beautiful countryside, which is wonderful if you plan to stick to your immediate surroundings, but can be a problem if you have some more serious sightseeing planned. If you plan on leaving your rented room or villa daily and touring a different part of Tuscany each time, then you should rent a house that isn't too far from the places you plan on touring. The truth is that Tuscany isn't that small; it takes about two-and-a-half hours to get from Pisa to the Val d'Orcia, two hours to reach Arezzo from Lucca, and two hours to drive from Florence to the Maremma. Also, don't choose a remote B&B from which you have to drive for 40 minutes just to reach the main road. Finally, if you are planning some intensive sight-seeing in different parts of Tuscany, consider booking two or even three different accommodations, rather than renting a place for an entire week. You could book a B&B south of Siena for touring Siena itself, the Val d'Orcia, the Maremma and even Chianti, and a villa near Lucca if you want to tour Lucca, Pisa, the Garfagnana, Bolgheri, and more. It will save you a lot of driving hours.

How to Plan the Perfect Tuscan Vacation

The top tips in this guide, together with the detailed day-trips suggested in the following chapter, are guaranteed to help you create a wonderful vacation in Florence and Tuscany. With the information provided, you will easily be able to discover hidden treasures and little corners of bliss that only the locals know about.

But before we get to the business of discussing what is **off** the beaten path, it's important to first understand what is **on** it. Over the years we've received numerous emails asking for our advice on how to build a solid Tuscan itinerary. Eventually, we decided to add a chapter to the book, dealing specifically with this issue. We've mapped out four highly enjoyable itineraries that focus on the "must-see" stops, quintessential Tuscany, if you may. These are itineraries that can be followed as is, or, better yet, serve as an initial base upon which to expand. Ideally, use our top tips and our off-the-beaten-path itineraries to personalize these recommendations and create a unique and memorable vacation.

Question: We are a couple, traveling to Italy for the first time. We have three days in Florence and Tuscany before driving south to Rome. We are keen on making the most of our vacation, and experiencing as much as possible, even if it means sticking to a tighter schedule. What would you suggest?

Answer: Three days isn't enough time to cover the entire region, but if you are prepared to follow a tight schedule, you'll be able to get a lot done. That said, we would highly recommend adding at least two more days to your itinerary—you will be able to see so much more of Tuscany in five days, and at a far more leisurely pace.

Day 1—Florence: Arrive by train in Florence (Santa Maria Novella train station), walk from the station to Florence's famous **Duomo**, visit the Duomo itself and then climb up to the Duomo's dome (or to the top of the adjacent bell tower) to enjoy a beautiful view. Next, walk to the **Accademia Museum**

(Gallerie dell'Accademia) to see Michelangelo's *David*, and stop for lunch at one of our top recommended restaurants (see top tips). Then visit the **Uffizi** and admire the incredible art work by Sandro Botticelli, Leonardo da Vinci, Michelangelo and others. Note that booking your tickets to the Uffizi and the Accademia online in advance is **essential**, or you'll end up spending your whole day in Florence queuing for these museums instead of touring the city. (Alternatively, purchase the Firenze Card: www.firenzecard.it). Next, cross the **Ponte Vecchio** (Florence's famous old bridge) from the Uffizi to the other side of the river, and tour this area, known as the **Oltrarno**, to discover its Florentine charm. Finally, walk or take bus number 12 (or a taxi) up to **Piazzale Michelangelo**, a popular piazza from which you can enjoy a truly stunning view of Florence, especially at sunset.

If you have an extra day in Florence, add the following museums and churches to your itinerary (listed in order of importance): the Medici chapels (near San Lorenzo, you must book your visit in advance), Palazzo Vecchio, the Church of Santa Croce (where Michelangelo and Galileo are buried), the Bargello Museum, and the former monastery of San Marco.

How to make even one day in Florence better, using our tips: Try the best ice cream in town (see tip 5), lunch like a local at one of the best and most famous panini shops (see tip 15), catch an opera performance (see tip 4), discover hidden gardens and museums (see tip 9), sip on a good cocktail while enjoying a mesmerizing view of the city (see tip 1), get some serious shopping done and find gorgeous leather bags (see tips 14, 19 and 20), and more.

Day 2—Option A: Chianti + Siena: The Chianti hills in central Tuscany, where the world-famous Chianti wine is produced, is one area that shouldn't be missed. Enjoying this delectable ruby-red wine is an important part of the Tuscan experience. You can book a guided tasting in a serious *enoteca* (wine shop) in Florence (see tip 8 for our top recommendations), but the best way to

discover the charms of Chianti wine is by heading out to the countryside, to visit the wineries themselves.

Early in the morning, leave Florence in your rented car and head to the classic Chianti region, which encompasses four towns: Greve in Chianti, Castellina in Chianti, Gaiole in Chianti and Radda in Chianti. **Greve** is the most accessible of the four and offers easier parking. There's a wine museum that can be toured (they offer wine tasting, too), and right above the town hides a tiny, delightful and ancient *borgo* (fortified hamlet) called **Montefioralle,** which is lovely to tour. On Saturday mornings there's a small but lively market on Greve's main square. **Radda** is more rustic, but the views that can be enjoyed from its walls are incredible, and there are a number of wonderful *borghi* (the plural form of *borgo*) in the vicinity that we recommend you visit. **Castellina** and **Gaiole** are both delightful; parking can be a problem, but the towns themselves are quaint. Specifically, Castellina offers visitors at least two excellent enoteche (wine shops) where you can do some serious wine tasting without driving out to the wineries (if you are on a tight schedule). For lunch, see our top recommendations in the Chianti chapter, and then make your way to **Siena**. Avoid the ZTL by parking at the Fortezza parking lot, or at the Siena train station Parking lot (and take the escalators up to the town center).

You'll need half a day to see Siena's most important sights—the astonishing **Duomo** (we are not exaggerating, it really is magnificent), the famous **Piazza del Campo,** the Palazzo Pubblico, and the **tower.** If you have some extra time, visit the former hospital of Santa Maria, the Pinacoteca, and the other sites that are included in the Duomo's ticket, such as the Museo dell'Opera, the Facciatone, or the crypt.

How to make even one day in Siena and the Chianti region better, using our tips: Skip the usual wineries where all the tourists go, and instead visit the top-rated wineries that local connoisseurs rave about (see tips 32, 35, 36 and 44); have lunch at a superb restaurant in the Chianti hills (see tip 36, 43 and 45); visit a hidden modern art park (see tip 31); book a walking tour of the countryside or go on a wild Vespa ride (see tip 37, 41, 48); join a hot air balloon ride (see tip 102); visit real castles and try glorious local olive oil (see tip 28 and 40); or discover the joy of Italian cooking with the best cooking classes (see tip 33 and 60).

Day 2—Option B: Pisa + San Gimignano + Volterra. Pisa needs no introduction; the Leaning Tower is a world-famous attraction that draws over 3 million visitors yearly (it's worth noting that if you plan on actually climbing up the tower, and not just taking your picture near it, it's best to reserve tickets in advance, and avoid the long lines). After your visit to Pisa, make your way to **Volterra;** it is one of the most ancient hill towns in Tuscany, and dates back to Etruscan times. Visitors come here to admire the Etruscan Museum (the display is a bit dated, but it's still one of the best collections in Tuscany), the Roman theater, the pleasant streets, and the many alabaster shops (Volterra is famous for its alabaster). Finally, visit **San Gimignano,** the most famous of the Tuscan hill towns. Loved for its impressive medieval towers, picturesque little piazzas and small but stunning Duomo, San Gimignano can easily make you feel like time stopped here some 700 years ago. Because this little town is so exceptionally preserved, it has become a serious tourist magnet, and in the

summertime the sheer number of visitors sometimes can and does ruin t
magic. If you hope to avoid the crowds, consider skipping San Gimignano a
visiting Pisa, Lucca and Volterra, instead.

How to make even one day in Pisa, Volterra and San Gimignano better, using our tips: Eat lunch at the best restaurant in Pisa (and forget about those touristy joints near the tower! See tip 98); find the best wine tastings near San Gimignano (see tip 104); shop for the best alabaster souvenirs (see tip 107), enjoy an authentic lunch with a spectacular view near Volterra (see tip 108); and more.

Day 3: Val d'Orcia. When you think of Tuscany—soft rolling hills and sun-kissed vineyards, centuries-old stone villages and fabulous food—you are in fact thinking of an area in southern Tuscany known as the **Val d'Orcia** (Orcia Valley). This picturesque area has been immortalized in numerous books and films (*Gladiator*, featuring Russell Crowe, and *The English Patient* are just two famous examples). When it comes to scenic drives, this area has very few competitors. A typical tour of the Val d'Orcia will start off at **Pienza**, widely considered the gem of the valley, where you can admire the delightful stone alleys, visit the beautiful Renaissance Duomo, taste the famous Pienza pecorino cheese, and soak up the views (see tip 81 to find out more). From Pienza drive to **Montalcino** (a spectacular drive through the valley, have your camera ready). Montalcino is best known for its wine, the **Brunello di Montalcino**, which is produced here exclusively and is considered one of Italy's best reds. To end your day in the valley, visit **Bagni Vignoni,** a town whose central piazza is in fact a large thermal pool, and around it sit hotels and spas offering various treatments using these nutrient-rich thermal waters.

How to make even one day in the Val d'Orcia better, using our tips: Skip the usual tourist stops in favor of a magical dip in the thermal pools of Bagni San Filippo (see tip 90); find out exactly where to find the best pecorino cheese for foodies in Pienza (see tip 82); visit multiple award-winning wineries and enjoy the best Brunello in the valley (see tip 85); enjoy a romantic evening and a wonderful view in the tiny village of Monticchiello near Pienza (see tip 80), visit the best spas in the area for a romantic nocturnal dip (see tip 55 and 84); and more.

As you can see, in three tightly packed days, you can get a lot done! Naturally, there's much more to discover. If you can stay in Tuscany longer, we highly recommend you explore other parts of the region, which are less touristy and absolutely beautiful. Specifically, check our top tips for the Maremma, Garfagnana, Lucca and Arezzo to find out more.

Florence

☐ 01 | Enjoy an *Aperitivo* with an Unmatchable View of Florence

It is clear that during just one vacation a person cannot follow all of the suggested tips in this guide. There simply is not enough time! Also, tips are a matter of taste. Some of our suggestions may be your style, others won't. But if there is one tip that is surely worth considering, it's this one.

The *aperitivo* (pre-dinner drink and snack) is one of the best parts of an Italian vacation. A perfect way to get your appetite working, it is a light and informal tradition that sets the ambiance for the rest of the evening. Since it is typically served before dinner, you will enjoy the view of Florence in the soft afternoon light. Depending on the location you pick, you'll see the incredible Duomo and the historic city center, or you can look down at busy people rushing by in the ancient streets.

So, where can you go for an *aperitivo* to remember? Here is a list of our favorite spots to enjoy a romantic, stylish, and memorable drink with a view.

The SE·STO Restaurant at the Top of the Westin Hotel

The Westin Hotel is famous for its restaurant with glass walls and a 360-degree view, making it perfect for an early dinner or, of course, an *aperitivo*. The contrast between the restaurant's clean, modern architecture and the colorful, rounded medieval and Renaissance buildings and piazzas below provides the perfect setting for a relaxed pre-dinner drink.

The Westin also offers a €28 lunch deal, which means you can enjoy the scenic restaurant even if you don't want to spend a sizable sum on a 4-course dinner. Booking in advance is not obligatory, but is recommended in high season, as this place is very popular. Obviously, there is not much point in coming here in bad weather, when you can't see anything because of rain and fog.

La Terrazza at the Stylish Hotel Continentale

The Continentale prides itself on its two restaurants—the Fusion Bar and Borgo San Jacopo—but we are here to recommend their terrace experience. *La Terrazza* Bar is located at the top of the medieval Consorti Tower and looks out onto Florence's most famous bridge, the *Ponte Vecchio*. Sipping a cocktail above the Arno River at sunset is an experience not to be missed. Book a table well in advance, and as close to the edge as possible.

The Panoramic Terrace at Risotrante Alla Torre De' Rossi

There are many wine bars in Florence, but very few of them can compete with the spectacular view from the Terrace at Alla Torre De' Rossi. This recently opened wine bar is not only smart and affordable, but also perfectly positioned, right on the Oltrarno. Just two minutes from the Ponte Vecchio, this venue is surrounded by shops and fun attractions just waiting to be discovered. The menu here is modern and well prepared, the wine list is extensive, and the views will enchant you. In high season, make sure you book in advance a table on the terrace, to make the most of your *aperitivo* or your meal. And, because Alla Torre De' Rossi is so centrally located, this spot is perfect for a good lunch, too, after your visit to the Uffizi, Palazzo Vecchio or Palazzo Pitti, all of which are less than five minutes away.

Divina Terrazza at the Grand Hotel Cavour

The Panoramic Divina Terrazza at the Grand Hotel Cavour offers one of the most jaw-dropping backdrops for an pre-dinner cocktail in Florence. Perfectly positioned, guests here see the city laid out in front of them, and the majestic dome of the Santa Maria del Fiore Cathedral is so close, you can reach out and touch it.

The terrazza draws in a crowd of locals in the know and savvy tourists. This is the perfect place to end your day of Florentine sightseeing.

The Popular and Panoramic Vip's Bar at Piazzale Michelangelo

Vip's is located right next to the famous and scenic Piazzale Michelangelo, and, as you can

imagine, offers quite a view. This spot is not as sophisticated as the other suggestions in this tip, but what it loses in style it makes up for with unparalleled views. To reach Vip's from Piazzale Michelangelo, walk down the stairs, turn right, and you'll see the terrace, called "Terrazza delle Cinque Paniere" and the bar itself.

SE•STO Restaurant (Westin Excelsior Hotel) ★★★★★
Piazza Ognissanti 3, Florence.
Tel: 055.2715.2783,
www.sestoonarno.com.

The Grand Hotel Continentale, ★★★★
Vicolo dell'Oro 6r, Florence.
Tel: 055.27262,
www.lungarnocollection.com.
The terrace is open daily, 4:00 p.m.-11:00 p.m., except during bad weather. Advance booking is recommended for groups larger than four.

Alla Torre De' Rossi–Ristorante Wine Bar, ★★★★
Borgo San Jacopo 3, Florence.
Tel: 055.2398711,
www.allatorrederossi.com.
The restaurant is open daily, 1:00 p.m.-3:00 p.m. & 7:30 p.m.-9:30 p.m. The wine bar is open 12:30 p.m.-10:30 p.m.
Off season, the wine bar is open from 4:30 p.m.

Terrazza Divina-Grand Hotel Cavour, ★★★★★
Via del Proconsolo 3, Florence.
Tel: 055.266271, www.hotelcavour.com.
Open daily, 16:00-21:00 (may close down in bad weather).

Vip's Bar, ★★★
Viale Giuseppe Poggi 21, Florence.
Cell: 334.345.5559,
Open March-May, 9:30 a.m.-8:00 p.m.;
June-September, 9:30 a.m.-midnight;
October-November, 9:30 a.m.-8:00 p.m.
During bad weather Vip's closes down, even in high season.

🍴 02 | **Savor a Meal** in One of the Best Restaurants in Florence

La Bottega del Buon Caffè is a fantastic restaurant and a personal favorite, so we were not in the least bit surprised when this refined venue recently received its first Michelin star. The owners believe that fresh produce is at the heart of any good kitchen, and focus on local, seasonal dishes with a very modern twist. A classic lunch tasting menu will cost about €65, and in our opinion, is worth every cent. A 6-dish dinner tasting menu will cost between €95 and €115 (wine pairings included).

We especially enjoyed their veal tartar, served with vegetables and olive oil ice cream, the roasted squid served on a cream of chickpeas, and the ravioli made with chestnut flour and filled with parmigiana cream. (Note that the menu is seasonal, and changes often.) If you are celebrating a special occasion, or looking to enjoy an intimate, sophisticated and modern meal in a beautifully designed setting, this is one of the best choices in Florence.

Next, both **L'Osteria di Giovanni** and **Trattoria Pandemonio** are favorite stops with well-informed tourists.

Both restaurants offer excellent pasta dishes, hearty antispasti platters and some of the most memorable steaks in town (their Bistecca Fiorentina is fantastic!). Because both restaurants are so popular with international visitors, they do run the risk of seeming more 'touristy' than local, but we can assure you that their food is 100% deliciously Tuscan.

In L'Osteria di Giovani, don't miss the massive Bistecca Fiorentina and the delicious home-made pasta. In Trattoria Pandemonio, don't skip the crostoni Toscani, the ravioli, the steak, and the fantastic tiramisu, one of the best we've had.

The atmosphere in both restaurants is vibrant and friendly, and the tables fill up very quickly, so reserving a table in advance is highly recommended.

Finally, For something different in style, try **Konnubio**. Konnubio's menu is far more contemporary-Mediterranean than classic-Tuscan, which is perfect for those who'd like a break with the typical Florentine fare. This is one of the very few places in Florence in which you can enjoy a full, rich breakfast instead of the usual cappuccino and cornetto, and best of all, there are usually at least five or six dishes here that are suitable for vegan and vegetarian clients.

L'Osteria di Giovanni ★★★★
Via del Moro 22, Florence.
Tel: 055.284897,
www.osteriadigiovanni.it.
Open daily for dinner, 7:00 p.m.–10:00 p.m; Saturday & Sunday open for lunch, too: 12:30 p.m.-2:30 p.m.

Trattoria Pandemonio, ★★★★
Via del Leone 50r, Florence.
Tel: 055.224002,
www.trattoriapandemonio.it.
Open Monday-Saturday, 12:30 p.m.-2:30 p.m. & 7:30-11:30p.m. Closed Sunday.

La Bottega del Buon Caffè, ★★★★★
Lungarno Benvenuto Cellini 69r, Florence.
Tel: 055.553.5677,
www.labottegadelbuoncaffe.com.
Open Tuesday–Saturday, 12:30 p.m.-3:30 p.m. & 7:30 p.m.-10:30. Sunday, open for lunch only. Closed Monday. Closed for the entire month of November. Reservations are highly recommended. Those who prefer to stop by for a lighter snack, will enjoy the restaurant's adjacent lounge bar.

Konnubio, ★★★★
Via dei Conti 8R Firenze.
Tel: 055.238.1189. www.konnubio.it.
Open daily from 7:30 a.m.-midnight.

03 Book an Apartment with the Best View Imaginable in Florence

The **Florence with a View** apartments offer scenery that few can compete with. Staying in the Santa Maria apartment, it feels like you can reach out and touch the Duomo just by opening the shutters. A quiet evening glass of Chianti shared with someone special and soaking in the night's ambiance from this exceptional viewpoint is one of the most tranquil experiences this beautiful city has to offer. The San Giovanni apartment is very impressive, too.

You can get a sense of each residence from the pictures on their website. On top of the view, the apartments themselves are stunning. They are spacious, eminently comfortable, and classically designed, and the furnishings are the definition of elegant luxury. This, in our opinion, is better than any hotel. The fact that so many of the apartments' original, 150-year-old features have been preserved, including beautiful hand carved Indian ceilings, marble work, and wood floors, certainly adds to the charm. Surprisingly,

prices here are still within reason, making Florence with a View one of the best accommodation options in town. Make sure you book well in advance, as it is rare to find an opening in high season.

If you can't find an opening, but are keen on waking up each morning with a view of the glorious Duomo outside your window, try the **Hotel Duomo.** Perfectly positioned, beautifully decorated and romantic, this may be "just" a 3-star hotel, but the superior double rooms with a full Duomo view, priced at around €180, are simply lovely and offer an excellent value.

Florence with a View Apartments,
★★★★★
Via Roma 3, Florence.
Tel: 055.582.961,
www.florencewithaview.com.

Hotel Duomo Firenze, ★★★★
Piazza Duomo 1, Florence.
Tel:055.219.922,
www.hotelduomofirenze.it.

⚡ 04 | Catch an Opera Performance at the Best Venues in Florence

St. Mark's is a beautiful Anglican church in Florence. It's not just lovely to visit; it's also quite famous, thanks to the series of performances it hosts, which have drawn thousands of opera fans over the years.

The most famous operas, such as La Bohème, Tosca, La Traviata, Rigoletto, The Marriage of Figaro, Carmen, and Don Giovanni form the basis of their repertoire, but they also perform traditional Neapolitan songs. All performances feature professional opera singers in full costume, and while this isn't exactly comparable to a real opera performance at La Scala in Milan, it certainly is fun. Another excellent option for music lovers is a night at with **Musica in Maschera** at the historic Palazzo Arrighetti-Gaddi. The repertoire here is classic, and a 16th century noble lady will accompany you into the ornate hall where the shows take place. Combo tickets for the opera and a rooftop apertivo are available, too. And what better way to start your evening than

sipping on some bubbly champagne while gazing over the Duomo? If you are interested in a more professional performance, consult the yearly program at **Maggio Fiorentino**, the main opera hall in Florence: www.operadifirenze.it (in English, too).

St Mark's English Church, ★★★★
Via Maggio 16, Florence.
Tel: 055.294.764,
www.stmarksitaly.com.
Find out more about the monthly program and book here: www.concertoclassico.blogspot.co.uk.

Musica in Maschera,
www.musicainmaschera.com,
cell: 328.356.2380. Tickets must be reserved in advance.

🍴 | 05 | **Try some of the Best Ice Cream** in Florence

There is a heated debate about the best ice cream shop in Florence. Each of the big name *gelaterie* has hordes of fans that fight for the honor of their personal choice. Without wanting to get involved in the conflict, we're willing to raise our heads above the parapet long enough to present a short list of our favorites. Four names are included here, in no particular order; they are simply our recommendations after years of tasting. As it should be, each has its own unique style and taste. From delicious, modern concoctions to the usual beloved traditional flavors, these are the parlors that do it best for us. The rest is up to you to judge.

La Strega Nocciola is our newest obsession in town. The gelato here is creamy, decadent and smooth, and the flavors range from perfectly made classics (don't miss the Nocciola and the Chocolate) to original creations such as the Lavender, blood orange and mascarpone cheese gelato. La Strega Nocciola is centrally located (just two minutes from the Duomo) and while the prices are slightly higher than what you may find in nearby shops, we can guarantee that the quality of their gelato justifies this tiny splurge.

Vestri is easy to miss, a small unassuming shop located on a street not far from the Duomo. But if you pass by, do enter—when it comes to ice cream and chocolate, they have a bit of a magic touch. Don't be surprised that no ice cream is on display. Instead, like many of the best *gelaterie,* they store their gelato in closed aluminum cans that are only opened to serve customers, keeping the ice cream fresher and smoother.

Carraia is one of the more popular ice cream shops in Florence. The location is a little away from the heart of the centro storico, just off the Carraia Bridge, but they do have a second shop in Via dei Benci, just meters from Piazza Santa Croce and Gelateria dei

Neri (see below). And while its gray exterior isn't particularly attention-grabbing, inside awaits a fine selection of rich, smooth-tasting flavors. Try their cioccolato fondente, or dark chocolate. Trust us, it's worth the indulgence.

Last but absolutely not least, **Gelateria Dei Neri** is our personal favorite as well as a Florentine institution. Named after the street where it is located, this place is very popular with the locals, and for good reason. All their delicious treats and delectable ice creams are charmingly laid out behind the counter, and the general feel here is that of a neighborhood *gelateria* that hasn't changed much since the '60s. Their ice cream is a little on the heavy side, very traditional, but also exceptionally good, especially the "classic" flavors, such as caramel cream, chocolate and stracciatella. Their semifreddi (a half-frozen dessert resembling an ice cream cake) are excellent. Whatever flavor you choose, be sure to grab a few extra napkins on your way out—you'll need them to get their sweet-tasting chocolate ice cream off your lips!

Gelateria La Strega Nocciola, ★★★★★
Via Ricasoli 16R
Tel: 055.217375, www.lastreganocciola.it.

Gelateria Vestri, ★★★★
Piazza Gaetano Salvemini 11, Florence.
Tel: 055.234.0374,
www.vestri.it.
Open Monday-Saturday, 10:00 a.m.-7:00 p.m. Sunday closed. August usually Closed. Hours may vary off-season.

Gelateria La Carraia, ★★★
Piazza Nazario Sauro 25r (just off the Carraia bridge), and Via Dei Benci 24r.
Tel: 055.280.695,
www.lacarraiagroup.eu.
Open daily, 10:00 a.m.-midnight (hours may vary, or shop may close, off-season).

Gelateria Dei Neri, ★★★★★
Via dei Neri 9r. Tel: 055.210.034.
Open daily, 10:00 a.m.-midnight (hours may vary, and shop may close off-season or in late August for a week).

¶¶ | 06 | Enjoy a Delicious Lunch at a Reasonably Priced and Authentic Trattoria in the Heart of Florence

Michelin-starred restaurants aside, finding a reasonably priced, delicious and inviting local restaurant is one of our great pleasures. And in Florence, finding such a venue is a particularly easy and pleasurable task.

Our first choice for a good lunch would have to be **Ristorante La Maremma,** which is located just a few meters from Piazza Santa Croce. Their lunch menu deals, ranging between €10 and €12, are an excellent value, La Maremma's pasta is good, for the most part, but the restaurant's forte is the *secondi,* meat-based main dishes. This isn't surprising, given that they are named after Tuscany's southernmost region, the Maremma, famous for its delectable meat. Try their delicious *peposo,* a tasty beef stew, or the *scaloppine al pomodoro fresco e capperi* (escapole with fresh tomatoes and capers). If you prefer a *primo,* try the *ribollita,* or the *tortelli* or *pici,* which are even better than the regular pasta dishes.

Next, In the same area, just off Via dei Neri, you will find **Francesco Vini,** a charming trattoria with outdoor seating. We love their hand-made pasta and the antipasti platters, but the pizza and even the Florentine steaks are all very good, too, and the general ambiance is friendly and welcoming.

For a more traditional meal, try **Club Culinario di Osvaldo.** This venue is geared more towards a local clientele, and the menu lists only classic, time-honored regional dishes from across the country. Try their antipasti platter of Umbrian charcuterie, which is excellent, the various pasta dishes (especially the Tortelli di Firenzuola and the Umbrichelli) and for dessert, don't miss the creme brule' topped with a Bourbon caramel.

Slightly pricier but very highly recommended is **Caffè Coquinarius**—an easygoing and popular restaurant and *enoteca.* Caffè

Coquinarius is perfectly positioned, right behind the Duomo and in front of the American book shop. The menu is varied, and ranges from large, fresh salads and delicious *antipasti* platters of fish and meat (probably the best antipasti platters in Florence, by the way!) to various classic staples of the Tuscan kitchen. This restaurant is particularly famous for its pasta dishes—don't miss their burrata-filled ravioli, served on a bed of red onion cream and topped with pistachio pesto, and the *ravioli cacio e pera* (cacio cheese and pear-filled ravioli). Their desserts, especially the cheese cake, are also excellent and the wine selection, as you might expect, is serious and tempting. If you plan on stopping by for dinner, be sure to book a table in advance, as this popular eatery is booked solid every night of the week.

Ristorante La Maremma, ★★★
Via Giuseppe Verdi, 16r.
Tel: 055.244.615,
www.ristorantelamaremma.com.
Open daily, 12:00 p.m.–2:30 p.m. &7:00 p.m.–10:30 p.m.

Francesco Vini, ★★★★
Two locations, half a block from each other: Borgo De' Greci 7R & Piazza Dei Peruzzi 8R.
Tel: 055.218737, www.francescovini.com.
Open Monday-Saturday, 9:00 a.m.–11:00 p.m; Off season closed on Monday.

Club Culinario Toscano da Osvaldo, ★★★
Piazza de' Peruzzi 3R
Tel: 055.217919, www.clubosvaldo.com.
Open daily, 12:30 p.m.–2:30 p.m. & 7:30 p.m.–10:30 p.m.

Caffè Coquinarius, ★★★★
Via delle Oche 11r, Florence.
Tel: 055.230.2153,
www.coquinarius.it.
Open daily, 12:30 p.m.–3:30 p.m. & 6:30 p.m.–11:00 p.m. Reservations are recommended.

¶|07 | **Enjoy the Best Pizza** in Florence

Florence is replete with sophisticated restaurants, and today it is easier than ever to enjoy a great meal in town. But highbrow restaurants aside, sometimes, we just want pizza. Not just any pizza, of course—we want the real thing. When we are in the mood for an authentic slice of Neapolitan goodness, this is where we go:

Santarpia' is widely considered a Florentine institution. Modern, centrally located (near Piazza Santa Croce) and 100% delicious, this spot enjoys a following among food critics and locals. The pizzas here are strictly traditional, and the dough is left to rest and rise for 48 hours, which results in a savory and easily-digestible slice. The toppings are the restaurant's forte, and range from the classic fresh mozzarella (delivered daily from the south) to imaginative ingredients such as Lampredotto.

Alternatively, try **Pizzeria Bistro Giotto.** This spot is a personal favorite, and has recently been listed by the Gambero Rosso, Italy's prominent culinary magazine, as one of the best pizzerias in the country. Giotto is geared towards locals, and as such, it's located outside the tourist-filled centro storico. This means that to reach it, you'll have to take a cab from the Santa Maria Novella train station.

Giotto's pizza is traditional, strictly Neapolitan, with a thick, fragrant crust and high-quality toppings. Try one of the more creative options on the menu, such as the Pizza Bouquet (the dough is filled with ricotta cheese, and topped with Fiordilatte cheese and thinly sliced prosciutto), or Pizza Tartar (the dough is filled with a Chianina beef tartar), or the truffled pizza, an autumn favorite. Those who are in the mood for some pasta or dessert will find both on the menu, too (The tiramisu is especially good!)

Pizzeria Santarpia' ★★★★
Largo Pietro Annigoni 9/C, Florence.
Tel: 055.245829, www.santarpia.biz.
Open Wednesday–Sunday for dinner
only, 7:30 p.m.–11:00 p.m.; Tuesday
closed.

Giotto Pizzeria Bistro , ★★★★
Via Francesco Veracini 22, Florence.
Tel: 955.332332, www.pizzeriagiotto.it.
Open Saturday–Sunday, 12:00 p.m.–2:30
p.m. & 7:00 p.m.–11:15 p.m.; Monday,
Wednesday–Friday open for dinner only;
closed Tuesday. Advance bookings are
highly recommended.

FLORENCE

♥ 08 | Taste Some Excellent Tuscan Wines in a Real *Enoteca*

Wine tasting is, in our opinion, one of the greatest pleasures on offer for tourists visiting Tuscany. That is why we have listed in this guide several recommendations for the best producers and wineries in the region, everything from delicious Chianti to exclusive Brunello to smooth Montepulciano Nobile (see tips 33, 36, 43, 56, and 94, for example). But if you have no intention of leaving Florence and touring the countryside, you can still enjoy some fantastic wines by simply spending a couple of hours in a good *enoteca* (wine shop) that offers various *degustazioni* (wine tasting) plans.

Cantinetta Antinori is one restaurant and *enoteca* that tends to divide people. Some say this spot is overpriced for what it offers, while others rave about their excellent wines. We find ourselves somewhere in the middle. On the positive side, the restaurant's setting is beautiful. It is located in Palazzo Antinori, a historic 15th-century edifice, and the

layout inside is quaint, comfortable, and spacious. The real draw is the wine, of course—the Antinori family is one of the greatest wine producers in Italy, and boasts a remarkable history going back hundreds of years, as well as several estates throughout Italy. They make wines of exceptional quality, many of which can be sampled here for a range of prices. On the other hand, the limited menu can be a little disappointing and certainly is overpriced. A simple solution would be to come here not for a full meal but rather, for a fun *aperitivo*, order a couple of starters, and ask the knowledgeable staff to make some good wine suggestions.

A far more easygoing option is **Enoteca Alessi.** This friendly, family-run *enoteca* and delicatessen is located just minutes from the Duomo and has been serving hungry and thirsty patrons since 1952. You can come for a quick (and recommended!) €15 *degustazione* that includes three of the region's most famous wines (Chianti, Vino Nobile di Montepulciano, and Brunello di Montalcino) or opt for a more elaborate tasting of specific wines from other regions in Italy.

Equally charming is the popular **La Divina Enoteca**, a serious yet fun *enoteca* near the *Mercato Centrale* (main market). Here you will find a particularly fine selection of excellent Tuscan wines, including many of the top producers in the region. The friendly staff will be happy to answer your questions and suggest a little nibble that will complement your wine.

Cantinetta Antinori, ★★★★
Piazza Antinori 3, Florence.
Tel: 055 292234,
www.cantinetta-antinori.com.
Open Monday–Friday, 12:30 p.m.–2:30 p.m. & 7:00 p.m.–10:00 p.m.; closed on weekends. Closed for the last 3 weeks of August. During the high season (mid-April to late September), may open for two Saturdays a month.

Enoteca Alessi, ★★★★
Via delle Oche 27r, Florence.
Tel: 055.214.966,
www.enotecaalessi.it.
Open Monday–Saturday, 11:00 a.m.–7:00 p.m. Closed Sunday.

La Divina Enoteca, ★★★★
Via Panicale 19r, Florence.
Tel: 055.292.723,
www.ladivinaenoteca.it.
Open Tuesday–Sunday, 11:00 a.m.–8:30 p.m. Closed Monday.

✗ 09 | **Discover Two Hidden Gems** off the Standard Museum Route

Is it possible that Florence, with its five million tourists a year, has any remaining hidden treasures, any concealed gems waiting to be discovered? Surprisingly, the answer is "Yes." Tourists in Florence, especially those who don't have much time, tend to go to the same well-known museums and attractions, while completely skipping other parts of town. But for the curious and adventurous, two surprises hide along the roads less traveled.

Both are located far enough from the center to deter the crowds, but make no mistake, they are both easy to reach and definitely worth visiting. One is a small museum, the **Museo Stefano Bardini**; and the other is the **Jewish Synagogue and Museum** (Sinagoga e Museo Ebraico).

Museo Stefano Bardini, named after its creator, the Italian antiquarian Stefano Bardini, is a secret many art lovers would gladly keep to themselves. The collection is housed in a convent that was

renovated and transformed in neo-Renaissance style in 1881 by Bardini to accommodate his collection and business. In his glory days, Bardini had a number of laboratories for the restoration of his precious items, and art lovers would come from afar to buy the antiques.

After Bardini died, the museum was left to the city of Florence. Today,

it houses a delightful, fascinating collection of over 2,000 antiques and crafts—ancient, medieval, Renaissance, and 18th-century art, paintings, medals, bronze sculptures, oriental rugs, and more. Much of the museum's charm comes from its intimate setting, and of course, Bardini's excellent eye in creating his collection. As you discover room after room of enchanting pieces in the elegant, refined space, you will be drawn further into its warm, inviting environment; you may even be reminded of the Poldi Pezzoli museum in Milan. The wonderful view of the city from the Bardini villa gardens is an added bonus. Watch for the events and temporary exhibitions that regularly take place here. Then, Villa Bardini is the perfect place to end your visit; stop for an afternoon snack or a relaxed *aperitivo* (often accompanied, in the summer months, by live music).

The Jewish Synagogue (known in Italian as Sinagoga or Tempio Israelitico) may seem a little difficult to visit—due to threats, the security detail around the site is strict. However, the effort is absolutely worth it. Once you enter, the chaos of the tourist-strewn city outside is forgotten, and you are engulfed in beauty. Built in Moorish style, with Arabic, Byzantine, and Romanesque elements, the synagogue was inaugurated in 1882, about 20 years after the emancipation of the Italian Jews.

The community set out to build a temple that would be worthy of the beautiful city of Florence, and they

certainly succeeded. The massive green dome, which can be seen from afar, was once gilded. Inside, the walls are decorated with Moorish arabesques and geometric patterns. Superior craftsmanship can be found in every corner. Interesting and informative organized tours of the synagogue and the museum are available daily (every half hour in high season). Tours are recommended, and need to be booked in advance.

Museo Bardini, ★★★★★
Via dei Renai 37, Florence.
Tel: 055.234.2427,
www.museicivicifiorentini.comune.fi.it/
bardini.
Open year-round, Friday–Monday, 11:00 a.m.–5:00 p.m.

The Jewish Synagogue and Museum, ★★★★
Via Farini 4, Florence.
Tel. 055.245252,
www.moked.it/jewishflorence/
synagogue-and-museum.
Synagogue: June–September, open Sunday–Thursday, 10:00 a.m.–6:30 p.m.; Friday and eve of major Jewish holidays, 10:00 a.m.–5:00 p.m.; October–May, open Sunday–Thursday, 10:00 a.m.–5:30 p.m.; Friday and the eve of major Jewish holidays, 10:00 a.m.–3:00 p.m.; Closed on Saturday and Jewish Holidays year-round. Last entry 45 minutes before closing time.

Museum: April–September, open Sunday–Thursday, 10:00 a.m.–6:00 p.m.; Friday, 10:00 a.m.–5:00 p.m. October–March, open Sunday–Thursday, 10:00 a.m.–3:00 p.m.; Friday 10:00 a.m. –3:00 p.m. Closed on Saturday and Jewish holidays year-round. Last entry 30 minutes before closing time. Guided tours are available, book in advance.

✗ | 10 | **Indulge your Senses** with a Relaxing Spa Treatment in the Center of Florence

Florence is a spectacular city, but after a day spent tramping around hot, busy streets, standing in lines for what feels like hours, and perhaps even ushering young children through the madness, it's a good guess that you'll be worn out. As you stare at your swollen feet, too tired to move or think about all the beautiful things you still want to see tomorrow, a good massage seems like the only viable solution. It's true that Tuscany's best spas, those that feature hot thermal water pools with a fabulous view and an endless range of treatments, are located outside the city, deep in the Tuscan countryside. But there are also a number of excellent urban spas less than 10-minutes from wherever you are staying in Florence, at a range of prices.

The very best hotels in Florence all have excellent spa services. None of them are cheap, but if you want to treat yourself to some extra pampering and soothe that

aching body, they are the place to go. Alternatively, book a session at one of the city's smaller private spas (there are many outside the hotels), which also offer simpler but enjoyable solutions for re-energizing the weary tourist in you.

Silathai is a lovely little spa near Piazza Pitti, offering Thai massage, reflexology, and relaxing Swedish massages, which are much gentler than traditional Thai massages. The spa features a pleasant decor

in warm golden hues and Eastern religious iconography. The staff here is friendly, and the many treatments are far more reasonably priced than at the hotels. They speak English, too, which is another useful advantage if you need to tell an overly enthusiastic masseuse to go easy on your aching shoulders!

Hotel Ville sull'Arno is a recently opened, stunning boutique hotel that offers a decadent spa for both guests and non-guests. Located within walking distance of the Duomo, this romantic venue prides itself on a list of fine massages, executed with the best ingredients. Try their signature body treatments, such as Ninfea—a 50-minute revitalizing body massage; at €95, it isn't cheap, but it's certainly far more affordable than at other hotels in the city. The hotel's wellness center comes complete with emotional showers and a caldarium, and certain treatments can be also be executed outside the spa, in the conservatory.

The **Four Seasons** is the most exclusive address in town, and has recently been elected as the best urban spa in Italy. Their top-notch treatments are all executed using products made especially for them by the Santa Maria Novella pharmacy, a historic Florentine institution. Guests enjoy high-quality treatments in elegantly designed rooms, as well as free use of the pool and hot tub. Be warned, though, that gifting yourself with a treatment in this 5-star luxurious setting does come at a steep price: The full body treatments average around €550, while the starting price for a massage is €100 for just twenty minutes. Consult their website to find out more.

Soulspace®, which is located just minutes from the Duomo, is a beautiful spa that offers reasonably priced massages as well as a large number of relaxation and beauty treatments—everything from aromatherapy to revitalizing treatments, water cocoons, four-hand massages and treatments designed specifically for pregnant women and new mothers. The space itself has a modern, comfortable design with an emphasis on neutral colors to help you relax. A number of special offers are available on their website.

Finally, at the more luxurious end of the scale, are The White Iris Beauty Spa in the Continental Hotel and Villa Cora. **The White Iris Beauty Spa** is run according to the Daniela Steiner method, and is in a perfect location right by the Ponte Vecchio. Massages start from €140, and a series of beauty treatments and facials are also available. If you fancy a drink to round off your relaxing experience, then head up to the hotel's terrace bar afterward for a refreshing glass of wine and views overlooking Florence. Alternatively, **Hotel Villa Cora** will immediately make you feel pampered. A historic mansion located near Piazzale Michelangelo, Villa Cora is first and foremost a magnificent (and pricey...) hotel, famous for its stylish décor, class and ambiance, and also for the glorious views of Florence it offers. Come here for their top-notch spa, relax with a professionally executed massage, enjoy a swim in the heated pool, and end your hours of indulgence with a drink in front of the vista in their rooftop bar. In the summer, the hotel also organizes *aperitivi* and mixers around the pool.

The Four Seasons, ★★★★★
Borgo Pinti 99, Florence.
Tel: 055.26261,
www.fourseasons.com.

Hotel Ville sull'Arno Spa, ★★★★
Lungarno C. Colombo 1, Florence.
Tel: 055.670.971,
www.planetariahotels.com.

SOULSPACE® Wellness Center, ★★★★
Via S. Egidio 12, Florence.
Tel. 055.200.1794,
www.soulspace.it.

Silathai Thai Massage Center, ★★★★
Via De Serragli 63r/65r, Florence.
Tel: 055.217.559,
www.silathaimassage.com.

White Iris Beauty Spa in the Continentale, ★★★★
Vicolo dell'Oro 6r, Florence.
Tel: 055.272.65966,
www.lungarnocollection.com.

Hotel Villa Cora, ★★★★
Viale Machiavelli 18, Florence.
Tel: 055.228.790,
www.villacora.it.

Please note that all these spas require booking in advance.

11 | **Join a Fun and Tasty** Cooking Class

So many B&Bs and *agriturismi* nowadays offer their guests some sort of cooking classes. In many cases, they are fun and worth trying. Most people don't suddenly plan on becoming a chef thanks to this class; it's just an enjoyable way to experience hands-on the Tuscan kitchen, and learn the Italian basics: from how to make pasta to how to correctly stir the bubbling ragu, just like a real Italian grandmother. A day of cooking can be not only a welcome break from all the sightseeing, but also quite a memorable experience from your Tuscan trip. Before booking your class, please note that there are a number of recommended classes outside of Florence, too (see tips 33 and 60, for example).

Let's Cook with Jacopo and Anna is a popular and excellent option— they offer a fun, educational and engaging cooking class, using fresh ingredients from the Florence market or from their own organic vegetable garden. If you select a morning course, you can book (for an extra fee) a guided visit to the market, to select the best produce together with Jacopo. Once you are back in the kitchen, you will roll up your sleeves and learn how to make fresh pasta, sauces, meat dishes, crunchy salads, and more. The setting is also delightful—courses take place either in the family's farmhouse (in the countryside near Montespertoli), or in Florence itself.

Let's Cook with Jacopo and Anna,
★★★★

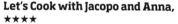

www.greve-in-chianti.com/
tuscancookinglessons.htm.

12 Find Monk-made Perfumes and Concoctions in Florence's Traditional Apothecaries

Today, most people buy their perfumes and cosmetics at the local drugstore or mall. But in Florence, it is still quite possible to seek out a traditional apothecary—those almost magical shops which are filled to the brim with quality products.

Antica Erboristica San Simeone is run by the friendly and knowledgeable Fernanda Russo, a pharmacist who specializes in phytotherapy (the science-based research of the medicinal properties of plants and herbs). Her intoxicating shop sits just minutes from the Duomo, and tempts visitors with a selection of organic creams and infusions. Our favorite products here, however, are the ambiance perfumes, each inspired by a famous Florentine work of art, or wine. Botticelli's Primavera, for example, is made with Jasmine and orange blossoms; the Brunello inspired fragrance, on the other hand, is deep and woody.

Next, towering above the city of Florence stands the abbey of San

Miniato al Monte (near Piazzale Michelangelo). Within the abbey hides the **monk-run San Miniato Al Monte Pharmacy.** Here you will find several organic products, made exclusively by the brothers, following centuries-old recipes. Creams, soaps and traditional infusions are all neatly placed in the hand-decorated ceramic vases that line the walls. And if you come at 6:30 p.m., you will be able to hear the monks chant the vespri prayer in the chapel, a wonderful experience that shouldn't be missed.

Antica Erboristeria San Simeone,
Via Ghibellina 190R, Florence.
Cell: 393.8393732, www.
anticaerboristeriasansimone.it. Open
Monday–Saturday, 9:00-20:00.

Farmacia Monastica–Abbazia San Miniato al Monte
(near Piazzale Michelangelo, take bus 12 from Firenze SMN). Open daily, 10:00–12:15 & 16:00–18:00. Cell: 348.992.5905, www.sanminiatoalmonte.it/farmacia.

13 Buy Beautiful, Hand-Made Paper
Products in Florence

For many people today it may be a rarity to put pen to paper for anything more than the weekly shopping list. However, it is impossible to deny the charm of a handwritten letter using the finest stationery. It is for this reason (and possibly because we are shameless romantics) that we keep a stock of high quality, beautifully designed notebooks, cards, and envelopes to hand. Who knows when you might need them? Thankfully, in Florence it is easy to fulfill this desire for lovingly designed paper products. The city boasts a plethora of specialist shops and the typical Florence printed paper can be found just about everywhere.

The real challenge, however, is to find a store that offers a genuinely unique touch. For something a bit more special, our favorite stop has to be **Papier Arti & Mestieri.** A tiny, family-run shop, this romantic and old-world studio is where Jackie O would do her shopping if she were on visit in town. There is much to choose from, but we especially love their elegant, lovingly-bound leather Tuscan diaries, the colorful postcards, and the creamy paper. You can find this shop just two minutes from the Ponte Vecchio (cross the bridge to the Oltrarno, turn left onto via de Bardi, and continue straight until you reach the tiny piazza S. Maria Soprarno, and the shop itself.)

For more regular goods at reasonable prices we recommend the chain store **Il Papiro.** Their shops stock good quality products and can be found in several locations in Florence and the rest of Tuscany; the likelihood is that you will come across one of their shops sooner or later. Their notebooks (decorated with a traditional Florentine pattern) and their photo albums are especially beautiful, and make for a graceful gift or souvenir.

Last but not least, **Sogni in Carta** is a small shop near Santa Maria Novella that's worth stepping into. Inside you'll find a selection of traditional Florentine stationery, most of which can be personalized; you can even have your name printed on one of their hand-made leather-bound diaries.

Papier Arti & Mestieri, ★★★★
Piazza S. Maria Soprarno, Florence.
Tel: 055.234.3670.

Il Papiro, ★★★
Piazza del Duomo 24,
Florence. Tel: 055.281.628,
www.ilpapirofirenze.it.

Sogni in Carta, ★★★
Via della Scala 65R, Florence.
Cell: 338.966.3650.
Open daily, 10:00 a.m.–7:00 p.m.

 14 | **Buy a Good-Quality** Italian Leather Jacket

Stylish leather jackets are a staple of the classic Italian wardrobe. We are not talking about those made-in-China, back-alley, not-quite-sure-it's-even-leather imitations, but something characteristic, timeless, and Italian.

While stores stocking authentic leather bags can be found dotted around Florence, finding a leather jacket specialist can be trickier. The shops in and around the famous **leather market near Piazza San Lorenzo** are usually the first stop for buyers, and the shops around the Santa Croce church are usually the second. Some of these shops are indeed worth exploring, but if you are looking for something special—an investment piece—you are unlikely to find it there. For a special item, head out to one of these well-known boutiques:

For mid-range priced jackets, **Borgo dei Greci**, the boutique-strewn street that leads from Palazzo Vecchio to the Santa Croce

church is your best bet. Here you will find a number of shops, the most interesting of which, in our opinion, are **Il Perseo Pelleteria** (quite popular with the locals), **Peruzzi Abbigliamento** (a huge shop with an ample selection) and **Leonardo Leather** (pricier, but full of interesting finds). Smaller and slightly more rustic, but with a few hidden surprises, is **Gruppo Gab** (across the street from Peruzzi). Even if you don't end up buying anything in these boutiques, you will still get a good idea of the price range and the kind of models you might expect to find in the better shops, and compare them with your finds in the San Lorenzo market.

A few minutes away, on via Lambertesca, we love stopping by the **Adam Leather Factory**, a simple looking shop that actually stocks quite a good collection. Lastly, when visiting this area don't miss **Bottega Fiorentina,** one of the best-known brands in Tuscany. Their showroom is located in an elegant 16th century

building, right next to Piazza Santa Croce, and the quality is excellent. The designs are smart, and most items are handmade by designers from Florence. Custom clothes are available, too.

For pricey but remarkable pieces, head to **Via de' Guicciardini,** on the Oltrarno (just a couple of minutes from the Ponte Vecchio). Two of the best known shops on this street are **La Pelle** and **Parri's**—both are very popular with well-heeled, fashion-loving tourists and locals, as they carry some of the most exclusive luxury items. Naturally, don't limit your visit to these two shops—many of the boutiques on this street are worth checking out before making your purchase. Then, don't forget to make a stop at **Il Fiorentino,** one of our personal favorite boutiques, where you will find a high-end yet still accessible collection, which can also be completely customized. Bags and leather jackets are all exclusively handmade by local artisans using top-quality materials. Stop here if you are interested in a classic but still vibrant look.

Finally, those who are looking for a quality jacket with a dramatic design should stop by **Janniderma**—a one-of-a-kind, wild boutique that offers custom designs for the creative (or the brave!). Whether you are a fearless fashionista with a passion for flair or an intrigued buyer on the hunt for

something different, Janniderma is worth stopping into. Check out their online collection to get a general sense of their style.

Il Perseo Pelleteria, ★★★
Borgo dei Greci 24. Open Monday-Saturday, 10:00 a.m.-7:00 p.m. Usually closed Sunday.

Peruzzi Abbigliamento, ★★★
Borgo dei greci 8r, Florence.
Tel: 055.289.039,
www.peruzzifirenze.com.
Open daily, 10:00 a.m.-7:00 p.m.

Adam Leather Factory, ★★★
Via Lambertesca 30r, Florence.
Tel: 055.283.286. Open Monday-Saturday, 10:00 a.m.-7:00 p.m. Usually closed Sunday.

Bottega Fiorentina, ★★★
Borgo dei Greci 5r, Florence.
Tel: 055.295.411,
www.bottegafiorentina.it.
Open Monday-Saturday, 10:00 a.m.-6:00 p.m. Closed Sunday.

La Pelle, ★★★★
Via Guicciardini 11r.
Tel: 055.292.031,
www.lapellesrl.it.
Open Monday-Saturday, 9:30 a.m.-7:00 p.m. Usually closed Sunday, but may open in high season (call first).

Parri's, ★★★★
Via Guicciardini, 18r, Florence.
Tel: 055.282.829,
www.parris.it.
Open Monday-Saturday, 10:30 a.m.-7:00 p.m.; Sunday, 11:00 a.m.-7:00 p.m.

Il Fiorentino, ★★★★
Lungarno Corsini 48r, Florence.
Tel: 055.239.8325,
www.ilfiorentino.com.
Open Monday-Saturday, 10:00 a.m.-7:00 p.m. Usually closed Sunday.

Janniderma, ★★★★
Via dei Benci 10, Tel: 055.234.6173,
www.janniderma.com.
Open daily, 11:00 a.m.-7:30 p.m.

🍴 15 | **Lunch like a True Italian**, with a Delicious Panino

For us, the perfect quick summer lunch has to be simple, authentic, and delicious. Choosing the right place can be tricky, though. After hours of walking around, it is more than tempting to crash, tired and swollen-footed, at the nearest pizza shop or bar and buy an even more tired-looking sandwich. But in a city like Florence, where one can choose from so many quality eateries, settling for such a mediocre solution would be a real shame. When picking a place for a light lunch on the go, we stick to one basic rule: The panini must be made using good quality *materie prime* (i.e., quality produce). When a spot has high-quality, fresh local produce, everything else just seems to fall into place. In Florence, there are four places in particular where we regularly seem to end up, and the quality of their *materie prime* is only the first reason.

Our current favorite spot in town is **Lo Schiacciavino**, a recently opened sandwich shop that is located just a few meters from Piazza Santa Croce (and two minutes from the famous All'Antico Vinaio, see below). Everything here is fresh, perfectly prepared and delicious. The reasonable prices and friendly service certainly add to the charm. Try their fantastic *Ci Credo* Sandwich (made with prosciutto crudo, Brie cheese and Truffle cream), served in a crisp *schiacciata all'olio* (thin, crumbly schiacciata bread, drenched in olive oil).

Behind the Uffizi, we like **Mangia Pizza**, which, despite the name, actually specializes in sandwiches. Prices are slightly higher than other locales in the area, but the quality here is good, and the sandwiches, served in ciabatta bread baked in the shop, are very tasty.

On the Oltrarno, we love **Il Santino**, in Via Santo Spirito. This tiny eatery has a warm, intimate atmosphere that makes us feel immediately at home. You can find a small but quality choice of cold cuts and cheeses, tasty sandwiches, and a nice wine list—perfect for a light lunch or an *aperitivo*. Seating is very limited, so try to go early before it fills up. Note that Il Santino is adjacent to Il Santo Bevitore, an excellent restaurant with the same owners.

Lastly, we can't end this tip without mentioning the most famous panini shop in Florence—**All'Antico Vinaio**. They are widely known and recommended in just about every tourist guide, and we can't deny that the sandwiches here really are packed with flavor (including the vegetarian sandwiches, which are just as delicious). The fact that most of their panini are priced at €5, and that you can wash it all down with a very reasonably priced glass of the house red wine, is a prospect that is sure to revive even the weariest tourist. This place is seriously popular, but the long line moves quickly, so don't despair. While you wait, you can always eavesdrop on locals fervently discussing politics and football.

Lo Schiacciavino, ★★★★
Via Giuseppe Verdi 6r, Florence.
Tel: 055.226.0133.
Open Monday, 11:00 a.m.–4:00 p.m.;
Tuesday-Thursday, 11:00 a.m.–midnight;
Friday-Saturday, 11:00 a.m.–2:00 a.m.;
Sunday, 11:30 a.m.–9:30 p.m.

Il Santino, ★★★
Via di Santo Spirito 60r, Florence.
Tel: 055.230.2820.
Open daily, 12:30 p.m.–11:00 p.m.

Mangia Pizza, ★★★
Via Lambertesca 24r, Florence.
Tel: 055.287.595,
www.mangiapizzafirenze.it,
Open daily, 12:00 a.m.–7:00 p.m. (off season opening hours may vary).

All'Antico Vinaio, ★★★★
Via dei Neri 74r, Florence.
Tel: 055.238.2723.
Open Tuesday-Saturday, 10:00 a.m.–4:00 p.m. & 6:00-10:00 p.m.; Sunday 10:00 a.m.–4:00 p.m. Closed Monday.

🏃 16 | Relax at One of the Little Known Gardens in Florence

The famous Boboli Gardens are beautiful and a must-see, but we have a special place in our hearts for the Torrigiani Gardens, which appear like a green mirage in Florence's chaotic historic center.

Spread across nearly 17 acres in the heart of Florence, this magical garden is still owned by two noble families who belong to the Florence elite of antiquity. It is also the largest private city-garden in Europe.

The area was once a much smaller botanical garden, but it was expanded in the 19th century and turned into an elegant English garden. The Torrigiani Malaspina and the Torrigiani Santa Cristina families do a marvelous job of preserving this special place, and a family member personally leads each tour. A visit includes a tour of the ancient botanical plots, with trees and plants from all over the world; the woods surrounding the family crypts; and a look at

some very suggestive sculptures. Activities such as painting classes and gardening lessons are occasionally organized; consult the garden's website to find out more.

Booking a private tour here may prove somewhat difficult; it will probably be easier to organize if you are a small group or hosting an event. If a booking seems to be an impossible mission, don't despair - there are a number of other good options in town:

In the summer months, we love visiting the **Giardino dell'Orticultura**, one of Florence's most interesting gardens. It was originally constructed as an experimental garden, commissioned by the local chapter of the *Accademia dei Georgofili*, in the 19th century. Today it is a pleasure to walk along the garden's paths, admiring the impressive glass and steel greenhouse, discovering the artistic sculptures that hide at the *Orto del Parnaso* (within the garden), and enjoying the many cultural events that take place here during the spring and summer months (there is even a summer beer garden!). On June 24, when Florence celebrates *la festa di San Giovanni*, in honor of the city's patron, this is one of the best places from which to enjoy the firework show. Find out more about the various initiatives organized yearly, here: www.giardinoartecultura.it.

Next, **Giardino Bardini** (also mentioned in tip 9). is a stunning little garden with an incredible vista over Florence. The garden also regularly hosts cultural and artistic events. Find out more here: www.bardinipeyron.it.

Also noteworthy are the **Iris and Rose gardens,** which are located near Piazzale Michelangelo. In the summer and spring, it is fun to walk down from the Piazzale, through the gardens, to the *centro storico*.

Lastly, once part of a private mansion that served pilgrims on their way to the San Domenico church in Fiesole, today **Parco di Villa Il Ventaglio** is an enchanting little garden that is open to the public. Majestic elm and chestnut trees line the romantic avenue that crosses the territory, and a small lake and several beds of flowers and shrubbery turn this park into a little corner of quiet magic. This is also where the headquarters of the Università Internazionale dell'Arte (international arts university) can be found.

Giardino Torrigiani, ★★★★
Via dei Serragli 144, Florence.
Tel: 055.224.527/ Cell: 349.286.8449, www.giardinotorrigiani.it. Call in advance to ask what tours are available.

Giardino dell'Orticultura, ★★★★
Via Vittorio Emanuele II 4, Florence. (There's a second entry from Via Bolognese 17). The garden is open daily, from 8:00 a.m.-sunset. Find out about the various events organized here: www.giardinoartecultura.it.

Giardino Bardini, ★★★★★
Costa San Girogio, Florence. Open Tuesday-Sunday, 10:00 a.m.-sunset. Closed Monday.
www.bardinipeyron.it.

The Rose garden, ★★★
Vialle Giuseppe Poggi (near Piazzale Michelangelo). Open year round, 9:00 a.m.-sunset. **The Iris garden** is open in May only.

Parco Villa Il Ventaglio, ★★★
Via G. Aldini 10, Florence. The park is open daily, 8:15 a.m.-4:00 p.m. (may close later in high season).

♈ 17 | **Treat Yourself to a Royal Brunch** or Relax with a Cocktail, at the Four Seasons Hotel in Florence

With its wonderful location, beautiful private gardens and two-star Michelin restaurant, the Four Seasons is considered one of the best hotels in Florence. The Royal Suite, which regularly hosts prime ministers and royalty, is probably one of the most incredible suites in the world; the stunning original frescoes and vaulted ceilings make you feel like you are nothing less than a member of the Medici family at the height of your power. Even the regular rooms are beautifully decorated and offer lovely views of nearby medieval streets or into the hotel's charming garden.

While a night in the Royal Suite is probably over budget for most people, there are ways to enjoy this luxurious hotel without breaking the bank. One way is to book a seat at their famous **Sunday Brunch**. Off-season, from October to July, the hotel offers delicious weekly brunches that have become very popular with locals and tourists alike. At around €90, the buffet brunch is still very costly,

honestly, but it's a fun experience. Call ahead on Monday to book for the upcoming Sunday, as places tend to run out quickly.

Alternatively, if you are visiting during the summer months, or if you prefer

an evening drink, afternoon tea or a glass of wine while listening to the soft piano playing in the background, then at the **Atrium Bar** is a must. The Atrium is one of the smartest bars in town, regularly drawing a crowd of businessmen, artists, well-heeled locals and sophisticated tourists. Sumptuously decorated with oak cabinets and elegant lamps that provide soft lighting, this space will help you quickly slip into the perfect mood. Naturally, the cocktails here are professionally prepared.

One last thing: the Four Seasons isn't the only place for a tasty Sunday brunch. The famous SE·STO Restaurant (see tip 1), located at the top of the luxurious Westin Hotel, also has a very popular Sunday brunch, as well as a jaw-dropping view (www.sestoonarno.com).

Four Seasons Hotel, ★★★★★
Borgo Pinti 99, Florence.
Tel: 055.26261,
www.fourseasons.com.
Please note that brunches are offered from October to late June, on Sundays only, in the (beautiful!) Il Palagio restaurant, between noon and 3:00 p.m. The Atrium Bar is open daily, 9:00 a.m.-midnight or 1:00 a.m.

18 | Stay in One of Florence's Historic and Magnificent Hotels - Palazzo Magnani Feroni

Palazzo Magnani Feroni has everything you would expect from a 5-star hotel; each room is meticulously decorated with luxurious antique furniture, the location is spectacular—just minutes away from the Ponte Vecchio and the Boboli Gardens—and the service is impeccable.

While there are more modern hotels in town, perhaps with better amenities, in our opinion, the Magnani Feroni makes up for whatever disadvantages it may have with heaps of charm. Architecturally speaking, this hotel is outstanding; it is located in a Renaissance palazzo, and guests enter a lobby (though the word "lobby" is really insufficient in this case) that is in fact an open art gallery, filled with antique statues and Renaissance works of art, as well as priceless frescos. The rooftop terrace and bar offer guests wonderful views of Florence and are the perfect place for a sunset *aperitivo*. The inner courtyard, filled with plants and bathed in sunlight, will make you feel as if you were a character in an E. M. Forster novel. In fact, all of the common spaces are majestic: chandeliers hang from the roof, gilded frames adorn the walls, and regal dark hardwood covers the floors. The rooms are equally beautiful, and the marble bathrooms are a little small but elegant. Off-season you will often find special offers.

Palazzo Magnani Feroni, ★★★★★
Borgo San Frediano 5, Florence.
Tel: 055.2399.544,
www.palazzomagnaniferoni.com.
Special offers are reserved for those who book directly through the hotel's website.

 # 19 | **Get Some Serious Shopping Done** in Florence

Florence is filled with tempting shops that grab the fashion lover's attention, everything from touristy little hubs packed with Florentine leather souvenirs to exclusive boutiques that sell the best Italian brands. In this tip we've tried to review the most important venues, ranging from top, high-end fashion boutiques to the more accessible, mid-range shops.

The very high-end options—such as Yves Saint Laurent, Bottega Veneta, Hermès, Salvatore Ferragamo, Gucci, and others—are concentrated in the area around Piazza della Repubblica, **Via degli Strozzi,** and the famous **Via Tornabuoni**.

Still expensive and high-end, but slightly less so, are the shops in **Via di Parione** (just off via Tornabuoni, near the church of Santa Trinita), **Via del Moro**, and, of course, the famous **Via della Vigna Nuova** (where every well-dressed Florentine goes). Specifically, don't miss **Zadig & Voltaire** (Via della Vigna Nuova 17), **Gianfranco Lotti** (at number 45), **Brunello Cucinelli** (next door, at number 47), and **Sartoria Rossi** (at number 51), a perfect stop for men on the look for smart suits and fashionable shirts. In the nearby streets, don't miss **Ottod'Ame**, in Via della Spada 19r, famous for their sophisticated, casual and urban-chic look, and **Pineider**, in Piazza de' Rucellai, who have been making classic, quality leather bags for more than 250 years. Additionally, there are a number of interesting shops along Lungarno Corsini and Lungarno Acciaiuoli, which are, sadly, often overlooked by tourists.

Another must-stop street is **Via Roma,** near the the Duomo, where you will find the well-known **Miu Miu** and **Luisa Via Roma** stores. Luisa Via Roma, specifically, is one of the hottest stops in town, and perfect for those looking for the latest trends, from Dolce & Gabbana and Armani to Marc Jacobs and Giuseppe Zanotti. If you are visiting Florence in July, during the famous *saldi* (seasonal sale), you are very likely to find a few interesting items for reasonable prices even here.

For mid-range options, hit the streets connecting Piazza Santa Maria Novella and the Duomo, which are lined with popular fashion brands such as **Stefanel, Sisley** and **Fratelli Rossetti.** The shops along Via Por Santa Maria (the street that connects Ponte Vecchio and Piazza della Signoria) are worth a visit, as are the many smaller (but interesting) boutiques in the surrounding alleys. You will also find several cool and fashionable items, from handmade jewelry to alternative, hip jackets to classic leather bags, in **Borgo San Jacopo** (on the oltrarno, one of the best shopping streets in Florence!), **Borgo SS Apostoli** (behind the Uffizi) and **Via dei Servi** (right off the Duomo). For nifty vintage finds, try one of these personal favorites: **Street Doing Vintage Couture** (on Via dei Servi 88); **Boutique Nadine** (Lungarno degli Acciaiuoli 22R,

near the Ponte Vecchio); the tiny but stunning **MarieAntoinette Boutique** (Chiasso dei del Bene 5), and **La Corte Vintage Store** (Via dei Fossi 7, near Piazza Ognisanti).

If you are looking for a one-stop shop, then you must visit **Coin,** a three-story mega-boutique, located on Via dei Calzaiuoli 56r, just 200 meters from Piazza della Signoria, and **La Rinascente,** in Piazza della Repubblica. Both stock many of the best-known local and international brands.

Naturally, don't miss the outdoor **leather market** near Piazza San Lorenzo (just a few minutes from the Duomo). Behind the leather stalls, at Via dei Conti 49, you'll find **Passamaneria Toscana,** a shop selling beautiful tapestries, that make for excellent souvenirs. If you are interested in Tuscany's finest outlet shops and villages, see tip 26.

 20 | **Buy Stunning Leather Bags** in Florence

Florence is famous for its leather industry. As we've mentioned before, the leather market near San Lorenzo Church is a popular stop for tourists, and there are numerous shops all around town competing for visitors' attention. Unfortunately, not all shops offer the same quality, and some merchandise is even fake. True Tuscan leather-making is an honorable local industry that has been a point of pride for hundreds of years. Knowing where to go to get the real thing is important. The best boutiques may be pricier, but at least they guarantee a beautiful, quality product, an investment piece that is not only fashionable but will last for years.

There are a number of excellent shops you should check out. All the shops listed in tip 14 (for good leather jackets) also sell bags, and are highly recommended. For beautiful modern bags, don't miss **I Nobili** (on Borgo Ognissanti) and **Kaitan** (just a couple of blocks away, on Via della Vigna Nuova). Both will appeal to fashion-lovers with a refined sense of style. For a different look try **Benheart**, which sits just around the corner. This is a completely different sort of boutique, but just as highly recommended. Their style is younger, much more colorful, and rustic. They have an ample selection of shoes, jackets and belts on display, and many of these can be personalized with your initials.

Don't end your search for the perfect leather bag without stopping at **Leo's**, located on the uber-popular Via dei Neri (the street which houses both the most famous panino shop in Florence - L'Antivo Vinaio, and the highly recommended gelateria dei Neri). Leo's have recently expanded their shop, and their style is a charming mix of Florentine tradition and modern urban lines.

For the serious shopper, the Scuola del Cuoio and Genten di Firenze are both unmissable stops, not just to see their collections, but mostly to admire the artisans at work. The **Scuola del Cuoio** is a Florentine institution. It is attached to Santa Croce Church, and people from all over the world come here to see masters in their workshops and to learn how to work leather. The school was opened after the Second World War by monks from the Franciscan order to teach orphans the tricks of the trade and turn them into skilled artisans. The quality is superb and prices are very high. Check their website to learn more. Guided tours (€14) are available, and need to be booked in advance, but you can also go in and briefly tour the workshops for free. The artisans are usually there and working Monday–Friday, 10:00 a.m.–5:30 p.m.

Genten Firenze is a Japanese brand with an all-Tuscan feel. They stock environmentally friendly pieces that are high-quality, handcrafted, and unique. The store is located in the most prestigious shopping area in Florence, near Via Tornabuoni, inside the 13th-entury Palazzo dei Cerchi. If you are ready to invest in handmade, classic, one-of-a-kind articles, consider making a stop here, too. On Saturday, the artists come to the shop to work, usually between 10:00 a.m. and 4:00 p.m. (also, sometimes on Tuesday at 10:00 a.m.).

Katian Firenze, ★★★★
Via della vigna nuova 65r, Florence.
Tel: 055.260.8136.
Open Tuesday-Sunday, 9:30 a.m.-7:30 p.m.; closed Monday.

Benheart, ★★★
Via della Vigna Nuova 97R, Florence.
Tel: 055.239.9483, www.benheart.it.
Open daily, 9:00 a.m.-8:00 p.m. (On Sunday the shop opens at 10:00 a.m.)

Leo's, ★★★★
Via dei Neri 64, Florence.
Tel: 055.274.1028.
Open Monday-Saturday, 10:00 a.m.-8:00 p.m.

Scuola del Cuoio, ★★★★
Via San Giuseppe 5r, Florence.
Tel: 055.244.533,
www.scuoladelcuoio.com.
Open Fall/Winter, Monday-Friday 10:00 a.m.- 6:00 p.m. Saturday 10:30 a.m.-6:00 p.m. Closed Sunday.; Spring/Summer, Monday-Sunday 10:00 a.m.-6:00 p.m. Closed Weekends.

Genten Firenze Boutique, ★★★★
Vicolo de' Cerchi 1 (at the corner of Via della Condotta), Florence.
Tel: 055.277.6472. Open daily, 10:00 a.m.-7:00 p.m.

 21 | **Explore the Most Exclusive Home Décor**
Boutiques in Florence

If you are like us, then you love finding one-of-a-kind items while traveling. Of course, it cannot be just any item, but has to be something special, even unique, stylish, and preferably handmade. Something original rather than a clone of the designs you can find in just about any tourist shop in Tuscany. When it comes to the right piece, we feel it is absolutely OK to splurge a little (or a lot...) on what will undoubtedly become a one-of-a-kind souvenir. If you are overcome by such an urge during your time in Florence, know that the boutiques in this tip have been attracting the local high society for many years.

Investing in a serious (and expensive) piece is not to be taken lightly, and not every shop in Florence can cater to the taste of the most demanding clients. But **Parenti** certainly can. An elegant, upscale family business that has served the Florentine elite since 1865, Parenti is a shop bursting

with history and luxury. As soon as you walk in, you are surrounded by a unique, beautifully displayed collection. This luminous store holds a selection of high-end articles from the likes of Saint Louis, Raynaud, Ercuis, Royal Crown Derby, William Yeoward Crystal, and many more. The price tags are not for the faint of heart or the light of wallet. However, there are not many places where you will find a baccarat chandelier designed by Philippe Starck side-by-side with Art Deco crystal glasses or vintage Van Cleef jewelry next to Alberto Pinto plates.

Next, ask any Florentine where to buy quality embroidered tablecloths or gorgeous nightgowns, and the answer will always be the same: **Loretta Caponi**'s atelier. Quality, as you might imagine, comes at a price, but do stop by if you are looking for a special piece to take home. It is no accident that clients like as Princess Diana, Jackie Kennedy and Madonna have been ·

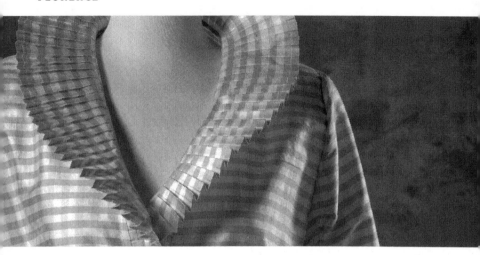

drawn to Caponi's sophisticated style. **TAF** is another must-stop for those looking for a special piece. Here you will find both traditional and modern handmade embroidered linen. Across the street you will find the TAF children's clothes shop, featuring some absolutely adorable items. On the Oltrarno, don't miss **B. del Secco**, a quality linen shop that has been serving Florence's finest since 1929. Here you will find a mix of modern craftsmanship and traditional Florentine items that make wonderful presents to bring to loved ones back home.

For silverware, we love the tasteful and elegant selection at **Argenterie Pagliai,** located in the artistic Oltrarno district right off the Ponte Vecchio bridge. Their work displays exceptional craftsmanship and a classical sense of style, but they also make simple, practical items for the household, from salt shakers to water servers for the kitchen table. Their tableware is particularly beautiful. Another fascinating silverware shop is **Argenteria Sacchi.** It is packed with one-of-a-kind pieces (quite literally–each piece is unique) that are fit for royalty. Though this

boutique does stock silverware from other manufacturers, their most prized pieces are those personally designed and produced by Sacchi's own artisans.

Chandelier lovers, or anyone who appreciates unique glass pieces, should go to **Gherardo degli Albizzi**, the most beautiful lamp and chandelier shop in Florence, in our opinion. This artistic boutique opened its doors in 1960, and is today run by the founder's daughter, Albiera, and her partner. The collection here is a feast for the eyes, including antique reproductions made using the finest materials, from bronze to crystal to gold. It is no surprise, then, that many noble family homes, embassies, five-star hotels and even museums pride themselves on having an original Gherardo degli Albizzi hanging from their ceiling. Prices, as you can expect, are far from cheap, to say the least. But then again, great art never is.

Alternatively, visit **Ugo Poggi**. The shop opened its doors in 1922 and has been selling delicate china dishes, high-class cutlery, and attractive dinnerware since Day One. This is the kind of place where wealthy Florentine families register for wedding gifts. Their elegant showroom is located in one of Florence's most expensive streets, Via Strozzi, ensuring its exclusive reputation. In the showroom, you can find their famous chandeliers, made with Murano glass, as well as traditional silverware and modern pieces, all of which are of superior quality and boast gorgeous designs.

Parenti, ★★★★★
Via Tornabuoni 93r, Florence.
Tel: 055.214.438,
www.parentifirenze.it.
Open Monday-Saturday 10:00 a.m.-7:30 p.m. Sunday 11:30 a.m.-7:30 p.m.

Loretta Caponi, ★★★★
Piazza Antinori 4r, Tel: 055.213.668 &
Via dlle Belle Donne 28R
Tel: 055.211.074)
www.lorettacaponi.com.
Open Monday, 3:30 p.m.-7:30 p.m.;
Tuesday-Saturday 9:00 a.m.-1:00 p.m. &
3:30 p.m.-7:30 p.m.

TAF, ★★★
Via Por. S. Maria 17r & 22r,
Tel: 055.239,6037 / 055.213.190,
www.tafricami.com.
Open Monday-Saturday, 10:00 a.m.-7:30 p.m.; Sunday, 11:00 a.m-2:00 p.m., 3:00 p.m.-7:00 p.m.

B. Del Secco, ★★★★
Via Guicciardini 20r, Florence.
Tel: 055.282.859,
www.bdelsecco.it.
Open Monday-Saturday, 10:00 a.m.-7:30 p.m.; Sunday, 11:00 a.m-2:00 p.m. & 3:00 p.m.-7:00 p.m.

Argentiere Pagliai
Borgo San Iacopo 41R, Florence. Open Monday-Friday, 9:00-13:00 & 15:30-19:30. Saturday open by appointment. Tel: 055.282840, www.argentierepagliai.it.

Argenteria Sacchi, ★★★★
Via Mortuli, 16, Florence.
Tel: 055.711.328,
www.argenteriasacchi.it.
Open Monday-Saturday, 9:00 a.m.-1:00 p.m. & 2:00 p.m.-7:00 p.m.

Gherardo Degli Albizzi, ★★★★★
Via Maggio 13, Florence.
Tel: 055.287.519,
www.gherardodeglialbizzi.com.
Open Monday-Saturday, 10:00 a.m.-1:00 p.m. & 3:00-7:00 p.m.

Poggi Ugo, ★★★★
Via Strozzi 26r, Florence.
Tel: 055.216.741,
www.ugopoggifirenze.it.
Open Monday-Saturday, 10:00 a.m.-7:00 p.m. Sunday closed. Off-season may be closed for lunch, from 1:00-3:00 p.m.

FLORENCE

 22 | **Visit the Best Gourmet Shops in Florence**
and Sip Some of the Finest Coffee in Town

Ideally, the best way to discover the joys of Tuscan cuisine is to drive around the countryside on long, leisurely day trips, hunting for the finest produce, popping into various vineyards and cheese shops, and buying wonderfully fragrant slices of prosciutto crudo and mortadella. However, even if your time is limited, and such trips are, sadly, out of the question, there are still a few shops in Florence that bring the countryside to you. These shops allow curious foodies and shameless hedonists to sample the best of the best, under one roof.

Eataly is a relatively recent addition to the Florentine scene, and a bit of a local institution. Despite the initial protests against this shop from critics who were enraged by the "commercialization of the Italian culinary tradition," so far, it seems that Eataly has done a good job of bringing many wonderful Tuscan (and Italian) delicacies to the attention of

shoppers who otherwise would not have been able to find out about them, let alone buy them. The convenient location (just 50 meters from the Duomo) means it's incredibly easy to stop by, roam the tempting aisles, and stock up on mouthwatering local produce (including the wine at the *enoteca* on the first floor). A food court at the back of the shop is open for lunch and dinner, and

a bookstore and a restaurant (Da Vinci Restaurant) on the top floor complete the experience.

If you are a fan of such markets, know that Florence's historic food market, the **Mercato Centrale**, has recently been expanded and renovated, and now includes a classy top floor filled with gourmet stands (tours and guided tastings are regularly organized here, usually on Sundays, check their website: www.mercatocentrale.it). The bottom floor continues to host the market itself, featuring several excellent gourmet shops, cheese stands, butcheries and various (mostly mediocre) eateries. Even if you don't end up buying anything, a tour of this market is highly recommended.

To conclude your hedonistic experience, stop by **Ditta Artigianale**, one of the best Caffès in Florence. This venue prides itself on a quality selection of coffee blends, a hip vibe, and a seriously professional staff. If you come in the morning, try their pastries (we especially love the pistacchio-cornetto), or the Turkish breakfast. The macchiato here is excellent, and the cold coffee beverages are equally good, especially the Mandor Latte—a double shot of espresso poured over a deeply aromatic almond syrup from Puglia, in southern Italy. If you come later in the day, try the selection of craft gin cocktails on offer.

Eataly, ★★★
Via dei Martelli 22, Florence.
Tel: 055.015.3601,
www.eataly.net.
Open daily, 10:00 a.m.–10:30 p.m.

Mercato Centrale Firenze, ★★★★
Piazza del Mercato Centrale, Florence.
www.mercatocentrale.it.

Ditta Artigianale, ★★★★
Via dello Sprone 3r, Florence.
Tel: 055.274.1541,
www.dittaartigianale.it.
Open daily, 8:00 a.m.-10:00 p.m. (until midnight in the weekends).

 # 23 | **Buy Quality, Handmade Gloves** and Shoes in Florence

For almost a century, **Madova Gloves** has produced classic designer leather gloves, and nothing else. Owned and operated by the Donnini family since 1919, the combination of tradition and highly specialized expertise ensures that if you are looking for gloves as a gift or as a souvenir of your visit to one of the greatest countries in the world for fashion, then you will not be disappointed.

For a pair of beautiful, traditionally crafted shoes, stay in the Oltrarno Quarter, which is famous for its artisanal shops and boutiques. One of the mainstays of this quaint area is the old-world workshop of the **Mannina** family. They have been crafting men's shoes since 1953 and are renowned for their skill, design ethic and precision. Another shop that is absolutely worth a visit is **Roberto Ugolini**. It is impossible not to immediately fall in love with the elegant creations of this artisan, who makes shoes to measure, and is keeping alive ancient Florentine

traditions in his studio on Piazza Santo Spirito.

Madova Gloves, ★★★★
Via Guicciardini 1r, Florence.
Tel: 055.239.6526,
www.madova.it.
Open Monday–Saturday, 10:30 a.m.–7:00 p.m. Closed Sunday.

Mannina Shoes, ★★★★
Via De' Barbadori 19r, Florence.
Tel: 055.211.060 & Via Guicciardini 16r (two locations). Tel: 055.282.895,
www.manninafirenze.com.
Open Monday–Friday 9:30 a.m.–7:30 p.m. Closed on weekends.

Roberto Ugolini, ★★★★
Via Michelozzi 17r, Florence.
www.roberto-ugolini.com.
Open Monday–Friday 10:00 a.m.–7:00 p.m. Usually closed on weekends.

 24 | **Load up on Traditional Italian** Kitchen Gear in Florence

We love that feeling of remembering that comes when you pull out a baking tray or saucepan that you bought in a little boutique in Florence, or when you chop the vegetables for a real Italian ragu with a handmade knife you bought in a hidden village in the hills of the Chianti region. Equipping yourself with Tuscan tools is one of the best ways to bring back home with you some of that Tuscan charm. Luckily, the region offers several good shops to choose from.

In Florence, we return again and again to **Bartolini**, a must-stop shop for the cooking enthusiast. Here you will find a huge collection of kitchenware, everything from pasta molds to knives to rolling pins to coffee makers. Naturally, we don't focus on international brands, but try to hunt for the occasional unique item and the classic Italian brands. If you choose just one kitchen gear shop to visit in town, this should be the one.

For a different kind of experience, visit **Coltelleria Galli**, just off Via Tornabuoni, and **Bianda Coltelleria**, in Via Vigna Nuova (which has been selling knives since 1820). These are two of the few traditional mom-and-pop shops that have survived the economic crisis, and still sell interesting, quality, handmade knives. A visit here can be fascinating, even if you don't end up buying anything.

Lastly, if you are a bit of a kitchenware enthusiast and feeling adventurous, drive up to **Scarperia,** a medieval village in northern Tuscany (about 50 minutes from Florence), that is famous for knife production. For details, see tip 30.

Bartolini, ★★★★
Via dei Servi 72r,
Tel: 055.291.497,
www.dinobartolini.it.
Open Monday–Saturday, 10:00 a.m.–7:30 p.m.

Coltelleria Galli, ★★★
Via della Spada 26r.
Tel: 055.282.410,
web.tiscali.it/coltelleriagalli.
Open Monday, 3:30 p.m.–7:30 p.m.;
Tuesday– Saturday, 9:00 a.m.–1:00 p.m. & 3:30-7:30 p.m.

Bianda Coltelleria, ★★★
Via della Vigna Nuova 86r.
Tel: 055.294.691,
www.coltelleriabianda.it.
Open Monday, 3:30 p.m.–7:30 p.m.;
Tuesday– Saturday, 9:00 a.m.–1:00 p.m. & 3:30-7:30 p.m.

Surrounding Florence

🏃 | 25 | Visit Two of the Most Beautiful Medici Villas in Tuscany

Not all of the grand villas built by the Medici family in Tuscany can be visited today, but of those that can, two in particular stand out as well-preserved architectural treasures. One is Villa La Petraia and the other is Villa in Poggio a Caiano.

Villa La Petraia is perfectly positioned in the Florentine countryside and offers an impressive view of the city from its Belvedere Terrace. This is the perfect place to get away from the crowds—take a tour of the villa itself or simply walk around the beautiful late-Renaissance gardens. This is where the Medici family spent many of their vacations, escaping the city's heat (and intrigues…) and enjoying quiet bliss, while still being close enough to the town to control their many businesses. The impressive tower is one of the oldest parts of the villa, a reminder of the mansion's past as a fortified residence, when it was still owned by the Brunelleschi family. The gardens and the beautiful frescoes were added in the late 16th century and early 17th century. The front gardens, which offer a panoramic view of Florence, are traditionally Italian, and the garden in the back is in the English style. Various rooms and hallways in the villa are still decorated with original frescoes and antique furniture, and priceless art adorns the walls, but the most impressively decorated space is the fresco-covered courtyard.

Like many Medici villas, this was later used as an official residence of Italy's royal family – the Savoias, and King Vittorio Emanuele II and his wife, Rosa Vercellana, spent many summers here. Come to visit and you'll understand why this estate was so loved. It isn't overly extravagant, just irresistibly charming, which is why we are willing to overlook the fact that the entire complex really could use a serious restoration and some TLC. Admission is free and the villa is easily accessed from Florence.

Additionally, note that just minutes from Villa Petraia is **Villa di Pratolino** (also known as Villa Demidoff), yet another famous estate built by the Medicis. And while the villa itself can't be visited, its beautiful gardens, famous for their wildly artistic tufa grottos and stunning huge statues, are open to the public and are a highly recommended stop to make.

Next, **Villa in Poggio a Caiano** is farther from Florence, located in a hillier part of Tuscany. Built under the orders of Lorenzo Medici (called "Il Magnifico"), the villa was designed by one of the leading architects of the time, Giuliano da Sangallo (he also designed the famous lion and griffin fountain in Montepulciano). The resulting villa was a huge success and the design was imitated by many architects working on other Tuscan mansions in the following years.

The inside walls are decorated with numerous beautiful works of art by artists such as Filippino Lippi, Andrea Sansovino, Pontormo and Andrea del Sarto. Two of the most significant and lavish political marriages in the Medici family took place here—Cosimo the First wed Eleonora of Toledo, and Alessandro de Medici wed Margherita of Austria. Francesco the First and Bianca Cappello were also married in this villa and died in it, both poisoned. This was even a favorite spot of Elisa Baciocchi Bonaparte, Napoleon's sister, who became the Grand Duchess of Tuscany in 1809.

Today the villa hosts a special museum with a wonderful collection of still lifes, which can be viewed by appointment only (but is often open during various holidays and festivals—call to find out more). The villa and the royal bedrooms are beautiful, and can only be visited by guided tour, which must be booked in advance. The residence has suffered somewhat from budget cuts, but now that the villa has been recognized as a UNESCO World Heritage Site, we hope it will be restored to its past glory. The best time to visit is during one of the festivals that take place in the villa, such as the *Assedio alla Villa festival* (www.assedioallavilla.it). Check the villa's website to see if anything is going on during your visit. The gardens can be visited freely without a booking.

Villa La Petraia, ★★★★
Via della Petraia 40, Località Castello, Florence. Tel: 055.238.8717, www.polomuseale.firenze.it/musei. Open daily: November-February, 8:15 a.m.-3:30 p.m.; March, 8:15 a.m.-4:30 p.m.; April, May, September and October, 8:15 a.m.-5:30 p.m.; June-August, 8:15 a.m.-6:30 p.m. Closed on major holidays. Last entry one hour before closing.

Villa di Pratolino (Parco Mediceo di Pratolino), ★★★★★
Via Fiorentina 276, Loc. Pratolino, Vaglia (about 13 km north of Florence). GPS Coordinates: 43.8596, 11.2981. The park is open April 25-November 1, Friday-Sunday only, 10:00 a.m.-8:00 p.m. (In October, the park closes at 7:00 p.m.).

Villa in Poggio a Caiano, ★★★
Piazza de Medici 14, Poggio a Caiano. Tel: 055.877.012. The villa complex (including the park, gardens and royal apartments) is open daily (closed on the second and third Tuesday of every month and on major holidays). The park and garden are open daily: October-March, 8:15 a.m.-4:30 p.m.; April-May and September, 8:15 a.m.-6:30 p.m.; June-August, 8:15 a.m.-7:30 p.m. Last entry is one hour before closing. Royal Apartments: Entry every hour, starting at 8:30 a.m. Last entry: November-February, 3:30 p.m.; March, October, 4:30 p.m.; April-May and September, 5:30 p.m.; June-August, 6:30 p.m. Entry to the Museo della Natura Morta (Museum of Still Life) is by guided tour only, and must be booked in advance. Tours leave once an hour (if a minimum number of people are present - usually around 10), starting at 9:00 a.m. (no tour at 1:00 p.m.). Last entry: November- February, 3:00 p.m.; March, October, 4:00 p.m.; April-May and September, 5:00 p.m.; June-August, 6:00 p.m.

 26 ## Hit the Best Outlet Stores in Tuscany
and Shop for Gorgeous Italian Fashion

Whether you're a fashionista or a shopaholic, if you're serious about shopping, then a visit to Tuscany's outlets is a must. Don't miss out on **The Mall**, which sits roughly 35 km from Florence. This isn't the cheapest outlet village in Tuscany, but it certainly is the most exclusive, and the perfect place to find stylish, high-end names such as Gucci, Salvatore Ferragamo, Miu Miu, Valentino and Armani. Note that right outside The Mall complex, there is also a **Fendi** outlet shop.

For leather items, you can visit the **Cuoieria Fiorentina Outlet Shop**, which is located approximately 20 minutes from the The Mall. The selection here is admittedly limited, but if you are already in the area, it is probably worth stopping by, especially during the *saldi* season.

If you have a craving for **Dolce& Gabbana** you can find just what you're looking for, along with some real bargains, at their outlet right next to The Mall.

Prada lovers should head to the company's outlet store in Montevarchi, on the way to Arezzo. Though not very cheap (discounts are usually around 30% of the wholesale price), you can sometimes find a good deal here, too. Come early, as the number of clients admitted daily is limited.

Fans of **Roberto Cavalli** will be interested in his outlet store in Sesto Fiorentino, about 20 minutes from Florence (right next to the popular shopping mall **I Gigli**). Fans of the Florentine designer **Ermanno Scervino** will want to check out his small but attractive outlet shop where the Ermanno Scervino Men's, Women's, and Junior's lines are all on sale. The store is located in Grassina, outside of Florence.

If you are looking for a mix of high-level and mid-level brands (like Levi's, Ralph Lauren, Adidas, and Wranglers along with popular Italian brands such as Guess, Motivi, and Elena Mirò), your best bet is to head out to the large outlet center in **Barberino di Mugello**, located half an hour north of Florence. Unlike the venues above, this is a quite large center, home to more than 90 shops, and it offers rather significant reductions. Another similar mid-level venue is the **Valdichiana Outlet Village**, near Arezzo, though it has a smaller and less varied selection.

The Mall, ★★★★★
Via Europa 8, Leccio Reggello (FI). GPS Coordinates: N 43° 42.130', E 011° 27.804'. Tel: 055.865.7775, www.themall.it. Open daily, 10:00 a.m.-7:00 p.m. (June-August, open until 8:00 p.m.). The Fendi shop is located at the same address, and has the same opening times.

Cuoieria Fiorentina, ★★★
Via dei Ciliegi 25, Ciliegi (Reggello). Tel: 055.866.2191, www.cuoieriafiorentina.it.

Barberino Di Mugello, ★★★★
Via Meucci (exit the autostrada at Barberino and follow the brown signs to the "outlet," not to the town of Barberino itself). Tel: 055.842.161, www.mcarthurglen.it/barberino. Open Monday-Friday, 10:00 a.m.-8:00 p.m.; Saturday-Sunday, 10:00 a.m.-9:00 p.m.

Dolce & Gabbana, ★★★★
Via S. Maria Maddalena 49, Incisa in Val d'Arno (FI). Tel: 055.833.1300. Open Monday-Saturday, 9:00 a.m.-7:00 p.m., Sunday, 3-7p.m. May be open on Sunday morning, too - call in advance.

Ermanno Scervino Private Outlet, ★★★
Via di Tizzano 169, Grassina (FI). Tel: 055.649.24395. Open Monday-Tuesday, 3:00-7:00 p.m.; Wednesday-Sunday, 10:00 a.m.-7:00 p.m.

Roberto Cavalli, ★★★★
Via Volturno 3, Sesto Fiorentino (Loc. Osmannoro). Tel: 055.317.754, www.robertocavallioutlet.it. Open Monday-Saturday, 10:00 a.m.-7:00 p.m.

Valdichiana Outlet Village, ★★★
Via Enzo Ferrari 5, Foiano della Chiana (AR). Exit the autostrada at "Valdichiana." Tel: 0575.649.926, www.valdichianaoutlet.it. Open daily, 10:00 a.m.-8:00 p.m.

Prada Outlet, ★★★★
Strada Regionale 69 (Levanella), Montevarchi. Tel: 055.978.9481. Open Sunday-Friday, 10:30 a.m.-7:30 p.m.; Saturday, 9:30 a.m.-7:30 p.m., Sunday, 10:30 a.m.-6:30 p.m. (Call in advance to make sure it is open. Hours may vary).

 27 | **Relax at the Stunning** Asmana Spa

Florence is home to some of Italy's most incredible artistic treasures. But after exploring the city's many churches, museums and exhibitions, even the most avid art-lover can feel exhausted. Luckily, we know the perfect place for travelers to recharge and relax.

Asmana is a multiple award-winning spa in the town of Campi Bisenzio, just 20 minutes from Florence. It's an easy drive if you have a car, or you can reach the facility by bus (during the day) or taxi (at night, 35 euro).

This is one of the largest spa complexes in Italy, and guests need only choose between the many services on offer, including the cocoon escape, the hay dream, the golden room , the salt room, and more. Your ticket will include entry to the Hammam, the herbal and the wine saunas, and the spa's salt pool, outdoor pool, cave pool and the foot bath. For an additional (and quite reasonable!) fee you can book one of the spa's signature massages or wellness treatments—the list of treatments is quite extensive (see their website to find out more). The on-site bistro, tropical juice bar, and the many relaxation areas complete the incredible experience.

Asmana Spa - Wellness World,
Viale Allende 10, Campi Bisenzio.
Tel: 055.776771
www.asmana.it.
Consult the detailed website to see which treatments and facilities must be booked in advance and which are free with your entry ticket and require no prior booking.

 28 | **Buy a Bottle of Laudemio** –the Highest-Quality Olive Oil

Praised by gastronomic experts and celebrities alike, Laudemio is considered by many to be the finest olive oil this part of the world has to offer. Traditionally, Laudemio was the name given to best part of any olive harvest, and it was especially reserved for the lord of the manor. For centuries, it has been said to represent the pinnacle of the taste and fragrance offered by the Tuscan oil industry. In the 1980s, twenty-one producers, many of whom could trace their lineage back to Tuscan noble families of antiquity, came together to ensure the continuing quality and exclusivity of production. To find out more about the history of the Laudemio, visit www.laudemio.it

Personally, we like the produce from **Castello di Poppiano,** home to one of the prominent members of the Laudemio Council. The Castello itself, owned by the Guicciardini family for nine centuries, is a 1,000-year-old medieval fort that was extensively renovated in the

19th century. Located between Florence and Siena in a wonderfully fertile and sun-soaked area, the estate produces olive oil that is particularly fruity and aromatic. It has won a number of prizes over the years, including the Ercole Olivario National Contest, one of Italy's most esteemed olive oil contests, securing its reputation.

Another great option is Frescobaldi Laudemio. The Frescobaldis are a centuries-old noble family with a fascinating history at the center of Florentine economic and political life. They are mostly famous for their award-winning wines, but their oil is fantastic, too. There are a number of Frescobaldi-owned estates throughout Tuscany, but **Castello di Nipozzano** is one of the most interesting, in our opinion, not least because it is also home to the much-heralded Nipozzano Chianti. Note that Frescobaldi oil (from this estate and from the charming San Donato in Perano estate) can also be tasted and purchased at the Relais Vignale agriturismo, in Radda in Chianti.

Lastly, you can also try the fine olive oil at the small, beautifully positioned **Fattoria Montecchio,** right in front of San Donato in Poggio. The farm also offers wine tastings, which are good, but overpriced, in our opinion.

Castello di Poppiano, ★★★
Via Fezzana 43, Montespertoli.
Tel: 055.82315,
www.conteguicciardini.it.
Oil and other produce can be bought directly in the castle shop, which is open Monday–Saturday, 8:30 a.m.–noon & 2:00-6:00 p.m.; Sunday, 2:30-6:30 p.m. (Though calling before leaving for the castello, especially off-season, is always highly recommended).

Castello di Nipozzano, ★★★★
Via di Nipozzano, Nipozzano, Pelago.
Tel: 055.831.1528,
www.hospitality.frescobaldi.it.
GPS Coordinates: N 43 47.091 - E 11 28.297. Tours and visits need to be booked in advance.

Fattoria Montecchio, ★★★
Via Montecchio 4, San Donato in Poggio.
Tel: 055.807.2907,
www.montecchio.it.

🏃 29 | Explore the Archeological Treasures
of Fiesole

Located just eight kilometers northeast of Florence, Fiesole is a town that bubbles with charm. Many visitors come here for the panoramic views, but in reality, there is more to see and do in town. Fiesole was founded 2800 years ago as an Etruscan stronghold. When the Romans conquered the area, they turned it into a thriving and powerful city, far larger than it is today. With time Fiesole evolved into a sort of highly exclusive "suburb" for the rich and noble folk of Florence, and many illustrious families built magnificent villas up in these hills. Today many of these mansions still exist, but are only open to group tours or on special occasions, which is why we won't review them on this itinerary. That said, if you come here between April and October, know that the Fiesole tourist office usually organizes weekly guided tours to some of these villas. Find out more here: www.fiesoleforyou.it.

Start your time in town with a visit to the **Archeological Museum** and the Etruscan-Roman Archeological Area and Amphitheater, located just a few meters from Piazza Mino. The archeological area includes the ruins of a 4th century Etruscan temple, a Langobard temple, an incredibly well-preserved Roman amphitheater dating back to the first century BC, and the ancient thermal baths. The small museum features finds from the excavations done here (though several items were moved to the much larger archeological museum in Florence). Then, walk up the steep and famous Via San Francesco, to enjoy the best views over Florence.

If you have some extra time, tour the Bandini Museum, too, which holds a small collection of medieval paintings, as well as glazed terracotta medallions and lunettes by the famous della Robbia family. Other attractions in this town are the Franciscan missionary museum and the gardens of the Peyron Villa, though in our opinion, they are somewhat less impressive.

If you find yourself here around lunchtime, our favorite spot in town is **Osteria Il Pentolino**. Tiny and very Tuscan in style, this place will conquer your heart with its reasonably priced and delicious home-made pasta, and its generous antipasti platters of prosciutto and local cheeses.

Finally, it's worth noting that in the summer months, Fiesole's amphitheater hosts several concerts and shows—see www.estatefiesolana.it for the full program.

Fiesole Archeological Park & Museum, ★★★★
Via Portigiani 1, Fiesole.
Tel: 055.5961.293, www.museidifiesole.it.
Hours: April–September, open daily, 10:00 a.m.–7:00 p.m.; November–February: Wednesday–Monday, 10:00 a.m.–3:00 p.m., closed Tuesday; March–October, open daily, 10:00 a.m.–6:00 p.m.

Osteria Il Pentolino, ★★★★
Via Matteotti 39, Fiesole.
Tel: 055.012.1125, www.ristorante.fiesole.fi.it. Open Tuesday–Sunday, 12:00 p.m.–2:00 p.m. & 7:00 p.m.–10:30 p.m. Closed Monday.

🏃 30 | Explore Hidden Corners of the Mugello Valley and Savor the Local Traditional Dishes

Parco Mediceo di Pratolino is located at the entryway to the Mugello valley and is the perfect antidote to the stress of a tourist-filled Florence in August. If you have a car, you can easily reach it in under 15 minutes. This large and delightful park was built in the 16th century by Francesco I de' Medici, Duke of Tuscany. In the past Il Pratolino was a mannerist jewel, complete with artificial grottos and labyrinths, fountains and beds of rare flowers. After the Duke's death several sections were stripped away (some were transferred to the Boboli Gardens in Florence) and the park fell into decay. Nowadays, while the park hasn't quite returned to its former glory, it does tempt visitors with manicured paths and lush green meadows, woodlands and large ponds, an ancient lemon grove, and most famous of all, the *Apennine Colossus*, a giant sculpture by Giambologna, that sits by the garden's main lake. Other, smaller works of art are scattered on the

grounds, too. The park's proximity to Villa La Petraia (see tip 25) makes it an even easier destination to include in your itinerary.

From the park, continue north to the Mugello Valley. The Mugello usually sees tourists zooming through, briefly stopping only to do some shopping at the popular Barberino di Mugello outlet shopping village (see tip 26). But curious travelers and foodies who are willing to venture off the beaten path will quickly discover that this area offers much more—pristine views, authentic Tuscan charm and a relaxing ambiance Your first stop in the valley will be **Scarperia**—a tiny and ancient village that was founded as a Florentine outpost, surveilling the road going north to Bologna. However, Scarperia quickly gained notoriety for something else—its high-quality knife production. In fact, Scarperia has been sharpening its tools since the 12th century, and over the past 900 years, it has become synonymous with top-quality cutlery.

The main attraction here is simply walking around and visiting the many knife shops, which sell some magnificent pieces. Our favorite boutique is **Coltellerie Giglio Scarperia**—their studio looks like something out of a fairy tale; heavy wooden tables are covered with gorgeous knives and blades, wooden spoons and beautiful copper pots, many of which were handmade by the owner's 90-year-old uncle.

The town's lesser-known but charming monuments are worth exploring, too, including the 14th century Palazzo dei Vicari whose façade is covered with family emblems of local noble families, and the quirky knife museum, which feature an eccentric little collection of scissors and knives. The best time to visit Scarperia is during one of the town's many festivals: on the first Sunday of September, the town celebrates Renaissance Day and is filled with colorful costumes and music; on Diotto (September 8), the town reenacts its founding by the Florentines; and on the last Sunday of May, during the Infiorata, the town is covered in flowers, and petals are used to create huge and colorful mosaics on various piazzas.

Once you have completed your tour here, it's time for lunch. There are a number of good restaurants in the area, but our absolute favorite is **Ristorante La Limonaia di Villa Senni.** This is not the sort of agriturismo and restaurant that would normally pique our curiosity, but somehow or other we ended up here, and what was supposed to be a quick lunch on the go turned into one of our best meals in this area. Everything we tried here was delicious (note that the menu is seasonal, and you may find completely different dishes, depending on the time of your visit): Their lemon tagliolini are fantastic,

and so is the peposo—a Tuscan version of Boeuf Bourguignon, made strictly with locally grown Chianina beef, cooked for hours in Chianti wine, and served with creamy borlotti beans. If you are visiting in the fall, try the polenta with fresh porcini mushrooms, the Tuscan ham cocoli, or the beef tartar.

Parco Mediceo di Pratolino (Parco Villa Demidoff), ★★★★
Pratolino, Vaglia. The entrance to the park is located across the street from the the Gigante Adventure Park. The easiest way to reach the park is to exit Florence along Via Bolognese, all the way to Vaglia. The park is open April–October, 8:00 a.m.–sunet.

Coltellerie Giglio, ★★★★
Via dell'Oche 48, Scarperia.
Tel: 055.846.9936,
www.coltelleriegiglio.it.

Ristorante La Limonaia di Villa Senni, ★★★★
Via Senni-San Carlo 5, Scarperia.
Tel: 055.845.7616, cell: 338.723.4233,
www.lalimonaiadisenni.com. Open Thursday–Sunday for lunch and dinner, Monday open for dinner only, closed Tuesday. Hours may vary off season, call before driving over.

Chianti

🏃 | 31 | Visit the Chianti Sculpture Park

The **Chianti Sculpture Park** was founded by Rosalba and Piero Giadrossi, a husband and wife team with a passion for contemporary art. This unique and beautiful open-air museum, located in the heart of the hills of Chianti just half an hour north of Siena, is filled with sculptures by artists from around the world. The park was opened in 2004, and is set on seven hectares of woodland. We love coming here in the late afternoon to stroll around in the fresh, scented air. The park is the first initiative in a process that is meant to eventually transform Pievasciata, the hamlet where it is located, into a B.A.C—Borgo d'Arte Contemporanea (contemporary art hamlet). The philosophy of this park centers on combining art and nature, giving voice to artists from 19 countries (and counting) from around the world who use different materials and styles to create their artwork. This is a true mosaic of art and nature. Among the artists who have their work on display here are Neal Barab and Benbow

Bullock from the USA, Jeff Saward and William Furlong from the UK, and Nicolas Bertoux from France.

From June to August, you can extend the day by attending the weekly classical and jazz concerts. Arrive early to get a good seat. You can also combine a visit to the park with a tour of Vagliagli (a tiny medieval *borgo* 11 kilometers north of the park, with gorgeous views of the entire area from the top of the hill), or a wine tasting session at one of the nearby estates in Castelnuovo Berardenga, Siena or Gaiole in Chianti.

Chianti Sculpture Park, ★★★★★
S.P. 9, Loc. La Fornace 48/49, Pievasciata (near Castelnuovo Berardenga), GPS Coordinates: Long. E. 11° 22' 53." Download detailed driving instructions from their website. Lat. N. 43° 23' 36". Tel: 0577.357.151, www.chiantisculpturepark.it. Open daily, March–November, 10:00 a.m.-sunset.; Off-season (November–March), it is recommended that you call first, as the park may be closed to visitors.

 32 Visit Castello di Ama for a Unique Experience, Combining Excellent Wine with Beautiful Modern Art

One of the region's finest wineries and also a contemporary art gallery, **Castello di Ama** is a personal favorite and a very special place that absolutely merits a visit. Since 2000, in collaboration with Galleria Continua of San Gimignano, the winery has commissioned a number of installations that are strategically placed throughout the estate by the likes of Louise Bourgeois, Anish Kapoor, Michelangelo Pistoletto, and Chen Zhen. The internationally renowned modern art in the castle gives a visit here a different kind of feel than you would encounter on any other Tuscan wine tour.

The current winery was founded by a number of local families in the 1960s. In those days before wine tourism, this was still a poor area, but the families involved believed they could restore the medieval castle to its former glory and create an exceptional product, an award-winning Chianti Classico. They were quite right, and since that time their

wines have won numerous accolades. Today the castle is run by Lorenza Sebasti and Marco Pallanti, who have continued the successes of Castello di Ama. They have received several honorable mentions, and in 2005, were even chosen as the winery of the year by the prestigious Gambero Rosso guide. Undoubtedly, their greatest claim to fame was when, in a blind tasting, their l'Apparita wine beat the world-famous Chateau Petrus.

There are a number of tours available, from the *Ama Anthology tour,* which offers exposure to the castle's various wines and olive oils, to the more specific *Discovering the Crus tour,* which focuses on various vintages of one of the estate's four specific crus: Castello di Ama, Vigneto Bellavista, Vigneto La Casuccia, and L'Apparita. Tours and tastings must be booked in advance. Though the tours are highly recommended, as they enable you to explore the grounds and see all of the artwork, you can also freely visit the estate, buy a glass of wine from the *enoteca* and wander around the property, soaking in its beauty. You can also stop for a tasty lunch at the estate's small diner.

Don't leave without picking up a bottle of their wine to take home with you (we love the Haiku 2009 and the Al Poggio 2011, but even an "entry level" wine like the Ama 2010 is excellent), and bottle of Castello di Ama olive oil, which is absolutely delicious.

Castello di Ama, ★★★★★
Località Ama, Gaiole in Chianti, GPS Coordinates LAT: 43° 26' 28" N e LONG: 11° 23' 21" E. Tel: 0577.746.031, Cell: 335.774.6188, www.castellodiama.com

🏃 33 | Book a Fun and Delicious Cooking Class in Chianti

Castelnuovo Berardegna is a delightful little town in the very heart of the Chianti region. Surrounded by vineyards that stretch as far as the eye can see, it is the perfect location for a fun and authentic Tuscan cooking class, such as the one offered by **Nonna Ciana.** It started small and was known to few, but over time it has become a popular attraction, thanks to the friendly owners and the very enjoyable experience they offer, so make sure you book your spot well in advance.

Lessons are held on the family farm, and are led by Grandma (*nonna*) Ciana herself. Your menu will include handmade and rolled pasta or gnocchi; various antipasti; a main dish, such as chicken in *vin santo*; and a delectable dessert such as pannacotta. Naturally, the menu is seasonal, and in most cases can be adapted to your specific dietary needs, should you have any.

Alternatively, consider the cooking lessons offered by **Tenuta Casanova.** This lovely agriturismo has built a reputation for itself, and today their cooking classes draw quite a crowd. The 20 hectares of vineyards and burnt yellow farmland is located between Poggibonsi and Castellina in the Chianti region. The drive up to the estate, along a winding road surrounded by vineyards and cypress

forest, will put you in the right mood for the culinary experience that awaits you.

The cooking classes here are a full-day activity. For six or seven hours, visitors learn many secrets of Tuscan cuisine, beginning with the preparation of fresh pasta such as ravioli and tagliatelle. You will, of course, also make a Tuscan *secondo* (main dish), usually meat-based; and a *contorno*—a side dish of cooked vegetables. Rita, the friendly chef leading the course, will even teach you the recipe for her famous tiramisù. All this is accompanied by tastings of the wines produced on this estate. To round things off, you even get a chance to try their 30-year-old balsamic vinegar served over ice cream. The classes cater to groups of eight maximum, so book in advance, as this attraction is popular. There is also an optional hour-long tour of the estate and the wine cellar, led by Silvano, which includes wine tasting as well as a chance to try their range of vinegars, olive oils, and honey. Remember, though, that the real highlight here is the cooking class. The wine is by no means bad, but it doesn't exactly rank among the top wines in Tuscany.

Finally, another fun cooking class absolutely worth considering is **Toscana Mia**. Run by two friendly Italian cooks, Simonetta and Paola, this is a laid-back and hands-on introduction to the magic of Tuscan cooking. During your half-day course you will prepare a five-course meal, featuring staples of the local kitchen. The best part, of course, is when you enjoy the fruits of your labor and feast on the meal you have prepared, accompanied by the good wine offered by the owners. Family cooking classes, and 3- or 4-day

cooking courses can be organized.

Nonna Ciana Cooking Class,
★★★★★
Farmhouse Le Pietre Vive di Montaperti di Nicola Guerrini, Strada di Monteapertaccio 1, Loc. Monteaperti, Castelnuovo Berardenga.
Cell: 333.466.3208,
www.lepietrevive.it /
www.cookingclassesnonnaciana.com.

Tenuta Casanova, ★★★
Località Sant'Agnese 20, Castellina in Chianti. GPS Coordinates: latitude 43°28'37.1"N, longitude 11°13'33.1"E (may appear in your GPS as "Caselle di Sant'Agnese"). Cell: 335.615.0760,
www.tenutacasanova.it

Toscana Mia, ★★★★
Podere Le Rose, Località Poggio S.Polo 2, Gaiole in Chianti. GPS coordinates: 43.446948, 11.378546.
Cell: 334.247.6098 (8:00 am - 9:00 pm CET), Paola and Simonetta.
www.toscanamia.net.

34 | **Visit Tuscany's Most Famous Butcher** and Stop for a Lively Dinner!

Dario Cecchini's **Antica Macelleria** draws quite a crowd, and not just because of the excellent meat. Cecchini's vibrant, larger-than-life personality has made this an institution in Italy. A true Tuscan host, he often welcomes his guests with a few lines from Dante's *Divina Commedia*. You may even be treated to a glass of Chianti and a piece of bread smeared with aromatized lard while you wait in line to get your teeth into one of his famous steaks. As the eighth generation in a long line of butchers, Cecchini comes from a strong tradition. It's just as well that the art of butchery is in his blood, as he had no choice but to enter the family business when his parents died at a young age, leaving him to take care of the family. Giving up his dreams of becoming a vet (a little ironic, perhaps, given the restaurant's defiantly carnivorous philosophy), Cecchini combined this long tradition with his natural charm and PR skills, making himself famous at home and abroad in the process.

In the evening, the small restaurant adjacent to the butcher shop opens and dinner is served. Here people feast on steak tartar, fondly called *"Sushi del Chianti"*, cold cuts, and, of course, the highlight of the meal—a traditional *bistecca Fiorentina*, Florentine steak; it is a huge undertaking, seared on the outside and almost rare on the inside. The dining experience resembles a medieval feast: Everyone sits together and gorges, wine is poured again and again into newly emptied glasses, and the smell from the roaring grill will, at some point, confuse your senses.

There are two seatings a day, for lunch (1:00 p.m.) and for dinner (8:00 p.m.), and, as Cecchini puts it, are recommended for those who have a hearty appetite. (Hours and days may vary, call first!). The fixed price is very reasonable at around €50 per person with wine included, though you can bring your own bottle if you prefer. There is also a vegetarian menu available, but it is very limited, and, to be honest, if you're looking for a vegetarian meal, this not the place to choose. Cecchini's is for proud meat-lovers, a self-proclaimed "Paradise for Carnivores." In any case, book well in advance, especially during high season, as this place is popular.

Serious foodies may also be interested in Cecchini's 3-hour workshop, which is held every Friday (very interesting but costly at €200). If you have rented a villa or apartment in the area, and interested in buying a *bistecca Fiorentina* to take home and cook ⅃ your friends and family, make sure you book it a few days in advance.

Antica Macelleria Cecchini, ★★★★
Via XX Luglio 11, Panzano di Greve in Chianti. Tel: 055.852.020, www.dariocecchini.com. Open daily, 9:00 a.m.–4:00 p.m., hours may vary off-season. Dinner is served at 8:00 p.m. and should be booked in advance.

🏃 35 | Visit the World-Famous Antinori *Cantina*
- An Unmissable Treat for Architecture Lovers and Wine Enthusiasts

Since 1385, the wines produced by the Antinori family have been a symbol of quality and class. Today the business is run by the Marquis Piero Antinori and his three daughters Albiera, Allegra, and Alessia, which are the 26th generation to run the family estates. The current owners stress both a connection to tradition and a desire to innovate and constantly improve the quality of their product. This is no small brand; just in Tuscany, the family owns a number of estates (and several others around Italy and the world), the most famous of which are Peppoli, Guado al Tasso and, of course, the world-renowned Tignanello estate.

Visiting the newly renovated **Antinori Cantina** is, in our opinion, a must-do experience. At €20 per person, including a tasting of 4 wines, it is also a very good deal. The cellar is highly recommended, not just for the wine, but also to admire the stunning and singular

structure itself. In fact, the design has drawn considerable attention from architects and critics around the world, and was elected as one of the most interesting *cantine* in Europe by several critics. The tour itself is serious and informative, and despite the size of the groups (up to 20 people), manages to maintain a certain intimacy. The tasting at the end, of course, is delicious. As far as the wines go, buying a few bottles from one of the Antinori lines is a guaranteed success. For a (relatively) reasonable price you can get an excellent bottle, such as the Cervaro Della Sala, or Solaia 2010, which received excellent reviews from just about every major wine critic. An equally good value is a 2007 Tignanello, or a Marchese Antinori Chianti Classico Riserva 2009, which is a wonderfully balanced, reasonably priced, delicious wine and one of our personal favorites. Visits

should be booked in advance, on Antinori's website: www. hospitalityantinorichianticlassico.it.

Should all that wine and art make you hungry, know that there is a restaurant on the premises, which is recommended for a quick lunch if you are visiting in September or October (when trucks come and unload the grapes into the winery right in front of your eyes). For a more serious experience, we would recommend dining at another Antinori establishment: Osteria di Passignano, a wonderful, delicious, Michelin-starred restaurant located just 20 minutes away from the estate (see next tip).

Antinori nel Chianti Classico (Bargino) Estate, ★★★★★

Via Cassia per Siena 133, Loc. Bargino, San Casciano Val di Pesa. GPS Coordinates 43° 36′ 43:30″, 11° 11′ 29.76″. The *cantina* is open daily April 1–October 30, 11:00 a.m.–6:00 p.m. (until 7:00 p.m. from June to late October); July 1–August 31, same hours, but the cantina is closed on Sunday; November 1–March 30, the *cantina* is open Wednesday-Monday, 11:00 a.m.–4:00 p.m., closed on Tuesday. Note: A visit to the *cantina* during its hours of operation will permit you to purchase wine and see the entrance to the building, but you won't be able to tour the entire facility or see its unique structure without **booking a tour** in advance. Tours usually leave 8 times a day, from 10:00 a.m. to 5:00 p.m., every hour on the hour, and are available in English, too.

🍴 36 | **Embark On an Exclusive Tour of the Antinori Badia a Passignano** Cellar and End with an Incredible Meal at the Osteria di Passignano

A visit to the vineyards and cellars of Badia a Passignano feels like a trip back in time. Located in the classic Chianti region, in a 700-year-old monastery and *borgo* that is still inhabited by Vallombrosan monks, this area is suffused with history.

The original Passignano Abbey was built in 395 AD and maintained its reputation for centuries. In fact, Galileo Galilei was once a teacher there. As such, a tour of the *Badia* is no ordinary afternoon spent wine tasting; it is a truly special experience.

The tours of the estate vary, and range from simple visits to more elaborate excursions that also include lunch. "Badia a Passignano and the great Antinori wines," for example, at €180, includes a 4-hour visit with an expert guide to the vineyards and the historic wine cellars in the abbey. You will learn about wine production, take part in some olive oil tasting and

have dinner at the Osteria on-site. Your meal will be accompanied by some of Antinori's signature wines: Chianti Classico Riserva Badia a Passignano, Tignanello, Guado al Tasso, Brunello di Montalcino, and Solaia (all considered some of the

best in Tuscany). Given the price of a dinner in the osteria and the price of the wines, this is actually a reasonable offer worth considering (do check the menu offered with this tour, first, to see if it is to your liking). Alternatively, a tour of the historic cellars in the abbey and a tasting of Chianti Classico Riserva, Solaia, and Guado al Tasso—all three are excellent, award-winning wines—can be organized daily for groups of at least four, at 4:30 in the afternoon, for around €80. Prices, dates, and timetables change, so do check everything on their website, book in advance, and take the time to read their cancellation policy.

Wine aside, whether you tour the estate or not, the **osteria** is a highly recommended venue, perfect for a special lunch or dinner. Situated in a lovely renovated farmhouse, it offers one of the best dining experiences in Tuscany, and justifies its Michelin star. Modern dishes, beautiful presentation and a very local menu are featured, and you can enjoy dishes such as cannelloni filled with lamb and served on a lemony zabaione; roast pigeon served with caramelized tropea onions; baccalà gnocchi; and more (note that vegetarian options in this restaurant are extremely limited). Whatever you order, you can expect a perfectly executed culinary experience. In fact, we can still remember a dish called "four versions of an artichoke," served in season, naturally, that we enjoyed a couple of years back in this osteria,

and it remains one of the best dishes we've had in Tuscany.

The small *enoteca* at the entrance of the restaurant offers guests the possibility of organizing a little impromptu tasting. Of course, you can also pick up a bottle to take home with you. The selection here is wide, including some rare bottles, but there is no need to spend a fortune; some mid-range wines are available, too. The shop is open Monday–Saturday, 10:00 a.m.–7:30 p.m.

Osteria Badia di Passignano,
★★★★★
Via Passignano 33, Loc. Badia a Passignano, Tavarnelle Val di Pesa. (The osteria is located right at the entrance to the tiny village of Badia di Passignano. You will see it immediately on your right.)
Tel: 055.807.1278,
www.osteriadipassignano.com.
Open Monday-Saturday, 12:15-2:15 p.m. & 7:30-10:00 p.m. Closed Sunday and for winter break (usually late January-early March, check website for details).

🏃 | 37 | Book a Moonlight or Early Morning Horseback Ride across the Rolling Hills of the Chianti Region

The **Berardenga Riding School** in Podere Santa Margherita offers day tours as well as moonlight tours across the rolling Chianti hills. Sadio and Donatella, the owners, have turned their passion for horses and country living into their profession by opening an organic farm holiday and riding center in a particularly beautiful part of Tuscany.

A variety of riding itineraries in the countryside are on offer, but we suggest talking to the owners, and based on your experience they will find the perfect tour for you, starting with an introductory lesson. The summer moonlight tour is especially romantic and recommended. A full-day ride and picnic will cost around €110. This place is no-frills, but packed with charm, and the surrounding views in this vineyard-covered part of Tuscany are spectacular.

Naturally, there are a few more options available. If you are leaving from Florence, you can book a horseback riding adventure with **Fun in Tuscany**, a popular tour operator that offers a variety of activities and tours throughout Tuscany, including horseback rides. Their tours are well organized and reasonably priced, and cater to various tastes and abilities.

Lastly, **Horses & Vineyards** offer riding adventures that are combined with some wine tasting, for a truly hedonistic adventure... Tours can be adapted even for those who have no previous riding experience. Tours leave daily (twice a day in high season), cost around €110, and must be booked in advance.

Berardenga Riding School, ★★★
Podere Santa Margherita, Strada del Ciglio 2, Castelnuovo Berardenga.
Tel: 0557.355071, Cell: 339.831.8519,
www.chiantiriding.it.

Fun in Tuscany, ★★★
www.funintuscany.com.

Horses & Vineyards, ★★★
www.horsesandvineyards.com.

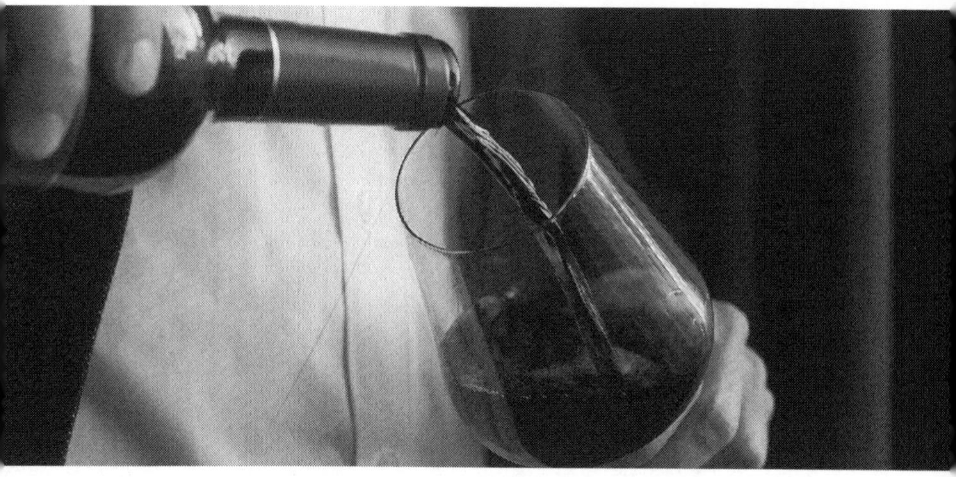

38 Soak Up the Authentic Tuscan Charm of Barberino Val d'Elsa's Two Historic Wineries

Castello Monsanto and Castello Paneretta are two of the most impressive estates connected to wine production in northern Chianti. They are located right next to each other, in the town of Barberino Val d'Elsa, just 20 minutes from Florence. Surprisingly, both estates have remained relatively off most tourists' radar, and that is perhaps a blessing. But those who do come here will be rewarded with beautiful views, fine wines, and an interesting visit.

Castello Monsanto was originally built in the 18th century but over the years it changed hands and fell into decay. In 1962 Fabrizio Bianchi and his wife Giuliana received the estate as a wedding gift from the groom's father, and took it upon themselves to breathe new life and energy into the land.

Your tour here will include a tasting, naturally, and a visit to the Monsanto cellar, which is without a doubt the highlight of any visit to the castle.

The Paneretta Castle sits farther up the same road, on a privileged spot overlooking the western slopes of Elsa valley. The castle's nucleus dates back to the 13th century, but the estate was expanded over the years, especially during the Renaissance. Historic documents show that wine has been produced here as far back as 1596, and the current owners pay their respects to this tradition by only planting local varieties of grapes, specifically Sangiovese and Canaiolo Nero, which they carefully select to maintain an autoctonous genetic profile.

Your tour here will include a guided visit to the cellar and the wine making facilities, followed by a tasting in the beautifully frescoed noble dining halls or outside, in the delightful garden. Visits must be booked in advance, and guests can choose between the standard wine tasting experience and the light lunch tour.

To complete your visit to this area, stop at the town of **Barberino Val d'Elsa** itself. Quiet, charming and delightfully Tuscan, this hilltop village makes for a nice break with the crowds. The greatest pleasure here is to simply wander around, discover hidden corners of beauty, pop into the occasional shop, and take in the views. History lovers will enjoy two more sights nearby—the church of Sant'Appiano, which is one of the oldest churches in Tuscany with origins that date back to Etruscan times, and the miniature church of San Michele in Fonte, which is an exact replica (on a scale of 1:8) of Florence's Duomo. Both churches are located outside of Barberino itself.

For lunch, Barberino offers a couple of fantastic choices for foodies. **Bird alla Pergola** is a modern farm-to-table restaurant with outside seating overlooking a spectacular view. Book (in advance) a table on the terrace, and enjoy fresh, light dishes such as the cheese antipasti platter, the ravioli with a fragrant ragu, and the tagliatelle with truffle shavings.

Meat lovers, on the other hand, might prefer the thick grilled steaks and generous cold cuts antipasti platter served at **I Nostrano**. This small eatery sits by the Staggia Fortress in the nearby town of Poggibonsi, and draws mostly a local crowd.

Castello della Paneretta, ★★★★
Strada della Paneretta 35 50021 Barberino Val d'Elsa
Tel: 055.8059003,
www.castellodellapaneretta.com.

Fattoria di Monsanto, ★★★★
Via Monsanto 8 Barberino Val D'Elsa
Tel: 055.8059000 Cell: 055.8059049,
www.castellodimonsanto.it

Bird alla Pergola, ★★★
Via Guidacci 35, Vico D'Elsa.
Tel: 055.807.3017.

I'Nostrano, ★★★
Via Romana 25, Staggia, Poggibonsi (near the Staggia Fortress).
Tel: 0577.174.1204.
Open daily for lunch,

🏃 39 | **Discover the Stunning Terracotta Art** of Impruneta

Ask any true Tuscan where to buy the best terracotta pots, reliefs, wine amphoras and tiles, and the answer will always be the same: Impruneta, of course. Terracotta is a reddish unglazed type of earthenware, and Impruneta, a sleepy town at the entryway to the Chianti region, has been famous for it since Etruscan times. But it was during the Renaissance that Impuneta truly gained notoriety, as leading artists came here in search for impeccable quality. Even famed architect Filippo Brunelleschi built Florence's famous Duomo dome with tiles from Impruneta, knowing that the local terracotta boasts a unique chemical composition that makes it particularly resistant.

There are several noteworthy workshops in town. Start at **Masini**, one of the oldest kilns in Impruneta, where the selection of hand-made objects is quite stunning. Next, don't skip **Sergio Ricceri**. This small shop is known for making reproductions of famous works by the Della Robbia family. **Pesci Giorgio** and **Ugo Poggi** are two more highly recommended shops, and both are located outside Impruneta itself (just a couple of minutes by car). Both offer a wonderful collection of objects of various sizes, and art lovers are sure to find a special piece to take back home with them.

Fornace Masini,
Via delle Fornaci 57, Impruneta.
Tel: 055.2011683, www.fornacemasini.it

Pesci Giorgio & Figli,
Via Chiantigiana per Ferrone 36.
Loc. Falciani, Impruneta.
Tel: 055.232.6285,
www.terrecottepescigiorgio.com.

Poggi Ugo,
Via Imprunetana per Tavarnuzze 16, Impruneta.
Tel: 055.201.1077, www.poggiugo.it.

40 | **Taste Great Wine** in a Real Castle!

When it comes to wine tasting, we personally love the smaller places—those intimate, family-run *tenute* (estates), where you can meet locals who have been working lovingly on the land for many years. In these little spots, you can often find excellent, award-winning wines as well as a warm local atmosphere. That said, it would be a shame to end your Tuscany tour without visiting one of the region's largest and most famous castles, too. These incredibly impressive estates have belonged to the oldest noble wine-producing families in the region for centuries, and still maintain a great deal of charm (as well as excellent products).

Both Castello di Brolio and Castello di Meleto are a notable and important part of Tuscan tradition. Both are citadels with histories that stretch back hundreds of years. These are places where tradition, history, and great wines come together. Of course, they are not small discoveries hidden from scores of tourists, but we still recommend them highly, as they offer visits that will certainly leave an impression.

Castello di Brolio is an enchanting place, even when groups of tourists come to visit, which is often the case during the summer months. Owned by the Ricasoli family since 1141, this stunning castle is the oldest winery in the world and today is a staple name in the Italian wine industry. You must taste their Chianti while in Tuscany for the simple reason that this is the family who first produced Chianti wine—in 1872, Baron Bettino Ricasoli, who also served as Italy's second prime minister during his lifetime, came up with the modern formula for Chianti wine: 70% Sangiovese, 15% Canaiolo, and 15% Malvasia bianca grapes.

The castle itself is very interesting from an architectural point of view. What you see today is a reconstruction in Gothic style that was ordered by Baron Bettino in

the 1800s. Before that, the castle had been destroyed and rebuilt a number of times due to its strategic importance to the city of Florence. The most recent damage was inflicted during World War II; shrapnel holes can still be spotted in the castle's façade. The setting is beautiful, with nature visible in every direction. The castle is surrounded by 240 hectares of vineyards, and beyond that are forests and rolling hills; on a clear day, you can even see Siena in the distance. Inside the castle are a chapel and the family crypt, as well as numerous wonderfully decorated rooms. You can also take a walk through the castle's well-manicured gardens, though you should be careful at night, as legend has it that the ghost of Baron Bettino still stalks the grounds when there is a full moon—and he is cranky!

There are a number of tours you can book, all of which require a reservation in advance. The classic tour allows you to delve into the considerable history of the Ricasoli family. According to their own account, they are the fourth oldest family in the world. Alternatively, you can take their wine production tour, which includes a visit to the cellars. Picking up a bottle from their *enoteca* is part of the fun, and you can choose from their many delectable wines, particularly the Rocca Guicciarda, the Brolio, and the Casalferro. You can stop here for lunch too, but to be honest, there are better options in the area, from a culinary point of view.

Castello di Meleto is smaller but offers a more personable visit. Like Castello di Brolio, this citadel is located in Gaiole in Chianti and has a history that dates back to the 11th century. Once the property of Benedictine monks, it later fell into the hands of a local noble family before eventually being given by Emperor Fredrick I to the Ricasoli-Firidolfis, which have owned it since the 1200s. In the intervening centuries, the castle has had an eventful history, largely due to its strategically important position between Siena and Florence.

Set among lush green trees and well-kept gardens, the castle is lovely. A grand stone structure replete with turrets on two of its corners, it is surrounded by cypresses and a number of smaller buildings. The grounds stretch for about 1,000 acres with 135 of that taken up by vineyards. Calm and serene, this is a truly stress-free location, perfect for a relaxing day out. Tours of the castle can be booked in advance, or you can just stop at their *enoteca* for a tasting. A 30-minute tour will take you to the beautifully frescoed rooms on the main floor, as well as the impressive 18th century wine cellar. A number of apartments and B&B rooms are also available—prices fluctuate greatly depending on the time of year, and are available on their website.

Lastly, **Castello Albola** is much smaller than the other two castles reviewed in this tip, but what it lacks in size it makes up for in rustic charm and authenticity. The wine produced here is fantastic (in fact, it was recently named one of the best 100 bottles in the world by Wine Spectator magazine), the tour is intimate, and the dramatic scenery which surrounds this small

castle makes it a stop absolutely worth making. Guided tours of the historic cellar and the vineyards are organized regularly during high season (April-November).

Castello di Brolio - Barone Ricasoli, ★★★

Loc. Madonna a Brolio, Gaiole di Chianti. GPS: LAT. 43° 24′ 56″ N LONG. 11° 27′ 31″ E (do not type Brolio into your GPS, use the coordinates instead). Tel: 0577.7301, www.ricasoli.it.
The castle itself is private property and cannot be toured. The gardens, winery, and other public spaces can be visited on a guided tour. Tours usually take place March-late October, daily. Consult their website to find out more.

Castello di Meleto, ★★★

Gaiole in Chianti. GPS coordinates: LAT. 43.44992 | LONG. 11.42302, Tel: 0577.749129, www.castellomeleto.it.
The enoteca is open April-October, 10:30 a.m.-6:00 p.m. Off-season, the enoteca is open occasionally, but on weekends only. Tours of the castle take place year-round, daily, and must be booked in advance. The 30-minute tour includes a visit to the castle itself, the historic cellar, and the small theater on the premises. Cooking classes, as well as other specific tours, can also be organized. Naturally, advance booking is necessary.

Castello Albola, ★★★★

Via Pian d'Albola 31, Radda in Chianti. GPS coordinates: N43° 31.33, E11° 24.22. Tel: 0577.738019, www.albola.it.
Tours of the castle and the vineyards are held April-November, daily, at 12:00 p.m. and at 5:00 p.m. Additionally, the castle's enoteca is open March-November, daily, 10:00 a.m.-6:30 p.m. (until 4:00 p.m. Off season). The castle may close down for a winter break (call before driving here off season). To book a tour call 0577.738019, or email: accoglienza@albola.it.

🏃 41 | **Rent a Bicycle, Electric Bike or Vespa**
and Hit the Chianti Hills for a Nature-Filled Day

Riding along the winding Chianti roads is a real pleasure. So the question, in our opinion, isn't "Should I do it?" but "Which transportation do I prefer?"

Whether you prefer a bicycle, electric bike or scooter, **Ramuzzi** in Greve in Chianti can help—they are a one-stop shop, and offer a variety of vehicles that can be rented for reasonable daily fees (including insurance). Consult their website to find out more and to book your vehicle of choice.

Chianti Bike in Tavarnuzze (northern Chianti, 20 minutes from Florence) offers a similar service and has a good selection of bicycles for rent (though they currently don't offer electric bikes). Guided tours with various itineraries can be organized, too. **On the Road In Chianti** (in San Casciano Val di Pesa, 15 minutes from Florence) offers Trekking bikes, electric bikes and hybrid bikes, and will be happy to recommend the best itineraries to explore.

Hello Florence & Chianti is a friendly tour operator located right on the main piazza in Greve in Chianti. They offer bike rentals and guided bike tours, as well as various other tours and activities, everything from wine tasting to horseback rides.

Experienced riders who seek a guided tour will enjoy the activities offered by Tuscany **MTB Guide**. These professional tours use the most panoramic trails in the region, and pass through top spots such as Badia di Passignano, Panzano, and Val di Pesa. Please note that these tours are not geared for inexperienced riders; the Chianti area is quite hilly and difficult to

ride. For the less experienced, an electric bike or Vespa would be a much better option.

Officina Ramuzzi, ★★★
Via Italo Stecchi 23, Greve in Chianti.
Tel: 055.853.037,
www.ramuzzi.com.

Chianti Bike, ★★★
Via Cassia 109, Tavarnuzze,
Tel: 055.202.0004,
www.chiantibike.com.

On the Road in Chianti, ★★★
Borgo Sarchiani 26, San Casciano Val di Pesa. Tel: 055.820.242,
www.ontheroadinchianti.com.

Hello Florence & Chianti, ★★★
Piazza Matteotti 11, Greve in Chianti.
Tel: 055.853.606,
www.helloflorence.net.

MTB Bike, ★★★
Via Quintole per le Rose 44, Impruneta.
Cell: 338.687.3530,
www.tuscanymtbguide.it.

🏃 42 | **Visit one of the Best Farmers' Markets** in the Chianti Hills

If you've rented a Tuscan Villa, or even an apartment, then buying fresh produce at a nearby farmers' market and cooking an authentic Tuscan meal on your own can be a real treat. The only trick is knowing where to go, and when. Luckily, this tip will point you in the right direction.

Each of the towns in the Chianti region prides itself on its very own (and very small) weekly market. Impruneta, Barberino Val d'Elsa, Greve in Chianti and Castellina in Chianti all hold their markets on Saturday mornings; Colle Val d'Elsa holds a slightly larger market on Friday mornings, and Gaiole in Chianti hosts its little market every two weeks, on Mondays. In our opinion your best bet is heading to Greve in Chianti, on Saturday mornings.

Greve hosts the largest farmers' market in the area, and since there are a number of specialty shops here, too, all conveniently located right off the main piazza,

you'll be able to find everything you might need for a real Tuscan feast. Additionally, in high season (between the months of June and August), Greve in Chianti also hosts on the third Thursday of every month a popular event known as Stelle e Mercanti. Half market half town festival, this event takes place in the evening and draws quite a crowd. Several stands line the main piazza, including food stands, artist booths and live music.

¶|43 **Enjoy a Splendid Meal** at One of the Best Restaurants in Tuscany–Il Ristoro di Lamole

Delicious food, an incredible view and excellent wine? Sounds like a plan to us. **Ristoro di Lamole sits** on a panoramic hill, eight kilometers outside Greve in Chianti and offers a perfect experience for lunch or an early dinner. The sumptuous vista is one of the restaurant's greatest assets; from the outside terrace you can see for miles over the green Tuscan countryside, and the sunsets here are stunning. Inside, the dining area is simple and comfortable. We also love their kitchen philosophy: good, fresh produce, prepared and presented in a modern, elegant style, while still maintaining that old-fashioned and authentic Tuscan charm.

Try dishes like rabbit with fried vegetables, tagliatelle with porcini mushrooms, and the pork. You can't go wrong, everything we tried here was excellent. Combine these with a bottle of Lamole's Chianti, and you are sure to have a lovely time.

This restaurant isn't cheap, but it isn't excessively expensive either, given the location and the standard of the cuisine. Make sure you book a table on the terrace to enjoy the view.

Ristoro di Lamole, ★★★★★
Via lamole 6, Greve in Chianti.
Tel: 055.854.7050,
www.ristorodilamole.it.
Open daily, 12:30 p.m.–3:00 p.m. &
7:00 p.m.–9:30 p.m. Days and hours of operation vary off-season.
Booking a table in advance is highly recommended

Visit the Beautiful Village of San Gusme
and Explore Little-Known Elite Wineries

44

The area that stretches between Siena and the minuscule village of San Gusme offers some of the most enchanting views in Tuscany, and this alone, in our opinion, is reason enough to drive here. Naturally, the fantastic wine that can be found on every corner, seals the deal.

Start your morning by driving from Siena east to the tiny hamlet of San Gusmè along the scenic SS73. Once you pass Castelnuovo Berardenga, continue on SP484, where the view becomes positively spectacular. Park your car at the main entry to the village (set your GPS to Via dei Fossi; there's a small parking lot there), and enter. What San Gusmè lacks in monuments (there's nothing much to actually see here), it makes up for with heaps of charm. The hamlet dates back to the 9th century, and in the 12th century it was given to the great Ricasoli noble family (famous for inventing the recipe for Chianti wine). It was later passed on to Siena, and remained

under Sienese control for centuries. The best time to visit this tiny fortified hamlet is during the first week of September, when the locals celebrate the Festa del Luca with a series of open air concerts, cultural events and markets (see: www. sangusme.it).

Interestingly, this festival was born to honor a small terracotta statue situated by the main entrance to the village, showing a man crouching down, "doing his business." A small plaque was set next to the statue that says: "King, emperor, pope, philosopher, poet, factory worker or farmer: a man doing his 'daily functions'. Don't laugh, think only of yourself!" Although it was once the object of much ridicule, today the people of San Gusme adore and celebrate the weird little statue.

Next, make your way to the beautiful **Felsina Winery** for some serious wine tasting. For more than 50 years the Poggiali family has been concocting magical reds and

whites, which perfectly reflect the essence and spirit of this corner of Tuscany. A favorite with many locals, including Matteo Renzi, former prime minister of Italy, the Felsina winery is a pleasure for visiting, tasting and looking. The main estate is surrounded by olive groves and vineyards, wild fields dotted with medicinal plants, and woodlands. A few little streams that run nearby complete the picturesque setting.

A tour of this winery will include a visit to the large vaulted cellar and then the aging room, where the huge oak barrels are stored. Finally, you will be invited into the estate's enoteca to taste some of their flagship wines. This tour is already a lot of fun, but if you want to add something extra-special, you can book their extended tour, which includes a Jeep ride across the vineyards, or even a light lunch.

So much good wine will surely put you in the mood for an equally excellent meal. Luckily, there are a number of worthy options in this area. For a rustic, zero-frills experience, drive back to Castelnuovo Berardenga and join the locals at the popular **Ristorante Quei 2**. This is where we come when we are in the mood for something simple—fragrant bruschette drenched in olive oil and topped with thick slices of tomato, bigoli pasta in boar sauce, chubby tagliatelle that are impossible to

eat without staining your shirt, and grilled slabs of beef. The service can be a bit neurotic, but the ambiance is usually friendly.

For a more serious meal, book a table at the **Le Pietre Vive restaurant**. This is one of our favorite spots in Tuscany, and for good reason—every dish on the menu in this quiet, farm restaurant is pleasantly rustic and delicious. The pici pasta, Sienese prosciutto and ricotta desserts are especially good!

Felsina Winery, ★★★★★
Via del Chianti 101, Castelnuovo Berardenga. Tel: 0577.355117. GPS coordinates: Lat. 43.349499 - Long. 11.501247. Tours and tastings should be booked in advance. The wine shop is open Monday–Saturday, 10:00 a.m.–7:00 p.m.; Sunday, 10.00 a.m.–6:00 p.m. Hours may vary off-season, call in advance. The tour and tasting cost 15 euro, there are additional charges if you book the Jeep ride, or an extended tasting that includes a light meal (see website).

Ristorante Quei 2, ★★★
Via del Chianti 28, Castelnuovo Berardenga. Tel: 0577.355433. Open Thursday–Tuesday, 12:30-15:00 & 19:00–22:00; Wednesday closed. La Bottega del 30, Via di Santa Caterina 2, Villa A Sesta, Castelnuovo Berardenga, GPS coordinate: 43.384951, 11.480284. Tel: 0577.359.226, www.labottegadel30. it. Open Wednesday-Monday, for dinner only. Booking in advance is highly recommended. Open for lunch.

Restaurant Le Pietre Vive, ★★★★
Via Martiri di Monteaperti 4, Castelnuovo Berardenga. GPS coordinates: 43.31471, 11.438044. Tel: 333.466.3208, www.lepietrevive.com. Open April-late October, daily, for dinner. Reservations are recommended.

45 | Enjoy the Perfect Meal, Followed by a Visit to the Chianti Astronomical Observatory

Start your evening at one of the best restaurants in Chianti, in our opinion—**La Locanda di Pietracupa**. This is the sort of modern, sophisticated venue that offers diners (including a few VIP guests such as Geroge Clooney...) the chance to enjoy a series of perfectly executed Tuscan dishes, from *tagliolini con fiori di zucca e tartufo* (homemade tagliolini pasta with zucchini flowers and a creamy, truffled sauce), to a delicious *filetto di manzo al vinsanto con millefoglie di melanzane* (a tender beef fillet, flavored with vin santo and garnished with eggplants).

If it is available during your visit, don't skip the restaurant's best dessert, a reinterpretation of the Sicilian *cannolo*, made here with a delicate wafer and filled with an incredible chocolate mousse.

Next, what could be more magical than to end a day of hiking, good meals, and wine tasting with a private visit to the Chianti Astronomical Observatory? The observatory organizes guided activities in the summer, which are popular with families, but what few people realize is that you can also book a reasonably-priced private viewing (you'll have to book well in advance, especially in high-season, as there aren't that many openings). Enjoying the stars after an adventure filled day is surely a special and romantic way to celebrate your time in Tuscany.

The Chianti Astronomical Observatory, ★★★★
Strada Provinciale Castellina in Chianti, Barberino Val D'elsa. GPS coordinates: 43.523099, 11.244836 (park outside the park and then proceed for circa 300 meters on foot). Tel: 339.755.4145 (call Monday–Friday, 9:00-19:-00; Weekends 9:00-13:00). info@osservatoriochianti.it www.osservatoriochianti.it.

La Locanda di Pietracupa, ★★★★
Strada Pietracupa 31 (appears on some maps as Via Madonna di Pietracupa 31), San Donato in Poggio. Tel: 055.807.2400, www.locandapietracupa.it.

🍴 46 | Buy High-Quality Meats, Sausages and Cold Cuts at Macelleria Falorni, One of the Best Butcher Shops in Tuscany

Combining Tuscany's glorious vistas with a tasting tour of the region's finest charcuterie is a meat lover's dream. Luckily, this dream can easily be made a reality, as Tuscany offers its fair share of *macellerie* (butcher shops) that will satisfy even the most discerning carnivore.

Antica Macelleria Falorni, located in Greve in Chianti's elegant central piazza, is one such stop. The Bencistà Falorni family has been selling their top-quality cold cuts and meat since the 18th century, and pride themselves on using local breeds, such as Chianina cows and Cinta Senese pigs, to prepare a variety of *salumi*. Here you can find *prosciutto dolce*, a sweeter version of Tuscan *prosciutto*, and *prosciutto di cinghiale* (wild boar prosciutto, which has a decidedly gamey flavor), along with a range of salamis. A wide array of pecorino cheeses, stored in a 17th century ventilated cave to preserve the taste, is also available. The best time to visit,

naturally, is on Saturday morning, when the weekly market is held, and the piazza comes to life as it fills up with stands and people.

Antica Macelleria Falorni, ★★★
Piazza G. Matteotti 71, Greve in Chianti.
Tel: 055.853029.
www.falorni.it.
Open Monday–Saturday, 9:30 a.m.–7:30 p.m.; Sunday and holidays, 10:00 a.m.–7:30 p.m. Hours may vary off-season.

47 Discover the Charms of the Rustic Countryside and Learn How to Make Cheese at Podere Le Fornaci Goat Farm

For us, goat cheese is the best of cheeses. It grabs all the senses—the creamy texture, the tart flavor, the distinctive smell and feel. Italy, being the land of *pecorino* (sheep cheese) and cow's milk cheese, offers a far more limited choice of goat cheese than France. But there are some wonderful little farms dotted across the region, serving up excellent artisanal goat cheeses, too.

Our favorite is **Podere Le Fornaci,** located right in the heart of the Chianti area, just two kilometers from Greve in Chianti. This farm is organic and puts an emphasis on animal welfare. Admittedly, it does look a little shabby from the outside, but don't be put off—their cheese is excellent. Our favorites include the charcoal goat cheese and the *crosta fiorita,* but if you let the owners know what type of cheese you prefer, they will match you to the perfect taste. To extend the day, you can take a tour of the farm and stay for a light lunch, or even book a cheese-making class and tour, which is a fantastic experience for kids! Calling in advance before your visit is highly recommended.

Podere Le Fornaci, ★★★
Via di Citille 74, Greve in Chianti.
Tel: 055.854.6010,
www.poderelefornaci.it.
GPS Coordinates: 43°36'10"N / 11°18'14"E

48 Tour Tuscany in Style in a Vintage Car or Even a Ferrari!

Driving around the gorgeous hills of the Chianti region is a peak experience in its own right. But driving a vintage Fiat 500 or a luxurious Ferrari makes it a very different adventure indeed—one that will provide plenty of photo ops and lasting memories. **Noleggio Chianti 500,** in Castellina in Chianti, is a rental company with a fleet of Fiat 500s. You can just rent the car, but you can also consult with the friendly staff, who will help you create your dream itinerary. Find out more on their website.

If you are set for a real adventure, or if you are hoping for a once-in-a-lifetime experience where everyone will be looking at you enviously as you drive through the gorgeous countryside, then **Driving the Dream** is the answer. This aptly named rental agency offers various Ferrari models (as well as other high-end brands like Porsches and Range Rovers, and even Harley-Davidsons) for just a couple of hours or a few days. And if you've always dreamed about driving a Ferrari on a race track, you can easily do that, too, thanks to a collaboration between this company and the Siena Racetrack. Here, you can gear up and see if you have what it takes to face off with Formula One drivers!

Lastly, Ferrari fans might be interested to know that just 90 minutes north of Florence (in Marenello, near Modena) awaits the famous **Ferrari museum**, where visitors can admire several vintage Ferraris, drive a simulator, and, naturally, rent a Ferrari and take it for a spin.

Noleggio Chianti 500, ★★★★
Via 4 Novembre 35, Castellina in Chianti
Tel: 0577.148.1001,
www.noleggiochianti500.it.

Driving the Dream, ★★★★
Viale Europa 61, Siena.
Tel: 0577.188.1250, Cell: 331.213.8311,
www.drivingthedream.it.

Museo Ferrari, ★★★★★
Via Dino Ferrari 43, Maranello.
Tel: 0536.949.713,
museomaranello.ferrari.com.
In addition to the museum visit, tours of the Ferrari factory can be organized, if booked in advance. Consult their website to find out more.

49 Book a Magical Tuscan Stay at a Good yet Reasonably Priced *Agriturismo* in Chianti

Tuscany is bewitching for tourists, and this is reflected in the number of hotels, B&Bs and country resorts in the region. In fact, Tuscany currently boasts the most *agriturismi* per region in Italy (over 4,000, according to a recent count). But while finding some kind of lodging in the region is easy, finding a very good yet reasonably priced *agriturismo* is much more challenging. Hopefully, the recommendations in this tip will help readers find just the right place for their Tuscan adventure.

Ancora del Chianti is a family-run, slightly rustic B&B, which offers good value and a serene ambiance, just five kilometers from Greve in Chianti. Choose between the double rooms and the suites, which are located in the refurbished barn or in the farm house itself, and enjoy the charm of a real Tuscan lodging. This B&B is famous for the activities it organizes for its guests, everything from painting lessons to cooking

classes to guided hikes along the scenic trails of the Chianti hills. Since the prices here are fairly low, the rooms fill up very quickly, so book well in advance!

Podere Campriano is a charming, family-run, sustainable farmhouse near Greve in Chianti, in the heart of the Chianti region. The *agriturismo* is known for its wines (tours of the vineyards are available), olive oil tastings and fun cooking lessons, and those who stay here will discover an authentic slice of the Tuscan countryside. Guests can choose between serviced apartments and B&B rooms (suites), all of which have been lovingly decorated. Outside there is a lovely garden perfect for lazing around, and even a salt-water pool with panoramic views!

Next, in San Casciano Val di Pesa, just 20 minutes from Florence, await two 'fancier' but absolutely worthy options—Il Poggiale Dimora

Storica and Villa i Barronci. These two stunning country houses are located next to each other, and offer magnificent views, excellent amenities, and a real sense of luxury at prices that are often far more affordable than similar lodgings in Florence, Siena or Chianti (book in advance, and consult both the hotels' websites as well as online booking websites to get the best deals. Note that many hotels will match the offers you find on websites such as booking.com.)

Villa Il Poggiale Dimora Storica is a Renaissance villa which has been converted into a gorgeous modern mansion while maintaining its historic charm. There is an outside pool overlooking the hills, the air conditioned rooms are spacious and tastefully decorated, and the staff is friendly and accommodating. **Villa i Barronci** is equally charming, and slightly more modern and upscale in style. The exposed wooden beams and stonework accentuate the modern décor, while the outside pool and gardens allow visitors to relax completely, and enjoy the scenic surroundings.

B&B Ancora del Chianti, ★★★
Via Collegalle 12, Greve in Chianti.
Tel: 055.854.044, Cell: 339.158.7642,
www.ancoradelchianti.it,

Podere Campriano, ★★★★
Viale Rosa Libri 36/a, Greve in Chianti.
Tel: 055.853.688, Cell: 339.273.9149,
www.poderecampriano.it,

Villa Il Poggiale, ★★★★
Via Empolese 69, San Casciano in val di Pesa. Tel: 055.828.311,
www.villailpoggiale.it,

Villa I Barronci, ★★★★
Via Sorripa 10, San Casciano In Val di Pesa. Tel: 055.820598,
www.ibarronci.com,

Siena

50 | **Stay at Siena's Lovliest Hotel**–Il Campo Regio Relais

Though there are some wonderful *agriturismi* located outside Siena, choosing a hotel within the city walls has its charms. If you love touring the town on foot, a room close to the center is a big advantage. Plus, there is something to be said for choosing lodging that is part of the city; you get a much more intimate experience of Siena when you immerse yourself in its daily rhythms.

Our go-to hotel in town is the **Residenza d'Epoca Campo Regio Relais**, which is located just minutes away from the famous Piazza del Campo. The views are the first thing that makes this place exceptional— eating breakfast on the terrace, you will be overwhelmed by the panorama of the city, a wonderful way to start your day of exploration. The décor is elegant and inviting, and maintains much of the old-world, charming ambiance Siena is famous for. It is worth noting that this is a boutique hotel with just six rooms, and they do fill up quickly in high season, so book well in advance and ask specifically for a room with a view of the town.

Campo Regio Relais, ★★★★★
Via della Sapienza 25, Siena.
Tel: 0577.222.073,
www.camporegio.com.

🍴 51 | Dine at a Delicious and Homey Restaurant in Siena

La Taverna di San Giuseppe is one of the most popular restaurants in Siena. There may be smarter places in town, but when it comes to good, hearty, traditional food, this venue is excellent. From the moment you walk down the stairs into the long hall, with its time-honored wood furniture, candlelit tables, and exposed brickwork, you get in the mood for some authentic Tuscan cuisine. The service here is accommodating and knowledgeable without being snobbish, and the food is mouthwatering. The meat dishes, anything with porcini and truffles, and the pasta are especially tasty. The location is also perfect, as the tavern can be found just 400 meters up the street from Piazza del Campo, and a short walk down from the Duomo. Reservations for this lovely restaurant are highly recommended; popular with visitors and locals alike, it's always full.

Alternatively, try **L'Oro di Siena.** This intimate, romantic trattoria offers one of the most enjoyable dining experiences in Siena, in our opinion. Chef Antonietta has created a short but focused menu, including many of the area's staple dishes, from Sienese pici pasta to excellent antipasti platters of local cheeses and prosicutto. The attentive service and the good wine list are an added bonus. Try the selection of affettati (cold cuts) and the lardo di colonnata; the gnocchi with pecorino cream; the fresh tagliolini with Chianina beef ragu; and the grilled ham, Siena style. Reservations are highly recommended, as seating is limited, and they are always full.

If it's just a quick sandwich that you want, then head to **Il Cencio**, located right on Piazza del Campo. The sandwiches here are tasty and cheap, and there is a tiny balcony on the second floor where you can sit on a (shabby...) bench, enjoy the splendid piazza and do some people watching while you munch away.

If, on the other hand, you are in the mood for some wine in a stylish and romantic locale, head to **Zest Wine Bar and Restaurant,** which is located on a particularly scenic street, near the Santuario di Santa Caterina and the San Domenico church.

Finally, for a sophisticated and modern meal, you can't go wrong with **Il Campaccio Food & Wine.** This is a relatively new addition to the local culinary scene and a surprisingly good one, too. The intimate, curated space is run by two young chefs who are determined to 'shake things up', and the menu certainly reflects their determination—rabbit filled tortelli served with coffee infused leeks; spaghetti with sea urchins, chives and smoked prawns; roasted suckling pig and smoked lamb shank are just a few of the tempting dishes on offer. Additionally, you will always find here a couple of fresh and well-prepared 'fish of the day' dishes. The restaurant is open for dinner only, and is almost always full, so booking a table in advance is highly recommended.

La Taverna di San Giuseppe, ★★★★
Via Giovanni Duprè 132, Siena.
Tel: 0577.42286,
www.tavernasangiuseppe.it.
Open Monday-Saturday, 12:00 p.m-2:30 p.m. & 7:00 p.m. -10:00 p.m. Closed Sunday. Closed for the last two weeks of July and the last two weeks of January.

L'Oro di Siena, ★★★
Via Giuseppe Garibaldi 61, Siena
Cell: 339.859.9420, www.orodisiena.it.
Open daily, 12:30 p.m.-3:30 p.m & 7:30 p.m.-10:30 p.m.; Sunday open for dinner only. Reservations are recommended.

Il Cencio, ★★★
Piazza del Campo 70. Open daily, 11:00 a.m.-8:00 p.m. (hours may vary off season).

Zest Wine Bar and Restaurant, ★★★
Costa Di Sant'Antonio 13, Siena.
Tel: 0577.47139,
www.zestsiena.com.
Open Wednesday-Monday, 12:00 p.m.-3.30p.m. & 6.30 p.m.-10:00 p.m. Closed Tuesday.

Il Campaccio Food & Wine, ★★★★
Viccolo del Campaccio 2 (near the church of San Domenico), Cell: 327.902.0623. Open daily for dinner only. In high season opening hours may be extended, we recommend calling first.

 52 | **Book a Walking Tour of Siena** with a Professional Guide

Though Siena can undoubtedly be enjoyed on a self-guided tour, it is also true that touring with the right guide can add unrivaled depth to the experience. It is a unique opportunity and pleasure, especially for history and art lovers, to navigate the medieval alleys of this fascinating town, from Piazza del Campo to the impressive Duomo to the San Domenico church, with a professional guide telling stories of the people who lived, worked, ruled and died here.

Costanza Riccardi is both a licensed guide for the city of Siena and a hiking guide, which means that whether you are looking to embark on a city tour or explore the countryside, she will be able to help you. Her knowledge of local art and history, and her passion for the traditions of her home town, make her stand out among guides.

We also love the philosophy of **Tours Around Tuscany,** which offer personalized and professional tours of specific areas of Tuscany. Unlike other companies that organize what are often superficial tours with large groups and try to cover too much ground in one day, this organization will happily take small groups, or even just a couple, on memorable and intimate tours of Siena, the countryside of Southern Tuscany, and the Chianti region.

Finally, for last minute activities, stop by the **Info Point and Tour** on Piazza del Campo. They offer daily walking tours (at 11:00 a.m., usually) as well as a range of budget friendly courses and activities, and tickets for various events (including the Palio).

Costanza Riccardi, ★★★★
Tel: 0577.281.605, Cell: 333.325.7717,
www.sienawalkingtours.com.

Tours Around Tuscany, ★★★★
Tel: 0577.185.1602, Cell: 347.245.0225,
www.tourintuscany.com.

 53 | **Embark on a Fun and Professional Wine Tour** from Siena

While the wine tours that leave from Florence are better-known, Siena stands its ground and offers its fair share of interesting excursions, too. This makes perfect sense—Sienese Chianti is famous and delicious, and is a joy to explore. Just a short drive from Siena you will find some glorious estates and wine-producing towns, such as Castelnuovo Berardenga, which lies 20 minutes west of Siena, or Gaiole in Chianti, which is 40 minutes away.

Though we love traveling around the wineries ourselves, touring with a guide has several advantages. The knowledge and experience of an expert guide are one obvious benefit, but we are also happy to know that we can taste whatever wine we want without having to worry about driving home after three (or six) glasses of wine.

Wine Tour in Tuscany is a popular tour led by Donatella, a knowledgeable guide and

sommelier, who is as passionate about wine as she is about her native town of Siena. Since she personally knows many of the area's producers, her tours are very individualized and give you perspective and closeness that others find hard to match. Donatella also offers cooking classes, organic food tours, city tours of Siena itself, and tours of castles, ancient hamlets (*borghi*), churches and other interesting sites in the region. The wine tour, however, is the main draw. Tours can be personalized, and we love the fact that Donatella suggests visits to historic wineries, too, which adds an interesting dimension to the day. Like most other tours, these excursions focus on the best-known wines of Tuscany—a separate tour is offered to follow the path of Chianti, Brunello, Vernaccia, and the Montepulciano wines (and even the super-Tuscans). The Sunset Chianti Tour, which includes a visit to two wineries, a sunset drive through the region and dinner in Greve in Chianti, is very pleasant and romantic.

If you can't find an opening with Donatella, or if you simply prefer a different tour, try **Grape Tours**—a small tour operator that offers fun, personalized and intimate visits to the many wineries surrounding Siena. Choose between the Vernaccia (in the San Gimignano area), Nobile di Montepulciano, and Brunello di Montalcino tours and, naturally, the classic Chianti tour, all of which include a typical Tuscan lunch on a farm. These tours are well-organized, fun and interesting, and add a 'special something' to any vacation in the region.

Wine Tour in Tuscany, ★★★★
Via Carlo Pisacane 166, Siena.
www.winetourintuscany.com.

Grape Tours, ★★★★
In front of the San Domenico Church, Siena. Cell: 349.866.2988,
www.siena-wine-tour.com.

🏃 54 | Taste Some of Siena's Best Ricciarelli

For locals, the debate about Siena's best *ricciarelli* is as heated as the debate among Florentines about the city's best *gelato*. Ricciarelli—a soft, moist, almond-based cookie, dusted with powder sugar—has been a symbol of Tuscany since the 14th century, and is the second most famous cookie in the region after the *cantuccino* (commonly known in English as *biscotti*).

Together with *panforte* (a heavy dessert loaded with dried fruit and nuts), *cavallucci* (a harder, sweeter, and more floury version of *ricciarelli*), and pici pasta (thick spaghetti, traditionally served topped with fried breadcrumbs), *ricciarelli* cookies have become a symbol of Siena. We have yet to meet a Sienese man, woman, or child who can't immediately tell you their favorite establishment for purchasing a fresh batch.

Pasticceria Sinatti is located on Via della Sapienza, near San Domenico church (about 10 minutes from Piazza del Campo on foot). Their ricciarelli are flavorsome, dense and very popular with locals and visitors alike. A second option is also our personal favorite–**La Nuova Pasticceria** located just behind Piazza del Campo. Their *ricciarelli* are especially moist and delicate, a perfect pick-me-up snack at any time of day. Closing our list of top recommended ricciarelli in the *centro storico* are the fantastic *ricciarelli* served at the historic **Bar 4 Cantoni (Fiore)**, located just a block away from the Duomo, at the angle of Via del Capitano and Via di Città. The owners here also offer a vast array of other hand-made sweet treats, including the famous *panforte*.

A good *ricciarello* should always be soft and never contain flour. It should maintain a natural moistness from the almond paste. If packed properly, *ricciarelli* can travel well and will make a great gift for loved ones back home.

Pasticcerie Sinatti, ★★★
Via della Sapienza 36, Siena.
Tel: 0577.41872,
www.pasticceriesinatti.it.
Open Monday–Saturday, 10:00 a.m.–7:00 p.m. Sunday 9:00 a.m.–1:30 p.m. Closed Tuesday.

La Nuova Pasticceria, ★★★★
Via Duprè 37, Siena. Tel: 0577.40577,
www.lanuovapasticceria-siena.com.
Open Monday–Saturday, 9:30 a.m.–7:30 p.m. Sunday 10:30 a.m.–7:00 p.m. (sometimes they open as late as 11:00 a.m. on Sunday).

Bar Quattro Cantoni (Fiore), ★★★★
Via di Città 137, Siena. Tel: 0577.280942,
www.almangia.it/4cantoni.

Surrounding Siena

🏃 55 | Experience Hiking Adventures Along the Stunning Roads of the Tuscan Countryside

We can't think of a better way to discover the beauty of the land than by walking it. And a good guided walking tour, personalized to your own taste and interests, is the perfect way to unearth hidden treasures, explore paths known by few, and add a memorable and unique experience to your vacation.

Sara Testi is a knowledgeable guide who leads walking tours around her native Tuscany. She is both professional and friendly, and offers a wide variety of tours to choose from, depending on what interests you most. And since she has a degree in anthropology, she will be able to add a unique historical and cultural perspective to your exploration of *Bella Toscana*. If you are traveling as a family, her tours come especially recommended (you'd be surprised how much kids can enjoy these activities), but couples and adult groups will have a great time, too!

Find out more about her various itineraries on her website.

Walk About Tuscany is a small touring company led by the friendly and knowledgeable Gianni Stanghellini. He offers a wide variety of one-day or multiple-day tours, in some of the most scenic parts of the region. Gianni emphasizes personal interaction and discovery, allowing visitors to get to know Tuscany in an intimate way. Naturally, tours can be personalized to include, besides a hike, various wine tastings, lunches on farms, visits to hill towns, and more. Find out more about his many activities on his website.

Sara Testi, ★★★★
www.saratestiguide.com.

Walk About Tuscany, ★★★★
www.walkabouttuscany.com.

 56

Enjoy a Romantic Evening in a Hidden Corner of Tuscany, Starting with a Nocturnal Dip at the San Giovanni Thermal Spa

If there's a perfect way to end a day of sightseeing in southern Tuscany, this must be it: dinner at a small, intimate restaurant, followed by a night dip at a spa that becomes magical after dark.

Terme San Giovanni (the San Giovanni thermal spa) is located in Rapolano, an area in southern Tuscany famous for its thermal springs. The spa has five pools inside and outside the complex, filled with mineral-rich water at 39° C. The outdoor pools are especially enjoyable, and are surrounded by grassy banks that afford fantastic views over the Tuscan countryside. While the spa is open every day, it becomes especially magical at night—on Saturday nights in the summer, San Giovanni Terme transforms into a wonderfully romantic place; come here before the sun sets and watch the light disappear on the horizon while soaking in the warmth of the pools. When dinner time comes, you will

be spoilt for choice—the spa itself has a nice restaurant, but there are also a couple of other excellent options nearby.

For a lively and rustic experience, and some of the best meat in the area, head straight to **La Toraia,** a restaurant that any carnivore will appreciate. Their chianina steak is excellent, as are the gourmet burgers, but various tasty pasta dishes are also available. For a more refined experience, drive in the direction of Arezzo, and about 30 minutes from the spa you will come upon **Il Goccino.** This cozy and intimate little restaurant, which is located in the tiny and romantic village of Lucignano may not seem like much from the outside, but it is actually one of the best restaurants in this part of Tuscany, in our opinion, and merits a 30 minute drive. The philosophy of this kitchen is tradition revisited, emphasizing seasonal and local produce. Everything we tried here was excellent: tasty lamb chops, fresh pasta, the *salumi*, which are mostly made with locally-bred Cinta Senese and Grigio del Casentino pigs, the various seafood dishes (we loved the braised scallops, served with a purple potato puree, and sprinkled with pistachios), and the delectable desserts. Though meat is a star in this restaurant, there are a number of very good vegetarian and vegan options available, too, and the chef will happily modify some of the dishes for vegetarian clients. Cooking classes can be organized for small groups, consult the restaurant's website to find out more. On a hot summer night, book a place in advance on their lovely terrace!

San Giovanni Terme, ★★★★

Via Terme San Giovanni 52, Rapolano Terme. Tel: 0577.724.030, www.termesangiovanni.it.
Hours vary–the night spa is open in high season only, until midnight. Dinner and an entry pass to the thermal pools will cost around €35 per person. Pool access without dinner (from 7:00 p.m.) will cost around €12 per person. Booking in advance is required (call at least 2-3 days ahead of your planned visit).

La Toraia, ★★★

Tenuta La Fratta, Sinalunga. Tel: 0577.678.204, www.latoraia.com.
Open Thursday-Friday, for dinner only, 7:30 p.m.-9:30 p.m.; Saturday-Sunday, 12:30 p.m.-2:30 p.m. & 7:30 p.m.-9:30 p.m. Booking a table in advance is highly recommended.

Ristorante Il Goccino, ★★★★★

Via Matteotti 90, Lucignano. Tel: 0575.836.707, www.ilgoccino.it.
Open Tuesday-Sunday, 12:30 p.m.-2:30 p.m. & 7:30 p.m.-10:00 p.m. Closed Monday. May close off season, call in advance.

 # 57 | Visit the Splendid Monte Oliveto Maggiore Abbey and Sample Traditional Tonics Made by Monks

There are two Tuscan abbeys renowned for their Gregorian chants: Sant'Antimo, near Montalcino (see tip number 83) and Monte Oliveto Maggiore, near Asciano. Both are captivatingly beautiful and offer visitors a unique experience, but personally, we prefer Monte Oliveto. The reason is simple—while Sant'Antimo is very impressive from an architectural point of view, it is also very popular with tourists. Monte Oliveto Maggiore, on the other hand, still manages to offer a relative sense of peace.

The abbey is surrounded by woods and silence, so traveling to Monte Oliveto Maggiore is like being transported to a different reality. Walking on the stone path from the parking lot down to the main church, you are surrounded by oak, pine, and cypress trees, the occasional chirping bird, bushes and wildflowers. The air is cool and crisp; it almost feels like time moves more slowly here. The abbey, which was founded in the 14th century by Bernardo Tolomei (of the famous noble Tolomei family of Siena), is most famous for its fantastic cloister decorated with frescos from Luca Signorelli and Giovanni Antonio Bazzi (better known as Il Sodoma), but the chapels and the refectory are equally stunning. Once you have completed your visit to the chapel, it is time for the second part: a genuinely hedonistic experience.

Take the path down from the abbey, following the signs directing you to the *cantina* (cellar) and the *Azienda Agricola* (farm). The monks here offer tonics prepared using recipes that are hundreds of years old. Their *Flora di Monteoliveto,* for example, is a liqueur made from 23 herbs and flowers that grow on the land around the abbey. Touring the cellar is fascinating—big wooden barrels sit under vaulted ceilings and the reddish brick walls evoke a wonderful sense of history. Guided tours and tastings are available, but you have to book those in advance. Check their website to find out more.

Monte Oliveto Maggiore, ★★★★★
Loc. Monte Oliveto Maggiore, Asciano (set your GPS to Loc. Chiusure, or to Asciano. The abbey is located along the SS451 road, 14 kilometers from Asciano). Tel: 0577.707.611, www.monteolivetomaggiore.it. The Monte Oliveto Abbey is open year-round. Summer months, daily, 9:15 a.m.–12:00 p.m. & 3:00 p.m.–6:00 p.m.; winter months, Monday- Saturday, 9:15 a.m.–12:00 p.m. & 3:00 p.m.–4:00 p.m., Sunday, 9:15 a.m.–12:30 p.m. Additionally, a mass accompanied by Gregorian chants is celebrated year-round on weekdays at 6:00 p.m., and on Sunday and holidays at 11:00 a.m. (Hours may vary, check the website before your visit). The Abbey's *Enoteca* and Cellar are open mid-March to late October, daily, 10:00 a.m.–1:00 p.m. & 2:30 p.m.–6:30 p.m.; November–mid-March, weekends and holidays only, 10:00 a.m.–1:00 p.m. & 2:30 p.m.–6:00 p.m. (However, it is recommended that you come before 5:15 p.m., as the guard tends to close shop earlier, at 5:30 p.m. to attend mass.) Visits take place 4 times a day, at 10:00 a.m., 1:00 p.m., 2:30 p.m., and 6:30 p.m. (6:00 p.m. in winter). Advance booking is recommended, and for groups it is mandatory. Find out more here: www.agricolamonteoliveto.com.

 58 **Spend a Day Exploring Charming Chiusdino** and a Night at the Romantic Petriolo Spa Resort

Just 40 minutes away from Siena hides a magical, fairy tale-like stone church. The **Abbey of San Galgano** in Chiusdino is a famous site, as much for its intriguing history as for the dramatic landscapes that surround it.

San Galgano was a functioning monastery until the bubonic plague hit Italy in 1348. This deadly epidemic decimated the monks, and the resulting crime wave that spread

across Europe forced the surviving monks to flee to Siena to escape local vigilantes. The last of the monks left towards the end of the 15th century, and when lightning struck in 1786, destroying the roof, the church seemed to be beyond repair. However, this apparent misfortune transformed San Galgano into an unexpected attraction as visitors came to the area to see the poetic, solemn yet elegant roofless church. After 6:30 p.m., you can't enter the site, but even from the outside it is impressive, especially on a moonlit night.

After visiting the abbey you can walk up the hill to the nearby **Eremo di Montesiepi**. This hermitage was home to Saint Galgano, a Chiusdino knight who retired here to spend his remaining days as a monk. He quickly realized that he no longer needed his sword and fiercely thrust it into a rock to signify his newfound pacifism. The sword in the rock, which resembles a cross, lies protected to this day and serves as symbol of peace and faith.

For an intimate and homey lunch, drive to **La Grotta di Tiburzi,** which is located in the village of Chiusdino itself. This is one of our favorite trattorias in the area. Rustic, authentic and very Tuscan in spirit, this is where the locals come to eat. The pasta is fantastic, as good as any Tuscan grandma might make, and the braised beef served with rustic french fries is excellent, too. The service can be a little uptight, but the food most certainly justifies seeking out this little gem. Then, to end the day in a truly decadent manner, pop into the **thermal baths** of nearby Petriolo. The baths are just 20 minutes away and have been in operation since Etruscan times. The Etruscans valued the numerous benefits of the thermal waters, as did later Medieval and Renaissance societies. The high sulfur level of the 43 °C water explains the particularly strong odor. The sulfur, combined with other minerals such as calcium and sulfate, is very good for various ailments (though you should always consult your doctor before entering any thermal baths if you have a medical condition).

One section of the baths is free, but we must admit that it is a pretty rustic experience (and there are better free thermal baths to enjoy in the area—see tip 90). For something slightly more sophisticated, skip the free pools and stop by the **Petriolo Spa Resort.** The breathtaking views (if you spend the night, ask for a room with a view, and take your breakfast out on the terrace) are just one of the reasons we enjoy coming here. There is a private pool exclusively for guests and a fine array of spa treatments is available.

San Galgano Abbey, ★★★★
Chiusdino (the abbey is located midway between Chiusdino and Monticiano, follow the road signs to reach it), www.sangalgano.info. Open April–May, 9:00 a.m.–6:30 p.m. (7:00 p.m. Sunday and holidays); November–March, 9:30 a.m.–5:30 p.m. (6:30 p.m. on Sunday and holidays); June–September, 9:00 a.m.–8:00 p.m. **Eremo di Montesiepi,** April–October, daily, 9:00 a.m.–6:00 p.m.; November–March, 9:00 a.m.–1:00 p.m. Hours tend to vary.

Petriolo Spa Resort, ★★★★
Località Bagni di Petriolo, Civitella Paganico. www.atahotels.it/en/petriolo. NOTE: the spa is open daily from April 16 to November 2. Non-guests can buy a daily entrance pass (which allows entry from 9:30 a.m. to 6:30 p.m.) or an afternoon pass (2:00 p.m.–6:30 p.m.). This pass includes use of the two outside pools, the inside pool and the spa (treatments are excluded). A weekday pass costs €40 (afternoon pass: €30), a weekend pass costs €60 (afternoon: €40). Book your day pass (and any treatments you might be interested in) 2-3 days in advance

La Grotta di Tiburzi, ★★★★
Via Paolo Mascagni 15, Chiusdino. Tel: 0577.752948. Open daily for lunch and dinner.

59 **Book a Memorable Stay** at the Beautiful Castello delle Serre

The deluxe suite at **Castello delle Serre** is one of the best-kept secrets in Tuscany. Located in Serre di Rapolano, halfway between Siena and Montepulciano, the entire hotel is like a dream. Homey yet graceful, this ancient castle dates back to Byzantine times. The castello's suite is perfectly positioned at the top of a medieval tower, and spreads over three levels. The top level has a private rooftop terrace with a spectacular 360-degree view, overlooking the magical hills of Asciano on one side and the endless vineyards of Castelnuovo di Berardenga on the other. The elegant sitting room and bedroom have a charming feeling of pastoral luxury, like something enjoyed by noble families of years gone by. Other rooms in the hotel are very comfortable, too, and the staff is friendly and professional. The hotel's proximity to Siena (about 30 minutes), the thermal baths of San Giovanni, the Val d'Orcia, Montepulciano and even the Maremma is an added advantage, and makes the hotel a great home base for those planning on exploring Southern Tuscany. As you might expect, booking this popular suite well in advance is essential.

Hotel Castello delle Serre, ★★★★★
Piazza XX Settembre 1, Serre di Rapolano.
Cell: (active from 9:00 a.m.–9:00 p.m.,
Italian time) – 338.7315802 (Antonio),
www.castellodelleserre.com.

🏃 60 | Enjoy a Day of Pampering
at the Incredible Fonteverde Spa

The **Fonteverde Tuscan Resort Spa** exudes luxury. Located in a renovated 17th century country estate that formerly belonged to the Medici family, the hotel has 66 rooms and 7 suites. Many of the rooms have been meticulously redesigned with sumptuous fabrics and deep colors, four-poster beds, and drapes framing private balconies. However, the real forte of this resort isn't the hotel rooms, but the spa (which is also open to outside guests).

The Fonteverde spa is built around a thermal spring discovered by the ancient Etruscans and offers over 100 treatments. Five indoor pools and two outdoor pools are at the guests' disposal. The thermal pools offer magnificent views of vineyards and olive groves crisscrossing the Siena hills, and are reason enough to choose this spa for a relaxing massage. Fonteverde really does go for the "wow factor," and for those planning on spending a day of true pampering, this is one of

the top choices in the area. Their medical treatments are also worth exploring, including salt therapy to aid respiratory problems, Ayurvedic massage, and even hydro massage. Beauty treatments include anti-aging treatments and natural facials, many of which are executed using locally sourced, antioxidant-rich products, such as honey, mud, and olive oil.

Alternatively, a visit to Fonteverde's night spa is highly recommended. Like many other spa facilities in the region, Fonteverde offers access at night as an after-dark treat. In our opinion, soaking in the thermal pool under the stars (and for a relatively reasonable entry fee of €28) and then enjoying the facility's beautiful bioacquam pool (thermal hydro-massage) is a perfect way to end a day of Tuscan adventures.

Prices here are obviously not cheap,

but they are much more reasonable than the fees at high-end spas in Florence and Siena. If you don't mind a bit of a splurge, Fonteverde is a venue worth considering.

Fonteverde Tuscan Resort & Spa,
★★★★
Loc. Terme 1, San Casciano dei Bagni.
Tel: 0578.57241,
www.fonteverdespa.com.

61 Book an Authentic and Unique Cooking Class in the Countryside

Are you looking for a hands-on Tuscan culinary adventure? Then don't miss the fun and professional cooking classes at **Giuseppina's Cooking School,** in Certaldo (near San Gimignano and Siena). friendly, original, reasonably priced and seriously delicious, these lessons are highly recommended, especially for families. A standard hands-on course will last about three hours, but longer classes, that include a guided visit to the market, or even a truffle hunting expedition, can also be organized. And, if you've always dreamed of cooking and tasting medieval delicacies, know that Giuseppina and her staff offer original medieval cooking classes, too!

Cucina Giuseppina. ★★★★
Cell: 348.003.4869.
www.cucinagiuseppina.com

Arezzo and Cortona

🏃 62 | Discover the Charms of Arezzo

Arezzo, in our opinion, deserves much more attention than it gets. On the whole this little town in eastern Tuscany is known especially by art lovers, who arrive in droves to admire Piero della Francesca's incredible cycle of frescos in the San Francesco church. But actually, Arezzo is in many ways an open air museum—a town filled with ancient *palazzi*, mysterious alleys and beautiful churches. If you know where to go, then half a day spent in Arezzo can be a day of exploration and discovery. And, best of all—you can enjoy your time here without the hordes of tourists that occupy more popular towns like Florence and Siena.

Any tour of Arezzo should begin with the impressive **Duomo,** and then include a stop at the Serene **San Domenico Church.** Small and deceptively simple-looking, this church houses Cimabue's cross, a seminal work of Italian art; it was one of the first to depict Christ's

death in a humanistic style. It is also the only wooden cross by the famous medieval artist to have survived to this day. Next, don't miss a quick visit to **Giorgio Vasari's home.** Vasari, a renowned painter and architect, is known for painting the *Salone dei Cinquecento* in Florence's *Palazzo Vecchio,* but he is most notably remembered as the author of "The Lives of the Most Excellent Italian Painters, Sculptors, and Architects, from Cimabue to Our Times", a foundational work which to this day is an important source of information for historians about the lives and daily work of the most famous Renaissance artists. Vasari's home merits a visit not only because of the man's historical importance, but also because the site itself is quite impressive—the walls and ceilings are covered in beautiful frescos, and the small and tranquil adjoining garden is a perfect place to sit, relax, and take it all in.

From here, continue on to the **Church of San Francesco**, to visit Piero della Francesca's world-famous cycle of Frescoes, "The Legend of the True Cross", commonly regarded as a masterpiece of Early Renaissance art. Note that only a limited number of people may enter the church at any given moment, so booking your spot in advance is mandatory, or you may find that there are no openings.

Then, don't skip one of the smallest yet most enchanting museums in Arezzo - **Casa Museo Ivan Bruschi,** where you will find an eclectic collection of sculptures, coins, archaeological artifacts, jewelry and so much more.

Finally, head to **Piazza Grande**, Arezzo's main square, and one of the most beautiful piazzas in Tuscany. The newest buildings here were constructed in the 1500s and some of the others date back hundreds of years before that time. The circular Santa Maria del Pieve church is particularly impressive, as is the *loggia* (the roofed corridor) designed by Vasari. As you tour this enchanting piazza, you will probably understand why Italian director Robert Benini chose to shoot scenes from his Oscar-winning film "La Vita è Bella" in this very location.

Sitting down for some coffee or an *aperitivo* in this spot is a highly recommended experience.

So much art and beauty will make a person hungry. Luckily, Arezzo offers an excellent selection of restaurants to please all tastes. For a traditional meal, try the family-run **Ristorante Dario e Anna.** The food here is genuine, and there are a number of Arentine specialties to enjoy—try the tender *bistecca*, the homemade *tagliatelle* with porcini, and ask if there are any specials on the menu.

Alternatively, if you prefer a more modern and inspired menu, Arezzo happens to boast a number of recommended dining options. **Le Chiavi d'Oro** is a sophisticated, Michelin-recommended restaurant, which also enjoys a coveted location, just half a block from the San Francesco Church. Run by a team of three brothers—Teresa, Giovanna e Francesco Stilo—the menu here is strictly seasonal, and every dish that we have tried, from the fresh homemade pasta to the excellent seafood, was perfectly executed. And, because this is Arezzo, prices here are far more reasonable than what similar restaurants in Florence or Siena would charge. Booking a table in advance is highly recommended.

Next, shopping enthusiasts will be interested to know that Arezzo is famous for its its many **goldsmiths**, who have been hammering away at their shops since the 14th century. The town's gold has been the favorite of noble families, including the legendary Medicis, and throughout history many exquisite religious pieces have been commissioned by the Vatican from Arezzo's leading artists.

Goldsmiths still make up an essential part of the local economy,

with over a 10000 studios in the town itself and in the surrounding province; the annual goldsmiths convention held in Arezzo every spring draws in a crowd of tens of thousands of professionals. However, many of these shops and studios aren't open for the public; they produce and sell directly to shops.

If you have a car, we recommend driving outside the historic center and visiting **Alberto Sanarelli**, who is famous for his unique pieces. In the *centro storico* itself, there are several shops to explore—try **Eclat** (two shops: Corso Italia 36 & Via Vittorio Veneto 85) and the many other shops along Via Garibaldi, and Cosro Italia. If you are interested in buying some unique pieces, and aren't intimidated by certain price tags, visit **UnoAerre**, one of the most renowned boutiques in all of Italy. Located on the decidedly uninspiring outskirts of Arezzo, UnoAerre have been making jewelry worn by the best known Italian movie stars for over 50 years. They also have an interesting little museum, attached to the showroom, housing a dazzling collection of over 2000 priceless pieces. A visit to the museum must be booked in advance.

It's a good idea to call ahead before going to the showroom, too.

To round off an activity-packed day head to **Vineria 10**. This chic little wine bar is nicely decorated with tables set in alcoves and wine racks covering the walls. With a good wine list and very popular platters of cheese, sandwiches and cold cuts, this is the perfect spot to take pleasure in a fine *aperitivo* and rub shoulders with the locals.

Finally, bear in mind that the best time to visit Arezzo is during the monthly **antique fair** (which takes place every first weekend of the month, see tip 131), or during the famous medieval jousting match and festival, **La Giostra del Saracino** (see tip 127, or find out more here: www.giostradelsaracino.arezzo.it)

Casa di Giorgio Vasari, ★★★
Via XX Settembre 55, Arezzo,
Tel: 0575.409040.

Church of San Francesco, ★★★★★
Piazza San Francesco, Arezzo,
Tel: 0575.352727,
www.pierodellafrancesca.it.
Open Monday-Friday, 9:00 a.m.-6:30 p.m; Saturday 9:00 a.m.-5:30 p.m., Sunday 1:00 p.m.-5:30 p.m. Only a certain number of people can go inside at once, which is why booking your ticket in advance is mandatory (off season, you will often be able to enter without booking, but it is worth calling in advance just to be on the safe side).

Casa Museum Ivan Bruschi ★★★★
Corso Italia 14, Arezzo
Tel: 0575.354.126
www.fondazionebruschi.it.
Open Tuesday-Sunday,
10:00 a.m.-7:00 p.m.

Ristorante Dario e Anna, ★★★
Via Vittorio Veneto 14, Arezzo.
Tel: 0575.902473,
www.darioeanna.it.
Open Tuesday-Sunday, for dinner only;
On weekends open for lunch, too; closed
Monday.

Le Chiavi d'Oro, ★★★★
Piazza San Francesco 7, Arezzo.
Tel: 0575.403313,
www.ristorantelechiavidoro.it.
Open Tuesday-Sunday, 12:30 p.m.-2.30
p.m. & 7.30 p.m.-10:30 p.m. Closed
Monday.

Unoaerre Museum and Showroom,
★★★
Loc. San Zeno, Strada E n. 5, Arezzo.
Tel: 0575.9251,
www.unoaerre.it.

**Sanarello Alberto-Laboratorio
Orafo Artigianale,**
Via Vittorio Veneto 196/A, Arezzo.
Tel: 0575.900.114,
www.sanarelli.it.

Vineria Al 10, ★★★
Piazza San Giusto 10, Arezzo.
Tel: 0575.1824.566,
www.vineriaal10.it.

🛏 | **63** | **Book a Night at the Exquisite and Historic** Castelletto di Montebenichi

High on a hill halfway between Siena and Arezzo, a 12th-century palace looks imposingly out on the Chianti valleys below. **Castelletto di Montebenichi**, with its medieval architecture and fresco-adorned walls, is filled with history and tradition. Fortunately for tourists, it has opened its doors to the public as a tremendously impressive hotel.

Although the castle is large and commanding, the owners have maintained a sense of intimacy and great charm. The exposed brick walls show warm flecks of terracotta, especially in the light of the open fire, and the *palazzo* is packed with paintings, tapestries, gilded mirrors, colorful rugs, and interesting antiques. The hot tub, sauna, and pool, as well as the kind and helpful staff, complete the experience.

This incredible hotel only has nine rooms, so it's important to book in advance. If possible, go for a deluxe room or suite. It should be noted that the castelletto is a bit remote, frozen in time in the rural and tranquil Valdambra region in eastern Tuscany. So perhaps it is more suitable as a relaxing countryside getaway rather than as your home base for exploration and day trips.

Castelletto di Montebenichi,
★★★★★
Piazza Gorizia 9, Loc. Montebenichi, Bucine. Tel: 055.991.0110, www.castelletto.it.

 64 | **Book a Romantic Picnic,** Etruscan-Themed Excursion or Cooking Class with Toscana & Gusto

Cortona, for very good reason, is a popular destination. Charming (though very steep) streets lead you around the town made famous by Francis Meyer's *Under the Tuscan Sun*, and discovering the hidden little secrets of this well-preserved medieval town is always fun.

Once you have toured Cortona's various sites (such as the Etruscan Museum, the wonderful Diocesan Museum, and the tranquil Franciscan hermitage, all of which shouldn't be missed), you will probably be looking for a great place to relax and dine. If it is a restaurant you are after, then Cortona, despite its petite size, will not fail you. There are a number of tasty options in town (see tip 66). However, a traditional osteria or trattoria is not the only option worth considering.

Toscana e gusto is a local touring company that organizes four-course picnics for a minimum of two people. Prices start from €25 per person and include everything you might need; guests who book the service simply show up and enjoy the food, the Prosecco, the view, and the tranquil and decadent atmosphere. Picnics are available from late March to late October, depending on weather conditions. Two other very popular attractions organized by this company are their Etruscan tour, which will lead you on mission to discover Cortona's ancient past, and the reasonably priced cooking class, which is fun and intimate. All of these activities can, naturally, be matched and booked together.

Toscana e Gusto, ★★★★
Tel: 0575.604110, Cell: 349.851.2115, www.toscanaegusto.com.

🏃 | 65 | Soak Up Anghiari's Medieval Charm
and Discover Piero della Francesca's Stunning
Art in Sansepolcro

Deep among the quiet hills of the
Arezzo province hides the medieval
village of Anghiari: A delightful maze
of narrow cobbled alleys, tiny artist
shops and ancient stone *palazzi*. It's
almost impossible to imagine that
anything dramatic ever happened
here, but Anghiari was in fact center
stage for one of the most important
battles of the Renaissance—the
Battle of Anghiari in 1440, between
Milan and Florence.

The bloody fighting was
immortalized by Leonardo da
Vinci, but the affresco mysteriously
disappeared. Today, researchers
believe that it is hidden behind a
double wall in Florence's Palazzo
Vecchio. The only testimony we
have of da Vinci's work is a sketch
of the painting, made by Peter
Paul Rubens.

There isn't much to do in Anghiari
in the way of tourist attractions—
the two museums in town are very
small—but honestly, that hardly

matters, since the real pleasure here
is to wander through Anghiari's
quiet and beautiful centro. For
lunch, our favorite stop in town is **Il
Feudo del Vicaro,** a restaurant which
sits within a medieval tower house.
(On the bottom floor there's a small
bodega and deli, where you can
pick up artisanal pasta, condiments
and cheese.) The food here is rich,
comforting and slightly rustic, but
in a good way. The home-made
pasta with pecorino and truffles
is especially good, and the meat
dishes are well prepared. For your
post-lunch espresso, walk to the
well-positioned **Caffe I Giardini del
Vicario**, on Piazza del Popolo. Take
your coffee outside, on the terrace,
to enjoy the beautiful panorama.

Then, before you leave, there is
one last thing that you must do
in Anghiari. Drive from wherever
you parked your car to Chiesa della
Croce (a small non descript church
that sits at the very beginning of
Corso Matteotti, one of Anghiari's

main streets). There's nothing special about the monument itself, but once you turn your back to the church, you will see one of the most famous roads in Tuscany, the SS43, which cuts through the town and climbs high into the mountains in a surreal manner.

Next, make your way to Sansepolcro. This town may bot be on the to-do list of most visitors to Tuscany, but in reality, it offers much more than immediately meets the eye. For art lovers, a visit here is a must, as this is one of the best places in Italy to appreciate the work of Renaissance master Piero della Francesca (after the church of San Francesco in Arezzo, of course).

Start your tour at the **Museo Civico**, Sansepolcro's main attraction. This medieval palace turned museum houses some beautiful pieces by Andrea della Robbia, Santi di Tito, and Pietro della Francesca, of course, including the *Polittico della Madonna della Misericordia and The Resurrection*. This last work, in particular, has quite a history behind it. Commonly considered to be some of della Francesca's finest work, it is an example of the artist's life long dedication to the theme of perspective. In fact, famous British author Aldous Huxley went so far as to define it as "the greatest painting in the world". During WWII much of the area around Sansepolcro was bombarded, but the Museo and the paintings inside it were saved thanks to a British artillery officer named Tony Clarke, who had read Huxley's words and refused to bombard the town. It later became clear that the bombarding was also unnecessary, as the German troupes had already retreated, and Clarke was declared a local hero.

Next, take the time to tour Sansepolcro's streets. Visit the impressive **Duomo**, a 10th century Benedictine monastery that was converted into the city's main cathedral, and hop into **Panifico La Spiga**, San Sepolcro's best bread and pastry shop, to buy some cantuccini (biscotti) to munch as you tour the city. If you have the time, visit the quirky but enchanting **Aboca Museum**, which is dedicated entirely to the history of herbs and medicinal plants. You don't have to be a botanist to enjoy this exhibition, and the museum's bookshop is a real treasure trove, with much more than just books on sale.

For lunch or dinner, book a table in advance at either Ristorante Fiorentino or L'Osteria in Aboca. Of the many venues in town, these two family-run trattorias do it best.

Ristorante Fiorentino is centrally located in the heart of Sansepolcro and is famous for combining a profound respect for local traditions (some of their recipes date back to Renaissance times!) with modern flavors. Try the creamy and delicate risotto, the homemade pasta with any seasonal sauce, and the pigeon. L'Osteria in Aboca sits outside the town center, and is very popular with locals in the know. Their homemade pasta Bringoli col sugo d'oca (pasta with duck sauce), Ravioli di patate e crescenza agli spinaci (ravioli stuffed with potato, creamy cheese and spinach) and sliced steaks, prepared exclusively with locally grown Chianina beef, are all very good.

If you happen to be visiting Sansepolcro on the third Saturday of the month, go early and take advantage of the farmer's market in Piazza Torre di Berta. And if you're lucky enough to be around for the second Sunday of September you must come to enjoy the town's famous medieval jousting match, archery competition and medieval procession—the **Palio della Balestra** (www.balestrierisansepolcro.it).

Ristorante I Feudo del Vicario, ★★★★
Vicolo del poeta 1, Anghiari.
Tel: 0575 787.105, www.antoniofanelli.it.
Open Thursday–Tuesday for lunch and dinner. Closed Wednesday.

Museo Civico Sansepolcro, ★★★★
Via Niccolò Aggiunti 65, Sansepolcro.
Tel: 0575.732218,
www.museocivicosansepolcro.it
Open June 15-September 15, 9:30 a.m.–
1:30 p.m. & 2:30 p.m.–7:00 p.m.; September 16–June 14 closes one hour earlier.

Aboca Museum, ★★★
Via Niccolò Aggiunti 75,
Sansepolcro. Tel: 0575.733589,
www.abocamuseum.it.
Open April 1–September 30, daily, 10:00 a.m.–1:00 p.m. & 3:00 p.m.–7:00 p.m.; October 1–March 31, open Tuesday–Sunday (closed on Mondays), 10:00 a.m.–1:00 p.m.; 2:30 p.m.–6:00 p.m.

Ristorante Fiorentino, ★★★
Via Luca Pacioli 60.
Tel: 0575.742.033,
www.ristorantefiorentino.it.
Open Thursday–Tuesday, 12:00 p.m.–2:30 p.m. & 7:00 p.m.–9:30 p.m.; Sunday, open for lunch only; closed Wednesday.

Panicifico La Spiga, ★★★
Via Santa Caterina 72.
Open Monday–Friday, 7:30 a.m.–1:00 p.m. & 4:30 p.m.–7:30 p.m.; Saturday open in the morning only; closed Sunday.

L'Osteria in Aboca, ★★★★
Frazione Aboca 11 (outside Sansepolcro).
Tel: 0575.749125,
www.losteriainaboca.it.
Open Tuesday–Sunday, 12:30 p.m.–2:30 p.m. & 7:30 p.m.–9:30 p.m.; Closed Monday.

Experience A Unique Wine Tasting
 near Arezzo, and End with Some Delicious Truffles!

There is something special about visiting **Villa La Ripa**. Perhaps because it is the private historic mansion of a charming couple who invite you into their home to taste their boutique wines, or maybe it is because of the setting—secluded and peaceful, so very different from most other tasting venues in the region. Whatever the reason, this is an interesting stop to make.

The adventure begins as soon as you drive up to the centuries-old Renaissance mansion. Inside awaits your host—Dr. Saverio Luzzi is a physician who has also been producing wine together with his family for many years. It isn't common to see neurologists who purchase crumbling Medici-built villas in the countryside to pursue their dream, but in this case, that is exactly what happened. Guests are invited to hear about the illustrious families who once owned the villa and the surrounding land, and tour the grounds. During your visit

you will of course taste the estate's delectable Chianti wine and fine olive oil. If you are searching for an alternative to the typical wine-tasting experiences in Chianti, this is certainly an option worth considering.

Next, it's time to get serious about truffles. **Boscovivo** is a small family-run company located in the heart of Arezzo Province. It is also, surprisingly, one of the best manufacturers of truffle-based products in Tuscany. They not only offer a wide range of dips, spreads, seasoning salts, and truffle-infused goods, but also arrange tasting tours and activities for curious foodies, and their products and activities have already won an honorable mention from the Italian Food Academy.

Currently run by the charming and friendly Silvia Landucci, daughter of Alfredo Landucci, the founder of the company (whose photo is still featured on many of their products),

Boscovivo is prepared to lead visitors on truffle excursions with professional truffle hunters and trained dogs, organize tastings, and recommend the best products for you. Their attentive and welcoming manner is just one of this company's advantages. Their website is very lacking, so we would recommend contacting the company by phone or email to inquire about the various activities.

To find out about other truffle hunting and tasting adventures in Tuscany, consult tip 98.

Villa La Ripa, ★★★
Loc. Antria 38, Arezzo. Tel: 0575.315.118,
www.villalaripa.it.

Boscovivo Tartufi, ★★★
Via dei Boschi 34, Civitella in Val di Chiana. Tel: 0575.410.388 / 0575.410.396,
www.boscovivo.it.
Open Monday-Friday, 8:30 a.m.–1:00 p.m. & 2:30 p.m.–5:30 p.m. Visits and tastings can be organized according to a visitor's schedule, booking in advance is required.

‖|67| Discover the Hidden Treasures of
Cortona and Its Environs

Cortona is one of Tuscany's best known hill towns, thanks to Frances Mayes classic book, *Under the Tuscan sun.* A typical day in Cortona will include a leisurely stroll up the steep streets, a visit to the Palazzo Pubblico, a hike up to the Giroflaco Fortress and a stop at the ancient and secluded Franciscan Hermitage. But don't end your visit just yet... There are a couple more secrets in town that are worth discovering.

The first hidden treasure is actually located in plain-sight. Nearly every town in Tuscany boasts a local Diocesan museum, but these museums are rarely worth your time or money, as the work on display is usually decidedly underwhelming. **Cortona's Diocesan Museum,** on the other hand, is a surprising gem, and absolutely merits a visit.

The museum's nine halls offer a selection of medieval and Renaissance works of art, the most notable of which are the Painted Cross by Pietro Lorenzetti, the

Virgin and Child by the School of Siena and the famous *Annunciation* by Fra Angelico. Downstairs, visitors will even find a frescoed chapel that has remained untouched since the days in which this museum was a monastery.

For lunch, head to **La Bucaccia**. This is Cortona's best restaurant, and not only are advance reservations required, we recommend that in high season you call at least a few days ahead, just to be in the safe side. Although La Bucaccia has been discovered in recent years by travelers, and is now a popular stop in Cortona, somehow it hasn't lost an ounce of its charm. The restaurant is located in a converted 13th century town home, on a particularly picturesque street. Exposed stone walls and beams and soft lighting set the mood. The owners, Romano and Agostina Magi, are connoisseurs of local cuisine, and the menu reflects their passion.

Try their meat dishes, which are prepared from locally-bred cattle—the Chianina, one of the oldest cattle breeds in the world. The ravioli and other fresh handmade pasta dishes are excellent, too. And the wine list and dessert are on par with the rest of the fantastic menu.

Next, if you are visiting the area between June and August, we recommend that you drive for about 10 minutes outside of town to the beautiful Romanesque **Abbazia di Farneta**. This Benedictine-built abbey dates back to the 10th century, and while it's interesting to explore year round (especially the mysterious crypt), summertime is when this site becomes a must see destination: The fields surrounding the abbey are in full bloom, and rows upon rows of bright yellow sunflowers stretch in every which direction.

To end your day with style, drive to **Lake Trasimeno**. Though technically in Umbria, not in Tuscany, the lake is only 25 minutes south of Cortona. A relaxed evening by the water offers a welcome respite from all the tourists and sights, and the chance to simply relax. There are several secluded beaches here, as well as little bars in which you can enjoy the last dancing rays of light on the water, while tasting a good gelato.

Cortona Diocesan Museum, ★★★★
Via Mura del Duomo (in front of the Duomo), www.museodiocesanoancona. it. Open Tuesday–Sunday, 10:00 .m.--5:00 p.m. Closed Monday. Hours may vary off season.

Ristorante La Bucaccia, ★★★★
Via Ghibellina 17, Cortona.
Tel: 0575.606.039,
www.labucaccia.it.
Open Tuesday-Sunday, 12:30 p.m.-2:30 p.m. & 7:00 p.m.-11:00 p.m. Closed Monday (except in July-August, when the restaurant is open daily). Reservations are highly recommended

⊢⊣ 68 | Spend a Special Night at Il Borro,
Arezzo's Most Chic Resort

Arezzo and the eastern Tuscan countryside have a certain silence and purity of the air that differentiates them from the Siena or Chianti hills. Maybe the sense of calm comes from the fact that this part of Tuscany isn't on the usual tourist circuit. Or maybe it's because certain corners of this region feel untouched by time. As with many parts of Tuscany, this area has many spectacular views; secluded *agriturismi* dot the landscape, muddled with unpaved roads and unkempt fields. Add in the monasteries, spiritual refuges (the most famous of which is La Verna), long-forgotten churches, and secluded forests (such as the famous Camaldoli forest) that further populate the region, and you get silence, tranquility and beauty.

Il Borro Resort Spa and Winery maintains this rustic tranquility. It is owned by Ferruccio Ferragamo, son of the famous designer Salvatore Ferragamo, who bought the property in 1985 from the Duke Amedeo D'Aosta. This resort offers luxury, sophistication and style, and is surrounded by seven hundred hectares of soft hills, woodland, vineyards, olive trees, and an assortment of animals that wander the land.

When he purchased the property, Ferragamo set about renovating and rebuilding the 1,000-year-old manor house and medieval village on the estate. Both were in a state of desperate disrepair due to damage inflicted by the Second World War and the passing of time. Today, fully repaired and restored to its former beauty, the village is particularly enchanting.

As you would expect from a high-end resort owned by one of Italy's top fashion industry families, Il Borro is suffused with luxury and sophistication. The amenities include horseback riding, bike trails, tennis courts, cooking lessons, and wine tours. Alternatively, you can simply relax by the pool overlooking the marvelous view and enjoy the wellness center and spa. The rooms are a chic blend of traditional Tuscan furniture and modern facilities. Prices here aren't cheap, but should you decide to make Il Borro your home away from home, you can choose between renting a villa on the grounds and staying in a suite or apartment in the village. The most demanding guests will settle for nothing less than the exquisite Il Borro Villa. This historic gem is located right at the center of the estate and once belonged to some of the more renowned Tuscan families. Osteria il Borro, the elegant restaurant on the premises, is perfect for a romantic dinner, accompanied by one of the red wines produced by this estate, such as the Pian di Nova Rosso or Il Borro Rosso, both of which are quite good.

Il Borro Resort, ★★★★
Località Il Borro 1, San Giustino Valdarno. GPS Coordinates: 43.541675, 11.715015. Tel: 055.977.053, www.ilborro.com.

The Maremma

🏃 69 | Relax, Unwind, and Enjoy the **Perfect Dip** in the Thermal Waters of the Saturnia Spa

Nothing compares with the restorative, tingling feeling of sliding into a hot thermal pool. The medicinal properties of thermal spas have long been touted by locals for relieving everything from skin disorders to respiratory problems. There are several thermal spas and pools in Tuscany but not many stand out. **Terme di Saturnia Spa** is very different. Situated in the municipality of Manciano at a central point in the wild Maremma, this magical, idyllic hotel and thermal spa is one of Italy's best resorts.

The elegant hotel offers many amenities, including the popular Michelin-starred on-site All'Acquacotta restaurant. But the best attraction, of course, is the healing 37.5 °C thermal waters, which are rich in calcium, magnesium, sulfur, sulfate and bicarbonate ions, and are frequently replenished from a volcanic spring.

Relaxing in the warm waters is the perfect relief for tired feet after days of sightseeing. The resort itself is effortlessly stylish, with 140 rooms spread across two floors of a converted stone villa. A golf course, a full spa, regular pools and the beautiful views complete the pampering experience.

If you don't plan on spending a sizable sum on a luxurious stay at the spa, know that it is also possible to visit the thermal springs **free**

of charge. Naturally, this is a far more rustic experience, but still enjoyable. To reach the free part of the springs, known as 'Cascate del Gorello' (or 'Cascate del Mulino', on some maps), drive to Saturnia (following the signs), and as soon as you see the tiny sign saying 'Cascate del Gorello', turn your car and park at the small parking lot. A small path will lead you from the lot to the springs themselves. A word of warning is due, however— we wouldn't recommend coming here on weekends or holidays, when the site is positively packed with visitors.

If you find yourself enchanted with this area, you can even stay for the night, at **Le Cascatelle**, a magical little *agriturismo* located just 500 meters from the thermal springs. Le Cascatelle offers guests comfortable rooms, a manicured property, and even a private section of the thermal springs, in which they can dip without any distractions.

Terme di Saturnia Spa & Golf Resort, ★★★★★
the resort is located about 30 minutes from Scansano, there are signs leading to it along the main road. GPS coordinates: 11.51435 East, Lat: 42.64949 North. Tel: 0564.600.111, www.termedisaturnia.it.

Agriturismo Le Cascatelle, ★★★★
Loc. Terme di Saturnia, Saturnia. Tel: 0564.620.083, Cell: 338. 869.0049 / 339.182.6911, www.lecascatelle.it.

🏃 70 Discover a Stunning Beach in the Maremma

The Maremma is an area of Tuscany that is perfect for nature lovers. There are little beaches here that are just magical to walk on at sunset, and if you combine that with a boat ride (see tip 70) or a hiking tour of the region (see tip 127), you are in for a very special day.

We have many beloved beaches here: When we are in the mood for a more sophisticated evening, we drive down to Porto Ercole or Porto Santo Stefano; when we are looking to spend a relaxing day in a secluded spot, we head out to Laguna di Orbetello (near Albinia). But when we want some Caribbean magic in Tuscany, there is just one place to go—**Cala del Gesso.**

The Cala is a stunning but somewhat inaccessible beach that locals swear by, often calling it the most beautiful beach in southern Tuscany. However, this hidden corner of tranquility and bliss comes with a price, and requires a short but steep hike to reach the water. If you aren't afraid of a little challenge, this is the place for you. Don't forget to wear comfortable walking shoes, though—paradise doesn't come easy!

If walking all the way here is too much of a hassle, make your way to the far more accessible **La Caletta Beach Club** in Porto Santo Stefano. Chic and friendly, this is the perfect spot to relax and work on your tan. The beach also features a fun little restaurant, in case all that dipping and sunbathing awaken your appetite.

Cala del Gesso, ★★★★
to reach the Cala, drive along the SP65 from Porto Santo Stefano, and turn right at km 5+900. There will be a small asphalt road on your right. Drive down it until you reach a gate, and from there hike about 20 minutes down a rocky road to the beach.

La Caletta Beach Club, ★★★
Via Civinni 6, Potro Santo Stefano. www.hotelcaletta.it.

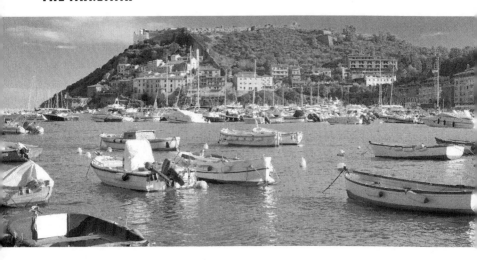

🏃 | 71 | Rent a boat (or even a yacht!) for a Day
and Sail the Tuscan Archipelago

Porto Ercole and Porto Santo Stefano are two seaports located in an area known as Monte Argentario—a peninsula in the Maremma, in southern Tuscany. **Porto Ercole**, famous for being the town where Caravaggio found refuge and eventually died alone and poor, is today a destination for Tuscany's rich. It's a glitzy place where the well-heeled moor their yachts before sailing out for a day tour of Giglio Island (recommended) or the Tuscan archipelago. Nowadays, unfortunately, Giglio Island is infamous for the horrible Concordia accident, but other than that tragedy, it is a beautiful place to explore.

In contrast to the glamor and glitz of Porto Ercole, Porto Santo Stefano is more of a beach resort town, with lots of tour operators offering guided boat rides. The tours take three or four hours, and the itinerary depends on your interests (though most make a stop at Giglio Island, the most popular attraction in the area).

Alternatively, you can be the captain of your own boat, rent a *gommone* (rubber dinghy) and take to the waters by yourself. The smaller boats don't even require a skipper's license and are inexpensive (about €120-€200). In fact, heading out for half a day with a picnic basket filled with cold water, fruit, and sandwiches and touring Tuscany by sea sounds to us like a perfect plan!

If you have a skipper's license or you want to rent a boat with a skipper, several companies are available. We particularly like **Zeurino Barche**, which both rents boats and offers guided tours, **Biba Boats, Argentarola**, and **Zen Yachts**, which runs a very professional service and rents both *gommoni* and yachts (everything between

€120 and €2,000 a day). If you are interested in renting your own boat instead of booking a short guided tour, we do recommend booking in advance. In high season it can be difficult to find an available spot, especially if you want a specific boat or date or if you are interested in renting the services of a captain. In any case, do look into a number of options before you choose the best company or tour for you.

Naturally, the companies listed above are not the only available options. As you walk along the water in Porto Santo Stefano, particularly along Viale Barellai and the promenade, you will see several signs for rentals and tours that are worth exploring. And Porto Santo Stefano and Porto Ercole aren't the only beach towns to offer boats for rent and tours—most nearby beach

towns, from Talamo to Orbetello, offer an array of such services.

Zeurino Barche,
Piazzale Candi 9, Porto Santo Stefano. Tel: 0564.818.728, www.zeurinobarche.com.

Zen Yachts,
Cala Galera BOX 4, Porto Ercole. Cell: 328.6658431 / 328.7038072, www.zenyachts.it.

Biba Boats,
Loc. Santa Liberata, Orbetello. Tel: 0564.820.116 / 335.234763, www.bibaboats.net.

Argentarola,
Via Orlando Carchidio 8, Monte Argentario. Cell: 338.7026.689, www.argentarola.com.

🏃 72 | **Rub Elbows with Tuscany's Who's Who** in Porto Ercole

Whatever your style on the open waters, we can guarantee one thing: After a day at the beach or out sailing, when you hit dry land again, you will have worked up an appetite. If you are looking for some glitz and glamour to add to your meal, choose Porto Ercole. Here you will find one of the best and most luxurious resorts in Tuscany—the **Hotel Il Pellicano**, which also features a Michelin-starred restaurant of the same name. At around €120 per person including wine, the food certainly isn't cheap (and, if we must be perfectly honest, there are better-value Michelin-starred restaurants in Tuscany). But the cuisine here is innovative, the setting is smart, and if you want to rub elbows with the Tuscan elite, this is the place to do so. (Well, this and the smart restaurants in Forte dei Marmi, see tips 118 and 120.) You can, of course, also spend the night in the hotel itself. A master deluxe suite, with an ocean view and your own private pool will cost you €2,500 a night; a double room with an ocean view is a 'steal' at around €1,000 (though special rates are occasionally available.) Naturally, you will be able to pamper yourself at the exclusive spa with treatments such as the citrus fruit antioxidant body ritual or the sea breeze massage and enjoy an array of beauty treatments, executed with products tailor-designed by the famous Santa Maria Novella antique pharmacy in Florence.

Alternatively, for a glamorous but more reasonably priced option in the Porto Ercole vicinity, try **Dama Dama**. This restaurant is part of the Argentario Golf Resort & Spa. It boasts a beautiful panoramic terrace overlooking the sea and surrounded by mountains—perfect for light lunches, cocktails, and sunset dinners.

Naturally, there are several accommodation options available at various prices. The elegant and inviting **Hotel Torre di Cala Piccola**, sits right on the cliffs of Monte Argentario, and is one of our favorite options in the area. The hotel terrace has a gorgeous view of the bay, the rooms are modern and pleasant, and guests enjoy access to the secluded and beautiful beach. Relaxing poolside, practically on the beach itself, is a delight. The restaurant is fine (though we prefer other dining options in the area).

Il Pellicano Resort, ★★★★
Località Sbarcatello, Porto Ercole.
Tel: 0564.858.111,
www.pellicanohotels.com.

Dama Dama, ★★★
Argentario Resort Golf & Spa, Via Acquedotto Leopoldino, Porto Ercole. Tel: 0564.810.292, GPS Coordinates: 42.416716, 11.184146,
www.argentarioresort.it.
The restaurant is open daily (in season), 12:30 p.m.–3:00 p.m. & 7:30 p.m.–10:00 p.m. May close off-season.

Hotel Torre di Cala Piccola, ★★★
Via della Cala, Località Cala Piccola, Porto Santo Stefano. Tel: 0564.825.111,
www.torredicalapiccola.com.
The hotel closes down off-season (from October to March).

73 Visit the Renowned Castello Colle Massari Estates and Taste Their Excellent Wines

Maria Iris and Claudio Tipa, the brother and sister team who run Castello Colle Massari, have a magic touch. Their winery is considered by some critics to be one of the best in Europe, and their work was once again officially recognized when they were chosen as the best winery in Italy by the 2014 edition of the influential *L'Espresso* guide. Maria and Claudio first united their knowledge, noses, and expertise in 1998 when they established the **Castello Colle Massari estate** in southern Tuscany, an area that was once snubbed by wine lovers and only in recent years is finally receiving the respect it deserves as more and more makers recognize its potential. Since starting this first estate, they have established two more, and all three are important in different ways.

The most famous is their **Poggio di Sotto estate** in Montalcino, where they make their excellent Brunello wine (see tip 85). Their Grattamacco estate in Bolgheri, on the Tuscan coast, is where they produce the famous Super-Tuscan Bolgheri DOC (see tip 94). All three estates can be visited and tasting tours can be booked in each. Although there are more laid-back estates in Tuscany, if you are passionate about wine and looking for a serious and professional experience, a visit to one of these is highly recommended.

The **Castello Colle Massari estate**, to which this tip is dedicated, is situated in the foothills of Mount Amiata, an area slightly out of the way for many visitors, who tend to stick to the central part of Tuscany and avoid the Maremma. But this is a beautiful region, perfect for nature lovers, with plenty of good food, pleasant hiking trails, beautiful beaches and a sense of tranquility that you can't always find in other, more crowded parts of Tuscany, especially during high season.

The huge 1,200-hectare estate is located just below the Brunello growing areas and is perfectly placed for growing Sangiovese grapes. A visit will include a chance to see their modern cellar, covering more than 6,000 square meters, and the beautiful *tenuta* (estate) itself, which somehow manages to be strikingly imposing and rustic at the same time. Booking forms for tours, and detailed directions to get to all three estates, including GPS coordinates, can be found on their website (one website for all three estates).

Colle Massari Società Agricola,
★★★★★
Loc. Poggio del Sasso, Cinigiano
Tel: 0564.990.496,
www.collemassari.it.

🍴 74 | **Enjoy a Delicious Meal** in Italy's Smallest Trattoria

La Tana dei Brilli (formerly known as La Tana del Brillo Parlante) is one of the most charming *trattorie* we've come across during our travels in Tuscany, and not just for its size. This tiny eatery, which can accommodate no more than 12 people at once, is intimate and magical. The décor is simple and enjoyably kitschy. Located just a minute from the impressive Piazza del Duomo, La Tana dei Brilli stands its ground in a town known for its fierce culinary rivalry (Massa Marittima, in northern Maremma, boasts a number of noteworthy restaurants, including Bracali, a two-starred Michelin restaurant, making this town and its surroundings a popular stop for foodies).

The menu is traditional but perfectly executed, and most dishes are modernized versions of owner Raffaella Cecchelli's father's recipes, which are over 50 years old. Here you must enjoy the fresh pasta (often rolled and cut right in front of you) in delicate pecorino sauce, the wonderful potato ravioli, generous *antipasti* platters filled with top-quality *salumi* that come directly from San Miniato (see tip 99), an all-cheese *antipasto* made entirely with cheeses from the nearby Saba farm (one of the best in Tuscany—see next tip), braised pork, quality veal *tagliata*, and much more. The restaurant uses seasonal, high-quality produce, and most pasta dishes are served in the large metal saucepans in which they were cooked. Don't miss the wonderful desserts, too—they may look rustic and simple, but wait until you actually taste them. Much like the rest of the menu, the list of

desserts changes often, depending on the chef's inspiration. We have yet to taste a bad dish here, but we do suggest you always ask Raffaella what she recommends, so you don't miss out on the best dish of the day. To walk off your lunch, tour Massa Marittima itself. The Duomo is beautiful, and the artifacts in the nearby archaeological museum are interesting, for the most part. Of course the best time to visit the town is during its famous medieval feast, the **Balestro del Girifalco** (see tip 127).

La Tana dei Brilli, ★★★★
Vicolo del Ciambellano 4, Massa Marittima. Tel: 0566.901.274. Open Friday-Sunday, 12:00 p.m.-2:00 p.m. & 8:00 p.m.-10:00 p.m. During the summer months, the restaurant is usually open daily (but do call in advance to make sure). Off-season, the restaurant may close down for a short winter break.

🏃 | 75 | **Visit Saba Farm** and Taste Some of the Best (and Healthiest!) Cheeses in Tuscany

You would be hard-pressed to find cheesemakers as professional, dedicated, and passionate as the siblings who own **Azienda Agricola Saba**. Angela and Antonio Saba attract visitors from all over Tuscany to their *caseificio* (cheese factory)—not just because of the excellent flavor of their products, but also because theirs is the first low cholesterol cheese in Italy. The sheep are fed a special diet that includes a significant quantity of flax seeds, a good source of Omega-3. The result is tasty Omega-3-rich milk. Clinical trials conducted by a medical team from the University of Cagliari (Sardinia), showed that those who regularly consumed Saba cheeses experienced 10% lower levels of cholesterol.

But the Saba family's cheeses aren't good just because of their health benefits; it is the taste that keeps visitors coming back here year after year. Originally from Sardinia, the Saba family has been in the business for more than 40 years and has become renowned across Italy for their creamy, refined, smooth pecorino cheeses.

The *Angelico* cheese is fantastic, as is the fresh cheese with pistachios. Note that since Saba only uses its own milk, the selection of available cheeses (as well as how aged and ripe they are) is closely connected with the production cycle of the sheep on the farm. From October to June, fresh milk is available, so you will find cheeses such as the 20-day-old pecorino (delicious!) and ricotta during this period.

Azienda Agricola Saba, ★★★★
Loc. Cura Nuova 74, Massa Marittima.
Tel: 0566.918.059, Cell: 340.304.2378,
www.sabaformaggi.it.
The cheese factory is open year round,
Monday–Saturday, 8:00 a.m–7:00 p.m.

🏃 76 Visit the Stunning Borgo of Pitigliano–
Tuscany's little Jerusalem

Pitigliano is one of the prettiest and most impressive *borghi* in southern Tuscany, towering above a steep gorge, and masterfully excavated into the tufa rock. Sadly, not enough tourists are aware of this *borgo's* existence. Hopefully this tip will spike the interest of some of our readers, and will inspire them to head south to visit this ancient village.

Pitigliano has been inhabited since Etruscan times, but it was during the Middle Ages that it truly flourished and even became a county capital. In 1293, it passed into the hands of the powerful Orsini family, who were interested in this strategically placed town mostly to help them in their constant battle against Siena. Some of the sights worth touring here are Palazzo Orsini (an impressive Fort, originally built by the Aldobrandesca family, rulers of the area during the high middle ages) and the towns many steep and colorful alleyways.

The best known attraction, however, is Pitigliano's tiny Jewish Quarter (or Ghetto). Pitigliano's small but vibrant Jewish community arrived during the 16th century after escaping from persecution and terrible violence in neighboring towns, which were controlled by the Papal states and filled with religious fervor as a result of the counter-reformation. The Jewish community sought refuge in this territory controlled by the Orsini family and greatly contributed to the social and economic development of the town. The Jewish Ghetto was founded in 1622 and continued thriving under the Medici family rule, earning the name "Little Jerusalem". Racial laws passed by Mussolini in 1938 changed everything for Jewish communities throughout Italy. Many families left Tuscany, seeking refuge in other cities or abroad. Others were caught and deported to concentration camps. Today, there are about 30,000 Jews living in all of

Italy and a number of tiny Jewish communities in Tuscany (mostly in Florence, Pisa, and Livorno).

Only one Jewish woman remains in Pitigliano today to keep the tradition alive, but the museum and the synagogue still draw quite a crowd. A tour of the museum will include a visit to the "Mikveh", the ritual bath house carved entirely into the tufa rock and resembling more of a biblical bathing house than something built during the Renaissance; a kosher slaughter room; a wine cellar; an antique matzo baking oven used during Passover, and more. During your visit to the Jewish Museum, you can also climb up and visit the synagogue itself, which was built in 1598 and completely renovated in 1995. End your tour of the old Jewish ghetto with a few baked goods that you can buy next door at the *Panificio del Ghetto* (the Ghetto's Bakery).

Other noteworthy attractions in the vicinity are the **Archaeological Park in Sorano** (9 kilometers away), and the charming (though minuscule) town of **Sovana**. The **Saturnia thermal springs** (see tip 68) are about 40 minutes away. For a good meal, our favorite restaurants in the area are **Hosteria di Pantalla** (fantastic local kitchen, the restaurant is situated outside of Pitigliano itself) and **Hostaria del Ceccottino**, which is perfect for a refined and sophisticated meal.

Jewish Museum and Synagogue, ★★★★

Vicolo Marghera (off Via Zuccarelli). Tel: 0564.614230. April-September, open daily, 10:00 a.m.-1:30 p.m. & 2:30 p.m.-6:30 p.m. Closed on Saturdays; October-March, open daily, 10:00-12:30 p.m. & 3:00 p.m.-5:30 p.m. Closed on Saturdays.

Hosteria di Pantalla, ★★★★

Loc. Pantalla, SP 25 Pitigliano-Farnese, Km 6, Pitigliano. Tel: 0564.616.117. Open Friday-Wednesday, 12:00 p.m.-2:30 p.m. & 7:30 p.m.-10:00 p.m. Closed Monday and Tuesday. Off season hours may vary, and the restaurant may close down for a winter break.

Hostaria del Ceccottino, ★★★★

Piazza San Gregorio VII 64, Pitigliano. Tel: 0564.614.273, www.ceccottino.com. Open Friday-Wednesday, 12:30 p.m.-3:00 p.m. & 7:00 p.m.-9:30 p.m. Closed Monday and Tuesday. Off season hours may vary, and the restaurant may close down for a winter break.

Montepulciano

 77 | **Discover Delicious Nobile di Montepulciano Wine** in Montepulciano's finest *Enoteche*

Underneath the beautiful streets of Montepulciano hides a second city of underground *enoteche*, where deep red wine flows from large wooden barrels and ancient cellars are stocked to the brim with wine from local producers. If you don't have the time (or the will) to leave town and drive out to visit the wineries themselves (see tip 78 to find out more about the best wineries in the area), then touring the *enoteche* is the next best thing.

A good *enoteca* (plural, *enoteche*), or wine merchant, is a place to cherish. Advice from an experienced wine lover from the area is invaluable. And in Montepulciano, the wine to hunt for in these shops is, of course, the ruby red, elegant and velvety Nobile di Montepulciano, one of Tuscany's most famous DOCG wines.

La Bottega del Nobile is an excellent choice. They have an extensive selection of wine from local producers, which you can taste by the glass. You can of course also pick up a bottle to go—perfect if you plan on a picnic or a dinner in your *agriturismo* or apartment. Alternatively, stay for a light lunch—the food here is quite good, too.

Enoteca La Dolce Vita is another fine choice. They have a wonderful selection of Nobile di Montepulciano (we like the smooth-tasting Salcheto and the vibrant Poliziano), as well as Chianti Classico (try something from Castello di Ama or Castello di Fonterutoli, both excellent producers), and, of course, Brunello di Montalcino. In fact, this *enoteca* stocks over 3,000 bottles in caves underground (including several good wines from other parts of Italy) and the staff is knowledgeable and happy to help. There is a small but top-quality selection of dishes and little nibbles to accompany your wine, too. Shipping can also be arranged if you are interested in buying several bottles and taking them home with you.

A third place to tempt wine lovers is the well-known **Cantina Contucci**, located right on Piazza Grande. Here, you will be taken down to the medieval cellar, which is stocked with huge wooden barrels filled to the brim with deep red Montepulciano wine. The Contucci family has been living in Montepulciano for more than 1,000 years, and has been producing wine since the Renaissance. Their Nobile di Montepulciano Riserva, at just €23, is both a bargain and delicious!

La Bottega del Nobile, ★★★★
Via di Gracciano Nel Corso 95, Montepulciano. Tel: 0578.757.016, www.vinonobile.eu.
Open daily, 10:30 a.m.–9:00 p.m. (Thursday until 7:30 p.m.), hours may vary off-season.

Enoteca La Dolce Vita, ★★★
Via di Voltaia nel Corso 80/82, Montepulciano. Tel: 0578.758.760, www.enotecaladolcevita.it.
Open daily, 10:00 a.m.–7:00 p.m. Hours may vary off-season.

Enoteca Contucci, ★★★
Via del Teatro 1, Montepulciano. Tel: 0578.757.006, www.contucci.it.
Open daily, 9:00 a.m.–12:30 p.m. & 2:30 p.m.–6:00 p.m. Hours may vary off-season.

¶¶ 78 Sink Your Teeth into a Quality Steak at
Montepulciano's Famous Acquacheta Restaurant

For more than twenty years, the cool, dark cellar of **Osteria Acquacheta** has specialized in satisfying the appetites of even the most ravenous carnivores. With a reputation as one of the best meat restaurants in Tuscany, Osteria Acquacheta's fame is perhaps rivaled only by Dario Cecchini's restaurant in Panzano, Chianti (see tip 32). The cellar that houses Acquacheta has been transformed into a hearty, informal setting—on cooler nights, a roaring fire is lit to complete the atmosphere.

Inspect your slab of steak before it is cooked and then watch as it is prepared in the brick oven at the end of the restaurant. The meat here is served in the Tuscan style, which to the uninitiated means rare, or at the very most medium; well-done is frowned upon. The house wine is reasonably priced and perfectly agreeable, though a nice bottle of Avignonesi Nobile di Montepulciano would certainly be better. You can also bring your own wine if you wish, and if it's a good bottle the owner, Giulio Ciolfi, will gladly waive corkage in exchange for a glass.

Osteria Acquacheta, ★★★★
Via del Teatro 2, Montepulciano.
Tel: 0578.717.086,
www.acquacheta.eu.
Open Wednesday–Monday, 12:30–3:00 p.m. & 7:30 p.m.–10:30 p.m. Closed Tuesday. Hours may vary off-season. Reservations are highly advised, especially in high season, and can be made by phone only.

 79 | **Visit an Award Winning Winery** and Taste Their Excellent Nobile di Montepulciano Wine

Choosing a winery tour can be tricky. Personally, we base our recommendations on a number of criteria, including the quality of the wine (of course), the professional information provided on the tour, the friendliness of the staff, and the beauty of the surroundings; ideally, we want to find a vineyard that offers tasting on a terrace with a gorgeous view.

When in Montepulciano and the surrounding area, we are usually drawn to a number of wineries that, in our opinion, offer both excellent Nobile di Montepulciano wine and charming views and ambiance.

The **Boscarelli** estate, run by the De Ferrari Corradi family, is definitely one of the best wine producers in the area. This estate is consistently mentioned on lists of top Italian wines, and a number of their wines have won awards. Pair that with the beautiful surroundings, a hospitable staff, and a very pleasant tour of

the vineyards and the production facility, and you will understand why this estate is high on our list. Since the 1960s, the family has been using the same traditional blend to make its flagship wine: Nobile di Montepulciano DOCG. We recommend picking up a bottle, of course, but don't limit yourself to the classics. Try a bottle of their multiple award-winning Nocio wine, too—a cru production, with select grapes from their very best vineyards.

Canneto has an interesting story. Unlike most vineyards in the area, which have been run by the same families for generations, this estate was bought by Swiss wine lovers in 1987 and has been run by this group of passionate winemakers ever since. The estate is nestled into the western slopes of Montepulciano and the vines benefit from this climate. The resulting wine is excellent but isn't sold on a large

scale, so it maintains a certain exclusivity. Expect the experience to be interesting, albeit pricey.

Avignonesi is another excellent choice, and one of our personal favorites—this estate offers tasting tours that are worth the drive! We recommend that you take advantage of the knowledgeable team and book a tour of the grounds in advance. The tasting at the end of the tour is particularly enjoyable, since the wine is served on the terrace with a panoramic view overlooking the hills. Avignonesi are known for both their Nobile di Montepulciano and their rich tasting Vin Santo, a centuries-old Tuscan dessert wine, usually served at the end of a meal together with *cantuccini*.

The team here takes their wine, and tradition, very seriously. Each lot is fermented separately, solely with indigenous yeast, to maintain as much as possible of the traditional taste and characteristics of the grapes' flavor. If you want to treat yourself to their best selection, go for the Nobile di Montepulciano Grandi Annate, a delicious, smooth, aromatic wine with a great finish. You can drink it right away, or let it age for a few more years and pop it open

on a special occasion. The Nobile di Montepulciano DOCG is excellent, too. Bookings aren't necessary for a basic wine tasting; you can simply stop by during open hours (see below) and taste some wine on the *enoteca* (free if you purchase a bottle). Cooking lessons, more elaborate wine tastings that include lunch on the terrace, and organized tours must be booked in advance.

Boscarelli-Marchesi de Ferrari Corradi, ★★★★
Via di Montenero 28, Cervognano di Montepulciano. Tel: 0578.767.277 / 0578.767.608,
www.poderiboscarelli.com.
Please note that weekend visits must be booked in advance. Weekday visits should preferably be booked in advance, too, especially off-season.

Canneto, ★★★
Via dei Canneti 14, Montepulciano.
Tel: 0578.757.737,
www.canneto.com.
Tours and tastings are available, and must be booked in advance.

Avignonesi, ★★★★
Via Colonica 1, Valiano di Montepulciano, GPS Coordinates: 43.17306 N / 11.93306 or 43° 10' 23" / 11° 55' 59".
Tel: 0578.724.304 or Cell: 346.580.5310,
www.avignonesi.it.
The Avignonesi cellar (cantina) is open May-October, Monday-Friday, 9:00 a.m.-6:00 p.m. & Saturday-Sunday 11:00 a.m.-6:00 p.m.; November-April, Monday- Friday 9:00 a.m.-5:00 p.m.

80 | **Dine at a Charming Restaurant** in the Heart of Montepulciano

Montepulciano is one of the prettiest hill towns in southern Tuscany—set on a high limestone ridge of almost two thousand feet, it is home to one of the best preserved historical centers in all of Tuscany. Famed for its wine production, Montepulciano also boasts a number of excellent restaurants along its pleasant streets that will surely tempt you with their delicacies. For lunch or dinner, try one of our favorites: **Ristorante La Grotta.** The combination of a perfect location (outside Montepulciano itself, overlooking the San Biagio temple), the attentive service and delicious food, not to mention their use of quality local produce and seasonal specialties, creates natural grace and charm. The restaurant is somewhat pricier than others in the area, but it also offers a serious and wonderfully-executed culinary experience. Try the pasta, which is the restaurant's forte, and let the knowledgeable staff recommend the right wine to accompany the day's dishes. The Tuscan croutons with fois gras and Vin Santo, the tagliatelle with goat cheese and artichokes, the saffron flavored pheasant ravioli, anything with white truffles, and the rack of lamb in a crust of bread and aromatic herbs are all excellent.

For something completely different, don't miss the delicious food and the fun wine tour at **Cantina Gattavechi**, our newest favorite spot in town. The setting is lovely, right next to the enchanting San Biagio Temple, the owners are friendly, and the food is rustic and excellent: large antipasti platters filled with salumi and local cheeses, homemade pasta and perfectly prepared meat. What is there not to love? Naturally, a visit here wouldn't be complete without touring the small historic cellar and tasting some of the family's good wines, which have been professionally and lovingly produced for four generations.

Ristorante La Grotta, ★★★★★

Via di San Biagio 15, Loc. San Biagio, Montepulciano.
Tel: 0578.757.479 / 0578.757.607,
www.lagrottamontepulciano.it.
Reservations are highly recommended. Open Thursday-Tuesday, 12:30-2:30 & 7:30-9:30. Closed on Wednesday and off season.

Cantina Storica Gattavecchi & La Cucina Di Lilian, ★★★★

Via Collazzi 74, Montepulciano (near the San Biagio Temple). Tel: 0578.757110, cell: 392.9252883 / 392.9012507. In high season (April-late November), the restaurant is open for lunch daily (12:30 p.m.-2:30 p.m.) and for diner Thursday-Sunday only (7:30 p.m.-9:30 p.m.); Off-season, the restaurant is open for lunch daily, and for diner on Saturday nights only. The Cellar is open daily, 10:00 a.m.-7:00 p.m. (in the off-season: 10:30 a.m.-5:30 p.m.).

Val d'Orcia

♨ | 81 | Indulge Yourself with a Magical Afternoon
Aperitivo or Meal in Monticchiello

In a tiny medieval village ten minutes from Pienza, you could have one of the most spectacular *aperitivi* of your trip. Naturally, there are quite a few spots in Pienza itself that offer a perfectly pleasant *aperitivo* of their own, but, simply put, the small hamlet of Monticchiello offers some of the most spell-binding views in Tuscany, the perfect accompaniment to a memorable meal or drinks. This fairy-tale village, whose history stretches well back into the first millennium A.D., and which is currently home to less than one hundred inhabitants, is an absolute joy. Its old walls surround houses that are superbly well-maintained, and its stone-paved streets are unusually wide for a settlement dating back so far. The only drawback is that finding parking here can be a real challenge, even more so than in Pienza.

If it's a simple pre-dinner *aperitivo* or an afternoon snack you are after,

then head to **La Guardiola**. It has the best location in town, with seating on the terrace overlooking the valley and providing an unforgettable view. The lengthening shadows and changing colors that come with the sunset are a mesmerizing sight to behold. The food is tasty, and while it may not be the right venue for a serious dinner, it is the perfect authentic spot for a light snack and *aperitivo*.

For a more serious meal, head to **Osteria la Porta**, which also has a terrace with a view (especially gorgeous at sunset). Housed in a quaint, historic *palazzo*, this restaurant offers food that is very tasty, even if slightly overpriced (which isn't a surprise, given the number of tourists who come here). The service is friendly and the general atmosphere is laid-back and fun. Try their tasty fresh pasta, particularly the *pici*, the *peposo* and the *maialino in crosta*. The wine list

is very good, featuring a number of top local producers. It goes without saying that a table as close to the view as possible is the best place to enjoy your meal here, so book in advance to secure your spot on the terrace! If you would like a longer stay to fully appreciate the views of this charming hill town, then ask the owners of the osteria about one of two perfectly comfortable rooms available for rent, or go to their website, where you will find details about all they have to offer.

La Guardiola, ★★★

Viale Marino Cappelli 1, Monticchiello (Pienza) Tel: 331.880.0443, www.barlaguardiola.it.
Open March-January, daily, 9:00 a.m.-11:00 p.m., though hours tend to vary off season, and they often close as early as 5:30 p.m.

Osteria La Porta, ★★★★

Via del Piano 1, Monticchiello (Pienza). Tel: 0578.755.163, www.osterialaporta.it.
Open Friday-Wednesday, noon-3:00 p.m. & 7:30 p.m.-9:30 p.m. Closed Thursday. January 10-February 5, closed for winter break (precise dates change yearly, sometimes they close down in mid December, too-call in advance to make sure before driving here if you are visiting off-season). Reservations highly recommended, especially in high season.

🏃 | 82 | Discover the Charms of Pienza

Located in the UNESCO World Heritage site of the Val d'Orcia, Pienza, which itself was declared a World Heritage site in 1996, is known as the jewel of this magnificent valley. A delight for the eyes, the commune is surrounded by vistas that will make you sigh with happiness. Pienza is a perennial favorite of travelers to Tuscany, and the views here define the romantic ideal of Renaissance pastoralism, with age-old farms, villages and towns nestled in the smoothly conical hills.

Pienza itself has undeniable charm. Once known as Corsignano, it was the birthplace of Enea Silvio Piccolomini, who later became Pope Pius II. Having spent many years away from his native town, the Pope returned after his papal coronation to find a village in which many of the inhabitants lived out a wretched existence. He dreamed of turning the settlement into the ultimate idyllic Renaissance town,

so under his orders, the town was completely rebuilt during the 15th century according to the principles of Renaissance architecture, as laid down by renowned architect Leon Battista Alberti. The work was carried out by Alberti's student, Bernardo Rossellino, and the results are magical. The only thing that ruins this marvel is the hordes of tourists who come every summer to admire the beauty of Pienza. If you can come off-season, in September or October, consider yourself lucky, as this is the best time to appreciate the charms of this town.

Pienza's wondrous buildings center on Piazza Pio II. Head straight for this charming town square, and begin your tour with a visit to **Palazzo Piccolomini,** the mansion that belonged to Pope Pius II's hugely influential noble family. Located on the west side of the piazza, this impressive construction was completed in 1463. The Italian gardens behind the mansion offer

a beautiful view; one can even spot Mount Amiata, a favorite sight for the Pope, far off in the distance. On the south side of the piazza adjacent to Palazzo Piccolomini sits the **Duomo.** The façade, one of the earliest completed in the Renaissance style, dominates the square. Inside you will find lovely altar paintings by famous students of the Sienese school, including Giovanni Di Paolo and Il Vecchietta. There are other impressive buildings that you can explore, such as the **Palazzo Vescovile** and the **Palazzo Comunale**, to complete the historical part of the tour. Naturally, don't skip a walk along Pienza's walls, to admire the splendid view.

Next, a tour of Pienza's charming alleyways must begin with a good cup of coffee, or even a glass of wine accompanied by excellent chocolate cake, to set the mood. For both, stop at **Piccolomini Caffè**. Service here can be hasty and even unfriendly at times, but if you manage to get a table in their tiny courtyard in the stone alley out back, it's the perfect place for a relaxing nibble. The sandwiches here are good, but if you have a bit of a sweet tooth, go straight for their chocolate cake.

Made by one of Florence's leading bakeries, **Pistocchi**, it's divine and goes particularly well with a nice, velvety glass of Montepulciano Nobile. A number of artisanal beers and good local wines are also on the menu, naturally.

For a tasty light lunch, try our favorite place in town, **La Taverna di Re Artù**. Its traditional, honey-toned exterior houses a very simple dining area and the décor—small circular tables under the exposed wooden crossbeams—is immediately inviting. The cold cuts, cheeses (including a tasty pecorino fondue) and bruschetta here are all delicious. The wine list is small compared to many other places in the area, but the quality of the wines they stock is undeniable. The same can be said for the range of micro-brew beers on offer, making this another perfect stop for an enjoyable *aperitivo*.

For a more substantial meal, that includes pasta and meat, we would recommend **La Buca di Enea**. Tiny and delicious, this friendly eatery is run by a husband-and-wife team who know their way around a good plate of pasta. Try their pappardelle,

pici and cold cuts, and then walk off your meal as you tour the panoramic walls of Pienza, enjoying a truly spectacular vista. If you prefer a more sophisticated and modern restaurant, **La Bandita** will be right on target with their innovative and perfectly executed menu.

Next, there are several alluring little shops in Pienza that sell the typical selection of Tuscan ceramics, produce, tablecloths and bags, but to be honest, we are reluctant to recommend any of them. Prices here are high—higher even than San Gimignano. However, if Pienza is your only stop, there are a few options worth considering. The town's main street, Corso Rossellino, is the place to go for some light shopping, and the selection here is far better than what you might find in other towns in the valley (such as Montalcino, San Quirico, Bagno Vignoni and more). We especially like the ceramic dishes at **Ceramiche d'Arte** in Piazza Martiri della Libertà (located at the very beginning of Corso Rossellino). They stock some delightful handmade items that you won't find in other shops. For the best cheese and produce shops, see tip 82.

A great place to stay in Pienza is **Agriturismo Cacciamici.** The setting is secluded and enchanting, the apartments are reasonably priced, comfortable and beautifully designed, and the owners are friendly and accommodating. Next, for a simple, welcoming, budget friendly stay in Monticchiello (15 minutes from Pienza), **In Toscana Affitacamere** is a perfect solution. You can rent a room, an apartment or an entire house in this magical little stone village. Alternatively, try the very popular **Agriturismo Cretaiole**, which is perfectly positioned outside of Pienza itself, allowing visitors to easily tour the area while still enjoying the magic of rural Tuscany. The owners, the Moricciani family, will make you feel right at home, and will be more than happy to recommend or organize themselves various activities to supplement your stay, everything from hikes to cooking classes to wine tastings.

Those who prefer a more stylish venue will be delighted with **La Bandita** (operated by the owners of the aforementioned La Bandita Caffè). This boutique country house has received rave reviews from a number of international publications such as Vanity Fair, The New York Times and Marie Claire, and it's easy to see why. Chic and stylish, La Bandita is owned by a New York couple who have made their home in the Val d'Orcia, and they have brought with them a sense of upscale sophistication unusual for this area. The location is stunning, with the obligatory views of the remarkable landscape, which can be enjoyed while sitting outside or swimming in the infinity pool. The rooms are graceful and elegantly furnished in modern style, and all have air conditioning. For other unique lodging options in this area, see tips 84, 87 and 88.

Piccolomini Caffè, ★★★
Corso il Rossellino 87, Pienza.
Tel: 0578.748.051. Open Friday-Wednesday, 8:00 a.m.–9:00 p.m. Closed Thursday. July–August, open daily.

La Taverna di Re Artù, ★★★
Via della Rosa 4, Pienza. Open Friday-Wednesday, 11:30 a.m.–8:00 p.m. Closed Thursday. May close down off-season

La Buca di Enea, ★★★
Via della Buca 10, Pienza.
Tel: 0578.748.653. Open daily, 11:30 a.m.–10:00 p.m., hours may vary, and the restaurant may close down off-season.

La Bandita: ★★★★
Caffè, Corso il Rossellino 111, Pienza.
Tel: 0578.749.005. In season, the restaurant is open for lunch Tuesday-Sunday, 12:30 p.m.–2:30 p.m. & 7:30 p.m.–9:30 p.m. Closed Monday. May close down of season for a short winter break.
Agriturismo: Podere La Bandita, Pienza. www.la-bandita.com.
Cell: 333.404.6704.

Agriturismo Cacciamici, ★★★★
Loc. Cacciamici, Pienza, Val d'Orcia.
Tel: 0578.754.006, Cell: 389.8058675 / 340.540.5873,
www.cacciamici.it.

In Toscana Affitacamere, ★★★
Monticchiello (Pienza).
www.intoscanacamere.it.

Agriturismo Cretaiole, ★★★★★
Pienza. Tel: 0578.748083,
cell: 338.740.9245 (Isabella),
www.cretaiole.it.

🍴 83 | **Buy Some Delicious Pecorino Cheese** or Become a Cheese Maker Yourself!

If you are an Italian cheese connoisseur, then you have heard of Pienza. The town's most famous industry is its cheese, and the pecorino here is a nationally known brand that has been produced in this area for centuries. And while production techniques are up-to-date, the core philosophy remains unchanged; in fact, when you are digging into some *pecorino di Pienza,* you can be almost certain that Pope Pius II, a Pienza native, enjoyed a very similar delicacy some 500 years ago.

Il Cacio di Ernello is one of our favorite cheese shops in town. Located just a few minutes from Pienza's main street and a few meters from the town's main parking lot, this small, inviting shop sells cheese produced by Ernello Armellini and his family at Podere San Polo, a farm located just four km away. They have a delicious array of pecorino cheeses aged with different methods, as well as a surprisingly creamy yogurt, made with a mix of sheep's milk and goat's milk. If you are interested in learning more about the cheese-making process, tours of the farm and tastings can be organized.

Podere Il Casale is an excellent choice for foodies and nature lovers. This organic, self-sustained farm at the heart of the Orcia Valley offers a variety of highly recommended activities for cheese lovers. Choose between a guided tour of the farm and the land, a traditional cheese tasting, or even a fun cheese making workshop. If you've always dreamt of peeking behind the curtains and learning the secrets of the trade, this two-hour long activity will provide the perfect introductory experience.

For some excellent ricotta that is fresh, full-bodied and will leave a delicate flavor of creamy sheep's milk lingering in your mouth, head to **SOLP**. You can visit their shop outside of Pienza (drive

six km on the SP146 towards Chianciano, you'll see the shop on your right) or simply go to their Pienza shop, on Via Dogali 6. You will also find a selection of pasta, marmalade, sauces, and pecorino cheese, naturally. In our opinion their marzolino cheese is especially good; this light, fresh cheese has been a favorite with Tuscans since Renaissance times and was especially appreciated by members of the Medici family. Today marzolino is immediately recognizable due to its slightly squashed, rounded shape. One of the best marzolino cheeses is the red variety (*marzolino rosso*). The red coloring comes from the tomato concentrate and oil wash used in production, which leaves a very delicate tomato aftertaste in the cheese itself. Don't forget to try their freshest available pecorino. SOLP's version is particularly delicate and rich tasting.

Lastly, for a selection of fantastic cheeses from many small producers in the valley, you really must stop by **La Taverna del Pecorino**—one of the best shops in town. The selection here is excellent, and the owners are friendly and they will usually insist

that you try a number of cheeses before you make your purchase. Those who prefer more mature cheeses with a more 'decisive' flavor will find this shop perfect for their needs; don't miss the *pecorino stagionato alle foglie di pera*, which is aged wrapped in pear tree leaves, and the pecorino tartufato, a creamy, truffled pecorino cheese.

Il Cacio di Ernello, ★★★★
Viale Mangiavacchi 37, Pienza.
Tel: 0577.665.321,
www.degustazionidipecorino.it.
Open Tuesday, Thursday-Sunday, 9:30 a.m-12:30 p.m. & 3:00 p.m.-7:00 p.m.
Closed Monday and Wednesday.

Podere Il Casale, ★★★★★
Via Podere Il Casale 64, Pienza
Tel: 0578.755109, www.podereilcasale.it
Classes and tours take place twice daily, and require advance booking. GPS Coordinates: Lat. 43.080901 - Long. 11.711618; N 43° 4' 51", E 11° 42, 42"

SOLP Caseificio Cheese Shop, ★★★
Via Dogali 6, Pienza. Tel: 0578.749.519,
www.pienzasolp.it.
Open daily, 10:00 a.m.-6:30 p.m., hours may change off-season.

La Taverna del Pecorino, ★★★★★
Via Condotti 1, Pienza.
Tel: 0578.749.412, Cell: 329.865.2763,
www.tavernadelpecorino.it.
Open daily, 10:00 a.m.-7:00 p.m., hours may change off-season.

🏃 84 Be Conquered by the Magic of the Val d'Orcia and Hear Gregorian Chants at the Sant'Antimo Abbey

A UNSECO World Heritage site since 2004, the Val d'Orcia is a part of Tuscany that oozes magic and charm and shouldn't be missed. The valley changes colors with the seasons—strong, vital green washes over the hills in spring and lunar yellow appears in the summer. But the most beautiful time is shortly after the harvest, between mid-May and mid-June, when golden wheat covers the valley, interrupted only by patches of wildflowers.

Numerous writers, poets, and artists have been inspired by the Val d'Orcia, as have many filmmakers. Among the movies filmed in the area are Franco Zeffirelli's *Romeo and Juliet*, Ridley Scott's *Gladiator*, and Anthony Minghella's *The English Patient*. When you drive through the area, it is easy to understand why the Val d'Orcia has been such a source of inspiration.

The valley has many great spots to visit. Pienza (see tip 81) is always popular, and the *enoteche* of Montalcino, featuring the world-famous locally produced Brunello wine, are a must-stop, of course (see tip 85). Two additional popular destinations are San Quirico d'Orcia, with its tiny streets bursting with charm, and Bagni San Filippo (see tip 90) with its fantastic thermal springs and pools. But one site that really shouldn't be missed is **Abbazia di Sant'Antimo**—the Sant'Antimo Abbey. This enchanting Romanesque abbey is located just 15 minutes from Montalcino and is cared for by Norbertine monks, who chant Gregorian hymns a number of times during the day. Listening to the chants, it feels like you are being transported back to the Middle Ages, the time when the church was built.

The Sant'Antimo complex was once much larger, and comprised 90 churches and 85 other buildings, including monasteries and hospitals. According to local legend,

the army of the Great Charlemagne stopped by the abbey, and many soldiers became very ill. During the night, an angel appeared before Charlemagne and told him he should prepare a potion for his soldiers, mixing the grass from the abbey with wine. Miraculously, the soldiers were healed after drinking the concoction, so Charlemagne decided to finance the rebuilding and expansion of the abbey to its current size. To hear the Gregorian chants, you'll have to come at 9:00 or 9:15 a.m., 12:45, 2:45, 7:00, or 8:30 p.m. on weekdays, or at 9:00 or 11:00 a.m., 12:45, 2:45, 6:30, or 8:30 p.m. on Sundays and holidays (hours may vary, do check their website before coming here). Before you leave, don't forget to drive to the Abbey's bookshop (two minutes by car)—even if you have no intention of buying a book, the shop is located on a hill with a picture-perfect **panoramic view** of the abbey and its surroundings.

Abbazia di Sant'Antimo, ★★★★
Castelnuovo dell'Abate, Montalcino,
Tel: 0577.835.659,
www.antimo.it.

🏃 85 | Treat Yourself to a Day at the Spa of One of the Most Stunning Resorts in Tuscany

Castello di Velona is, without a doubt, one of the most beautiful and exclusive resorts in Tuscany. With its effortlessly elegant rooms, magical suites (located within the ancient castle itself) and impeccable décor, this hotel is the very definition of luxurious, upscale accommodations. But even if a weekend here is out of your price range, you can still enjoy the resort's facilities, relax, and take in the incredible views (and they really are incredible!) by purchasing a daily pass to the hotel spa.

For about €50 (not cheap, but such a price can be expected given the venue) you will be able to enter the 1,500-square-meter, travertine marble cladded space, dip into the hotel's pools (including the infinity pool), spend some time in one of the five treatment cabins or the two Turkish baths, re-energize in the sauna or the 'emotional showers,' or book one of the various massages and treatments on offer (priced separately). Visit the Castello's website to find out more.

Castello di Velona, ★★★★
Località La Velona, Montalcino,
Tel: 0577.839.002,
www.castellodivelona.it.

 ## 86 | Discover the World-Famous Brunello Wine in Montalcino

It feels almost redundant to say that Tuscany is a part of the world that has an abundance of wineries and wine tours. In every area of the countryside, it is easy to find producers willing to open their gates and invite wine-loving tourists to admire their estates, cellars, and production facilities; and, of course, to buy their wines. This enviable oversupply means that choosing the right vineyard to visit, and the right wines to try, can be challenging. Should you go for a classic Chianti? What about the Super-Tuscans? How about the Nobile di Montepulciano? We love all of these wines, but we cannot ignore the fact that the Brunello di Montalcino is not only one of Italy's most famous wines, it is also a symbol of Tuscany. No oenophile should leave the region without touring at least one estate, and witnessing the making of this beloved wine at first-hand.

When we seek a place to enjoy a good Brunello tasting, we want an estate that combines excellent wines (preferably award-winning. Yes, we are spoiled that way...) with a magical location. Luckily, the **Col d'Orcia** estate offers just that. It's located near the petite, gorgeous hilltop village of Sant'Angelo in Colle, right outside Montalcino, and the winery grounds are picturesque, surrounded by hills, ancient cypress and olive trees. The tour itself is informative and interesting, and the staff here will leave you with a much deeper knowledge of wine than when you arrived. As for the wines themselves, their Brunellos rank among the best in the area, especially the Brunello di Montalcino DOCG Riserva. The Nearco San'Antimo Rosso DOC, a handpicked single cru made with the best grapes, is another must try, and one of our personal favorites. Book the tour, which of course includes tastings, in advance.

Alternatively, visit the cellar, taste a few wines and pick up a bottle to take home with you. The price of the tasting at the cellar varies according to the wines you want to try.

Naturally, Col d'Orcia isn't the only place that offers visitors the chance to taste top-notch Brunello wine. The **Casanova di Neri** estate was founded in 1971 by Giacomo Neri, who understood the huge potential of the area and began investing in what became a dream and a lifelong passion for him and his family. Currently, it is one of the hottest names on the Montalcino wine scene, after having scored fantastic marks from James Suckling, Robert Parker and a number of wine magazines. The Casanova di Neri wines are complex, exclusive and all-around wonderful, so stopping by their enoteca for an impromptu tasting or booking a tour (in advance) is highly recommended. Equally popular at the moment is **Il Poggione**, a remarkable little winery whose Brunello wine was recently listed as N. 4 on Wine Spectator magazine's list of the best wines in the world, 2015. The owners (who also run a small and very welcoming agriturismo) put their heart and soul into their wine, and the results speak for themselves. Tours aren't regularly available, but guests are more than welcome to stop by and purchase a bottle or two.

Alternatively, visit **Castello Banfi**. The narrow, cypress-lined road and vine-covered hills stretching out in every direction make just the drive up to the castle memorable. The 7,100-acre estate is magnificent, perhaps even more impressive because, up until about 25 years ago, the majority of the land was covered by forest. However, once the Mariani family acquired it, they set about transforming the land into not just one of the major producers of Brunello in Tuscany, but also a superbly luxurious resort. A walk through the grandeur of their vineyards is pleasurable, while the view of Monte Amiata, southern Tuscany's highest peak, is wonderful.

The jewel in the crown is the castle itself, originally known as Poggio Alle Mura (which, to this day, remains the name given to the Brunello produced by this estate). The castle isn't just one fortress; it is in fact a large complex—an entire medieval village to be exact—with roots stretching as far back as the Etruscans. The ostentatious Romanesque structure is now home to one of Tuscany's most exclusive hotels, **Il Borgo**. With just 14 uniquely designed rooms, it can be very pricey to stay here. However, an outdoor swimming pool with sumptuous views of the Tuscan sunsets, a perfectly manicured garden covered in delicate white roses, a peaceful reading room, top-of-the-line sports and spa facilities, cooking classes, and even hot air balloon rides all ensure that if you can afford it, your stay will be one you will never forget, for all the right reasons. Similarly, tours of the castle and its grounds or tastings in the beautiful enoteca aren't cheap, but they are interesting, impressive, and professional. The food in their

tavern is good, but, in our opinion, over-priced. Booking in advance is highly recommended, as this estate is popular.

Biondi Santi is another important contender for the wine enthusiast's attention. One of the most famous Brunello producers in the world, this is, in fact, the first family to produce this esteemed wine according to its modern formula. A visit to this estate is a special experience. The tour is quite short, but well-priced, interesting and informative nonetheless, and the setting is nothing short of magical—a tiny, romantic estate that is still inhabited by the noble Ricasoli family, where ivy-clad walls and hidden little trails come together to create a unique atmosphere.

Admittedly, the Biondi Santi Brunello is very expensive. It has been named one of the leading wines in the world by several magazines. (The 1955 Brunello was chosen as one of the 12 best wines of the 20th century, and you can still purchase one of the 228 remaining bottles from that year for the 'small' fee of €5,700.) A Biondi Santi Riserva (produced only during exceptionally good years with grapes that come from vines that are at least 25 years old) will cost a few hundred euro, and a 20-year-old Riserva bottle will easily cost a

couple of thousand euro. If you are unwilling to spend a fortune, you can still enjoy a nice classic bottle of a Biondi Santi Annata, produced yearly, which will cost around €80 a bottle. The Biondi Santi wines are produced according to very traditional techniques, and are aged in huge barrels, so that as little of the wine as possible comes in contact with the wood. Production is kept on a very small scale, and these wines are famous for their extraordinary aging potential (a good Riserva bottle will easily last for 40–50 years in your cellar).

Poggio di Sotto is another obvious choice. This is a name connoisseurs swear by—the winery is set between Mount Amiata and the Orcia River, and the view from Poggio di Sotto is alluring and calm. Production here has a rather low yield, mostly due to the very refined process of grape selection. Particularly notable are their 2006 and 2007 Brunello and Brunello Riserva; both won several awards and mentions. We also love their Rosso di Montalcino, which is, in many respects, very similar to the Brunello, but much more reasonably priced.

Lastly, we would recommend two additional producers that absolutely merit a visit, even if you only have time for a quick stop at their enoteca for a taste and to pick up a bottle. They may not be as world-famous as the other producers reviewed in this tip, but their wines will easily impress even the most demanding experts. These are also names to keep in mind when ordering a bottle of Brunello in one of the restaurants in the area. **Tenute Silvio Nardi** and **Lisini** both produce a memorable, deep, complex, and award-winning Brunello wine. Tastings and tours can be organized in both estates.

Col d'Orcia, ★★★★
Via Giuncheti, Montalcino
Tel: 0577.80891, GPS 42° 57' 59" N, 11°
26' 03" E
www.coldorcia.it.
The cellar is open Monday-Saturday,
9:00 a.m.-12:30 p.m. & 2:00 p.m.-5:00
p.m. Tours and tastings must be booked a
few days in advance.

Azienda Agricola Casanova di Neri,
★★★★★
Podere Fiesole, SP 14 Via Traversa dei
Monti, KM 31,800, Montalcino.
Tel: 0577.834.455,
www.casanovadineri.it.
The estate's enoteca is open for buying
and tasting Monday-Friday, 9:00 a.m.-
1:00 p.m. & 2:00 p.m.-6:00 p.m. Guided
visits to the cellar and the vineyards
can be organized, but must be booked in
advance, at: visit@casanovadineri.com.

Tenuta Il Poggione, ★★★★
S. Angelo in Colle, Montalcino.
Tel: 0577.844.029,
www.tenutailpoggione.it.

Castello Banfi ★★★★
(Castello di Poggio alle Mura), Montalcino.
Tel: 0577.840.111,
www.castellobanfi.com.
Guided tours and tastings must be
booked in advance. You will need your
own car to participate in the tour, since
the cellar is located about 5 km from
the castle itself and they don't offer
transport. Booking: 0577.877.505,
reservations@banfi.it. Alternatively,
taste some of the castle's best-known
wines in the handsome enoteca, which
is open daily, 10:00 a.m.-7:30 p.m. (until
5:30/6:00 p.m. in the winter months).

Biondi Santi, ★★★★★
Tenuta Greppo, Villa Greppo 183,
Montalcino. Tel: 0577.848.087,
www.biondisanti.com
(check their website for driving
instructions). Tours should be booked in
advance. Tastings in the cellar are not
available.

Poggio di Sotto, ★★★★★
Montalcino, GPS Coordinates: N 42° 59'
32.71" - E 11° 31' 30.45".
Tel: 0564.990.496,
www.collemassari.it.
Tours are available May-October,
Monday-Friday, 9:30 a.m.-6:30 p.m.
and Saturday 9:30 a.m.-1:30 p.m.;
November to April, Monday-Friday, 9:30
a.m.-5:30p.m. Tours last for about an
hour, and include a visit to the cellar, as
well as a tasting (of the Brunello wine
and the Rosso di Montalcino). Advance
booking is necessary.

Tenute Silvio Nardi, ★★★★
Casale del Bosco, Montalcino.
Tel: 0577.808.269,
www.tenutenardi.com.

Lisini, ★★★★
Podere Casanova,
Sant'Angelo in Colle, Montalcino.
Tel: 0577.844.040, Cell: 366.633.8677,
www.lisini.com.

¶¶ | 87 | **Tour the Streets of Montalcino** and Enjoy an Authentic and Tempting Meal

In the last two to three decades, as wine tourism has grown in popularity, Montalcino has transformed from a simple, often overlooked town to a prestigious wine-producing tourist destination. Today Montalcino attracts wine-lovers who want to sample the world-renowned Brunello di Montalcino wine and the lesser-known Montalcino Rosso.

This lively, hilly little town is filled with busy *enoteche* and tasty restaurants, and the multitude of choices can be confusing for visitors. However, a few places do stand above the others, and for the most part offer a rounded and authentic dining experience, paired, naturally, with excellent local Brunello wine.

Trattoria Il Pozzo isn't actually in Montalcino, but right in the center of the tiny, stunning village of Sant'Angelo in Colle. Positioned 10 kilometers north of Montalcino, far from the touristic chaos of the center, Sant'Angelo is like a breath of fresh air. The food here is authentic, though their menu doesn't maintain a consistent quality, and some dishes aren't as good as others. We enjoyed the fresh homemade pici and their bistecca Fiorentina and the pasta with wild boar ragù was lovely. Other dishes, such as the *bocconcini* in brunello sauce, were no more than OK. Another highly recommend option is **Il Leccio**. The food here is fantastic, and the setting is incredibly Tuscan and charming. Try the *bistecca Fiorentina* which is very good, the *sformatino di porcini con fonduta di parmigiano* (a porcini mushroom terrine, served with parmigiano fondue), and the salumi antipasto platter, which will satisfy any carnivore. For your *primo*, don't miss the pici pasta or the *tagliatelle*, both of which are served with *sugo di carne (ragù)* and are excellent, as is the pasta with fresh mushrooms (in season) and the grilled meats (all locally sourced, from Chianina cows). A good selection of vegetarian options is available, too.

Another excellent option is **Locanda Demetra**. This fantastic restaurant is a recent addition to the Montalcino culinary scene. It offers guests a combination of good food, a stunning vista, and an authentic setting. Booking your table well in advance is essential, as the number of openings is limited, especially if you want to sit outside and enjoy the sweeping views. Those who fall in love with the area can extend their visit by joining one of the Locanda's popular cooking classes, for a hands-on experience.

In Montalcino itself, our eatery of choice is **Ristorante Re di Macchia**. This tavern prides itself on its authentic Tuscan fare, and sticks to a simple and traditional but well-executed menu. Try the antipasti platters, with a selection of local charcuterie and sheep cheese, the chubby pasta with boar ragu or with porcini mushrooms, and pair it all with a good bottle of Brunello, of course.

To walk off you meal, make your way along the narrow streets of Montalcino to **Viale Strozzi** (just 5 minutes away from Piazza Garibladi). There is a small park here, complete with benches and trees, and the sweeping views that can be enjoyed from this point are nothing short of spectacular.

Should you feel the need to indulge in some extra shopping before heading back to your car, we would recommend you make a stop at **Abbigliamento 564 Via Mazzini,** a fantastic shop filled with surprises that any fashion lover would appreciate. Note that they have two locations on the same street, at number 25 and at number 39.

Trattoria Il Pozzo, ★★★
Piazza Castello, Sant'Angelo in Colle. Tel: 0577.844015, www.trattoriailpozzo.com. Open Wednesday-Monday, 12:00 p.m.-2:30 p.m. & 7:00 p.m.-11:00 p.m. Closed Tuesday.

Ristorante Re di Macchia, ★★★★
Via Soccorso Saloni 21, Montalcino. Tel: 0577.846.116. Open Friday-Wednesday, 12:00 p.m.-2:00 p.m. & 7:00 p.m.-9:00 p.m.; closed Thursday.

Il Leccio, ★★★★
Via Costa Castellare 1 (Piazza Castello), Sant'Angelo in Colle. Tel: 0577.844175, www.trattoriailleccio.com. Open daily (in season), 12:00 p.m.-3:00 p.m. & 7:00 p.m.-9:30p.m. Off-season hours may vary, or the restaurant may close down–call before driving here.

Locanda Demetra (restaurant & cooking school) ★★★★
Podere La Buca 221, Montalcino. Tel: 0577.150. 3199 www.montalcinocookingschool.com The restaurant may close down in August. In high season open Tuesday-Sunday, for lunch and dinner by reservation. Closed on Monday. Off season open Friday-Sunday only.

Abbigliamento 564 Via Mazzini, ★★★★
Via Mazzini 39 & 25, Montalcino Tel: 0577.847.050.

🏃 | 88 | Visit La Foce Villa and Garden–A Magical Destination and Iris Origo's Home in Val d'Orcia

La Foce villa and garden is one of the most magical points in the Val d'Orcia. The villa was once the home of writer and biographer Iris Origo, and the estate was a passionate obsession for her. Her book, *War in Val d'Orcia*, recounts her time in the valley during the Second World War and has enjoyed great success among critics and readers alike.

The estate is huge and includes multiple houses and annexes, cultivated fields, manicured gardens, woods teeming with wildlife, and a main villa that once served as a hostel for 15th century pilgrims on their journey to Rome. You can rent rooms, stay at their tastefully decorated apartments (absolutely recommended), and even rent the main villa. All accommodation options are pleasant, with beautiful views, adequate privacy, and spacious rooms. Each villa has a private swimming pool and there are tennis courts on the grounds.

The La Foce estate is midway between Pienza in one direction and the historic thermal bath town of Chianciano Terme in the other. In July, a chamber music festival is held nearby. Even if you don't stay here, consider touring the charming gardens, a beautiful sightseeing spot in and of themselves. The Italian garden was designed by Cecil Pinsent, who also designed parts of Bernard Berenson's garden in Villa I Tatti in Fiesole (Florence). Note that the garden is open to the public once a week: on Wednesday afternoon, year round, as well as the first weekend of every month from April to November. It can be toured on a guided visit only. A visit here wouldn't be complete without stopping at the adjoining Chiarentana estate (after Origo's death, her estate was divided between her two daughters—today Benedetta runs La Foce, and Donata runs Chiarentana), to taste some of their exquisite and award-winning olive oil. Visitors can choose between the various extra-virgin olive oils—monovarietal or blend—and take back home with them a decadent and authentic souvenir from this beautiful slice of land.

La Foce, ★★★★★
Strada della Vittoria 61, Chianciano Terme, Tel: 0578.69101,
www.lafoce.com & www.chiarentana.com.
Guided tours of the garden take place every Wednesday afternoon (3:00 p.m., 4;00 p.m., 5:00 p.m. and 6:00 p.m.) and on weekends (11:30 a.m., 3:00 p.m. and 4:30 p.m.

⊨ |89| Stay at a Wonderfully Inviting
and Reasonably Priced Agriturismo in
Montalcino

As Montalcino became a popular destination for tourists in the know, the number of B&Bs, *agriturismi* and hotels in the area grew exponentially. In fact, those who wish to make Montalcino their base for touring southern Tuscany will quickly discover that they are spoilt for choice, and that even a quick online search yields several interesting results. Finding a beautiful and romantic *agriturismo* that is also reasonably priced may reveal to be a slightly more difficult mission. But it certainly isn't impossible, and **Agriturismo La Casella** is a case in point.

Nestled among vineyards, on a particularly panoramic point overlooking the valley, this magical little *agriturismo* is just 500 meters from Montalcino itself. The apartments are large, well stocked, and very inviting. Marcella, who runs this family business together with her mother and sister, will make you feel immediately at home and will be happy to organize various activities to amplify your stay, from cooking lessons to landscape painting classes. The best apartment is, without a doubt, **La Terrazza apartment**—taking your breakfast out here, in front of views that we can only describe as breathtaking, is surely the best way to start your day. As you might imagine, early reservations are highly recommended, as this charming *agriturismo* is often booked solid months in advance.

Agriturismo La Casella, ★★★★
Loc. La Casella, Montalcino.
Tel: 0577.834.552, Cell: 348.3530320 / 349.284.3699,
www.lacasellamontalcino.com.

90 Book a Special Night at a One-of-a-Kind Historical Agriturismo in the Val d'Orcia

The **Sant'Anna in Camprena** *agriturismo* is unique—not many lodgings can boast such an impressive past as this former Benedictine monastery that dates back to the 15th century. As soon as you walk in, a sense of protective solace comes over you; it feels like a space where you can breathe and meditate. The interior maintains the delicate, simple style of a monastery and the rooms are quiet and elegant, reflecting that many of them used to be monks' cells. A treat few other *agriturismi* can compete with is the fact that the monastery's original cloister is not only still intact, but also covered with wonderful frescos painted by Antonio Bazzi, who is better known as "Il Sodoma," the same artist who decorated the Abbey of Monte Oliveto Maggiore (see tip 56).

The *agriturismo* is just six kilometers from Pienza, which means you will be close enough to visit the town but far enough into the valley to enjoy the stunning countryside. This is the magical location where director Anthony Minghella chose to shoot some scenes from his Oscar-nominated movie, *The English Patient*. Lastly, Sant'Anna in Camprena also organizes art classes and hosts concerts during the summer; contact them to find out what they have planned during your visit or to enroll in one of their classes.

Agriturismo Sant'Anna in Camprena, ★★★★★
Località Sant' Anna in Camprena (Pienza), Tel: 0578.748.037, Cell: 338.4079.284.
www.camprena.it.

🏃 91 | Visit the Fantastic (and Free!) Thermal Springs of Bagni San Filippo

The Thermal springs of Saturnia (see tip 69) are famous all over Tuscany, but we are here to recommend a completely different site. The Thermal springs and pools in Bagni San Filippo are one of the best kept secrets in the region. For years this quirky little nature reserve suffered from neglect, but a recent renovation following a storm brought it back to its former glory, and now it is a splendid place to visit. Come here to discover white natural pools excavated in the rock, uninterrupted nature, the healing properties of the hot, sulphur-rich water, and the magical ambiance of the forest surrounding the pools. Since these *bagni* are just 30 minutes from Pienza and Montalcino, they can be toured as a fun and alternative half-day trip from the valley. A word to the wise—avoid visiting the site on weekends and holidays, as the area is absolutely packed.

The Etruscan Coast

🏃 | 92 | Explore the Wonders of the Etruscan Coast: Charm, Good Food, and Great Wines

The *Costa degli Etruschi*, the poetic name given to the section of the coast that stretches from Livorno to Piombino, may not be as famous as the Chianti region or the hills of Siena, but it is one of our absolute favorite parts of Tuscany, a little slice of heaven just waiting to be discovered. So named because of the Etruscan settlements that once spread along its coastline, this surprisingly beautiful area offers a combination of fresh salty sea breezes, kilometers of tranquil, unspoiled beaches, and a number of charming little towns.

If you are a wine connoisseur, you are probably already familiar with this part of Tuscany, which has become a real hot spot in recent years. One of Italy's most expensive wines, the world famous Sassicaia, is made here, as well as a number of other famous Super-Tuscans. Naturally, wine tours in this area are not only highly recommended but also very easy to organize.

Any visit to the Etruscan coast, whether low-key or indulgent, must include **Bolgheri**. A small, sweet 900-year-old medieval village with no tourist attractions to speak of, it's a perfect place for a pleasant lunch followed by a stroll along its quaint alleyways. The drive leading to Bolgheri—along a stunning narrow road lined with over 2,000 cypress trees—is perhaps the most serene approach to a town in this part of Italy. (At the beginning of the road, on your left, you will find Bolgheri's tiny but very useful tourist office, where you can find out more about local tours, tourist attractions, and organized wine tastings.) When you reach the town, turn right and leave your car in the car park, as Bolgheri can only be entered on foot (ZTL). The castle, Bolgheri's most famous symbol, is today the main office of an agricultural company that produces wine and olive oil in the fields surrounding the village.

If you are looking for a place for lunch, we would recommend **Osteria Magona**. This is one of the best restaurants in the area, in our opinion. Meat is the real star here, and some of the dishes on offer, such as the Fiorentina steak, the tartare, and the Guancia di Manzo (slow-cooked beef cheek) and the tortino di erbe con Lardo di Cinta Senese (a delicate wild-herb flan served with a Stilton cheese fondue) are simply stellar. Of course there are also several bottles of excellent local wines on offer, to help wash everything down. Given that this is the most popular venues in the area, booking a table in advance is a very good idea. Those who prefer the tastes of the sea will enjoy **Osteria San Michele**, a wonderfully intimate little place, serving a seafood-based menu. Relaxed and with a full stomach, you will be ready to visit one of the leading estates in the area, such as Guado al Tasso, Ornellaia, or San Guido (see next tip for full details), to taste their world-famous Super-Tuscan wines.

Other sites worth exploring in the area include **Castagneto Carducci** and the Populonia Archeological Park. Castagneto Carducci is a small township and home to one of Italy's oldest families, the della Gherardesca, who lived in the 1,000 years old castle that dominates the town. There aren't many attractions to visit here, but the town itself is quaint. While you're there, take a walk to Piazzale Belvedere, which offers panoramic views over the landscape and right down to the sea. Castagneto Carducci hosts a number of *sagre* (food festivals) and fun little town events every year, find out at the local tourist office if anything special is happening during your visit. Another place of interest is the archeological site of **Populonia Archeological Park** (*I Parchi della Val di Cornia*), located right next to the minuscule, but charming town of the same name. Here you can see the remains of an impressive early Etruscan settlement, dating back to around 500 B.C. Particularly interesting is the site's necropolis, or large cemetery. Sadly, many of the original artifacts found at the site are displayed today at the Piombino museum (30 minutes away from Populonia), and not in the tiny archeological museum in Populonia itself.

Then, of course, there are the beaches. The nearby bay of **Baratti** offers a great spot for swimming, and the pine trees dotted along the edge of the beach provide the perfect spot for you to laze in the shade, protected from the hot afternoon sun. The **Vada, Punta Ala**, and **California** beaches are all wonderful too, and are filled with sea-loving Italians who prefer these more 'authentic' spots to the high-end beaches up in Pietrasanta, Viareggio, and Forte dei Marmi. Entire families and couples, naturally, come here to relax and work on one of the most important Italian points of pride: a perfect suntan.

Osteria Magona, ★★★★★

Via Bolgherese, Località Vallone dei Messi 199, Bolgheri. Tel: 0565.762.173, www.osteriamagona.com. GPS: 43.2178, 10.61076. Open Tuesday-Wednesday, 12:00 p.m.-2:30 p.m. & 7:30 p.m.-10:30 p.m.

Osteria San Michele, ★★★

Via Aurelia 199, Donoratico. Tel: 0565.774.478, www.osteriasanmichele.it. In high season, open Wednesday-Monday, for lunch and dinner. Off season, open Friday-Sunday only.

Populonia Archeological Park, ★★★★

Via Giovanni Lerario 90, Piombino. Tel: 0565.226.445, www.parchivaldicornia.it. Open March-May & October: Tuesday-Sunday, 10:00 a.m.-6:00 p.m. (until 5:00 p.m. in the last two weeks of October and the first two weeks of March), closed Monday; January 19-February 28, weekends only, 10:00 a.m.-5:00 p.m.; June-September, Tuesday-Sunday, 10:00 a.m.-7:00 p.m. (until 6:00 p.m. in the last two weeks of September), closed Monday. July-August, open daily, 9:30 a.m.-7:30 p.m. Closed November 1-December 31.

93 | **Discover the World-Renowned** Super-Tuscan Wines

Bolgheri and the surrounding countryside are world-renowned for producing many of the Super-Tuscans (read more about the Super-Tuscans in our introduction). A visit to the high-end, famous producers of Super-Tuscans in the area will surely focus on three names: Tenuta Ornellaia, Tenuta San Guido and Guado al Tasso.

The Antinori family, which founded the magnificent **Tenuta Ornellaia**, was one of the first families to recognize the potential of Bolgheri. Today, Ornellaia is owned by the equally celebrated Frescobaldi family, and is still a name that wine lovers speak with reverence, as the estate continues to produce some of the finest wines this region has to offer. But quality does come with a steep price tag—a good bottle of *Bolgheri Rosso Superiore* from this estate will cost around €130. Additionally, each year the estate creates a limited edition vintage, in collaboration with a prominent

modern artist who designs that year's label. A bottle from this vintage can cost up to $1,000 at auction. The 2010 vintage, which was enveloped by a beautiful spiral sculpture designed by leading contemporary artist Michelangelo Pistoletto, sold for more than $120,000 at auction. Other artists who have designed previous labels include Rebecca Horn, Zhang Huan, Ghada Amer, and Luigi Ontani.

Tenuta Ornellaia can be visited in a number of ways. You can, theoretically, stop by the elegant cellar to pick up a bottle (call first), but it would probably be preferable to book in advance a guided tour of the grounds. The classic tour is available Monday to Friday, lasts three hours, costs around €80, and includes a visit to the production facility and the vineyard, as well as a guided tasting. A number of personalized tours are also available, focusing on specific wines. The most famous of these is the Vendemmia d'Artista tour, which focuses on a tasting of five years of the Ornellaia, from 2006 to 2010. Only ten of these exclusive tours are available a year, so book ahead!

Tenuta Guado al Tasso is a 750-acre estate famous for its flagship wine, the Guado al Tasso, a superior Bolgheri DOC. Try the 2010 bottle; it isn't cheap at €85, but it enjoys a fantastic reputation among critics. Other notable wines are the *Bruciato*, a lesser-known but much more reasonably priced (yet still wonderful) wine, fondly described as the Guado al Tasso's younger brother. The estate's light and mineral Vermentino, is also very good—a fresh and crisp white that is the perfect companion for an *aperitivo*. Tours are usually not possible, as the Tenuta only opens its gates to the public on special occasions. Still, be sure to stop by the estate's *bottega* and pick up a bottle, or buy some of their products; a range of cured hams and sausages, organic tomato sauce, and more are available alongside the world-class wines. Bottles by this estate can also be found at any self-respecting *enoteca* in Tuscany, especially in Lucca, Siena and Florence.

Even more famous than the Guado al Tasso is the prestigious Sassicaia wine, the best-known Super-Tuscan of them all, produced by **Tenuta San Guido**. Made with 80% Cabernet Sauvignon grapes, the Sassicaia boasts qualities that have consistently put it in the top 10 lists of Italian wines. The winery itself sits on a beautiful estate named after Saint Guido della Gherardesca, who lived in the area during the 11th century. Though a bottle of Sassicaia may be out of reach for most people, visitors can try other wines produced by this estate, such as the 2009 Guidalberto, or a bottle of Le Difese from the same year. Today the estate is also famous for an impressive World Wildlife Fund bird sanctuary on its grounds (also known as the Bolgheri Oasis), which is a great sightseeing destination for nature lovers. To combine your visit with a hike in the WWF reserve, check the info on their website, and call ahead to plan your visit, as reservations are required.

Tenuta Ornellaia e Masseto, ★★★★★

Località Ornellaia 191 (the estate is located along the famous Via Bolgherese), Bolgheri. Tel: 0565.718.11, Coordinate GPS: Lat: 43.211596 Long: 10.61157, www.ornellaia.com.

Tenuta Guado al Tasso, ★★★★★

Strada Aurelia Km. 267, Loc. Scalabrone, Donoratico. Tel: 0565.749.735, www.antinori.it. e-mail: guadoaltasso@antinori.it.

Tenuta San Guido, ★★★★★

Loc. le Capanne 27, Bolgheri, GPS coordinates: 43° 13' 46.90", 10° 35' 7.86". Tel: 0565.762.003/762.026, www.tenutasanguido.com. The WWF Oasis is open from November to April, Saturday and Sunday, with two entrance times: 9:30 a.m. and 2:00 p.m. Reservations must be made by 5:00 p.m. at least two days before the chosen date. Reservations made by e-mail are valid on receipt of confirmation. E-mail: bolgheri@wwf.it, www.wwf.it/oasi/toscana/padule_di_bolgheri. cell: 338.4141698 - 389.9578763

94 | Savor the Wonderful Super-Tuscans
without Breaking the Bank!

The wines sold by the estates mentioned in the previous tip are indeed world-famous, but they are also pricey. Luckily, Tenuta San Guido and Ornellaia are not the only options competing for the wine enthusiast's attention. In fact, some of the lesser-known brands in this area are not only more reasonably priced, but are, in some cases, better, more complex wines that are slowly gaining a wonderful reputation. In short, for more mid-range touring, consider visiting the award-winning Grattamacco, Le Macchiole, Tua Rita, Michele Satta or the Mullini di Segalari estates. All of these produce highly recommended, excellent wines.

We love **Podere Grattamacco** wines, which have received several notable mentions and prizes. Currently owned by the Collemassari family (see tip 72), this estate was originally opened in 1977, at the beginning of the Super-Tuscan frenzy. The small estate (just 35 hectares, with 14 of

those given over to vineyards and three to olive groves) sits on a hill between Castagneto Carducci and Bolgheri, with a view of the sea off in the distance. Despite, or perhaps because, they have such a small plot of land to work with, the wines produced here are top-notch and can stand proudly among the finest Super-Tuscans. Visits and tastings are available, and can be booked via their website.

Next, **Azienda Agricola Le Macchiole** is not only an excellent choice, but also a personal favorite, and one of the best producers in the area, in our opinion. This is another small estate at only 22-hectares, and the producers here are proud of their low yield, which is made from painstakingly chosen grapes. Try their flagship bottles, the Bolgheri Rosso DOC and the Paleo Rosso IGT, particularly the 2008 vintage. If you are prepared to spend a hefty sum, try their Messorio IGT 2008, too, which received a perfect score of 100 from the Wine Spectator magazine—no mean feat!

The estate today is run by Cinzia Merli, who continues the family tradition after her husband passed away. Her passion and enthusiasm about the production of high-quality vintages is obvious. In fact, Le Macchiole takes pride in experimenting with different techniques, and their hard work continues to pay off as they turn out delectable wines year after year.

In the middle to high range, you will find **Tua Rita**, a company that isn't yet as famous as it ought to be. Though it is already esteemed among wine lovers, the general public is still not fully aware of this winery's product. However, they are steadily receiving more attention and have received top marks in recent years from a number of important tasters and magazines.

This is a family enterprise that has gradually grown over the last few years due to their endless effort and passion. Tua Rita's wines have a strong presence and complexity, thanks to the conditions in the area—they grow on hills from which the Etruscans once extracted iron, and many critics say this gives the wine an iron-like nuance. You probably won't be able to try the Redigaffi 2000, the first Italian wine to be given a perfect grade of 100 by Robert Parker, as this wine is often sold at auctions for more than €500 a bottle. Still, for much less than that you can get your lips around the Syrah 2010, which also received high marks. It is made with a single variety grape grown in their vineyards around the medieval town of Suvereto and is definitely recommended. Naturally, you can also taste the equally lovely Giusto di Notri, their flagship wine.

Tours and tastings are possible, but must be booked in advance through their website, or, better yet, by phone. Tours cost around €20 per person and include a visit to the cellar, the vineyards, and a tasting of four wines. If you are interested in tasting one of the more prestigious labels (such as the Redigaffi), prices change considerably (about €70 per person).

Next, consider the **Michele Satta's** estate. His wines are delicious and complex yet very drinkable, and for this reason, rank among our favorites. Of course, the fact that his product provides great quality for reasonable prices (€12-€25, typically) also helps sweeten the deal. A tour of the small estate is can be booked, but to be honest, it is short and very basic. Instead, we recommend stopping by their *enoteca* and picking up a bottle (or two...). Try the excellent Piastraia, a smooth and delicious red, or the Costa di Giulia, a fragrant white made with a mix of the local Vermentino grapes and Sauvignon grapes. Satta also produces a lovely Vermentino, the quintessential Etruscan coast wine, which is what the locals have been drinking for years. This is (usually) a single-variety wine, very typical in these parts of Tuscany, and its fresh, flavorful, and slightly acidic tones make it a perfect choice for an *aperitivo* or a dinner picnic on the beach.

Next, if you've had enough of the manicured, slightly snooty estates, we would recommend heading to **Mullini di Segalari.** This place is very different from all the others mentioned above. Their wine is good, and the estate itself is exactly the kind of rustic, charming, local little winery that will conquer your heart. A tiny untamed farm with a stream running through, hidden inside the forest, this place is characterized by a wild and unspoiled essence, a far-cry from the other strictly ordered Tuscan wine estates. Take their tour to see a perfect example of how a small family vineyard is run, and the passion with which they produce their wines. To reach the estate, get in touch with the owners for directions, or see if they can meet you in Castagnetto Carducci and drive there together.

Lastly, if you are not looking for a guided tour, but rather, a pleasant *enoteca* where you can enjoy a glass or two of some of the best wines in the area, we highly recommend **Enoteca Tognoni**. Located right at the entrance to the charming village of Bolgheri (turn left immediately after you've walked through the stone arch), here you will find a wide selection of excellent wines, from Guado al Tasso and Paleo to Solaia and others, and at any given moment there are 10 open bottles from which you can buy by the glass and taste without committing to just one brand.

Podere Grattamacco, ★★★★
Castagneto Carducci, GPS coordinates: 43° 11' 10.51", 10° 37' 40.91".
Tel: 0564.990.496,
www.collemassari.it.

Le Macchiole, ★★★★★
Strada Provinciale 16B Bolgherese, 189/A, Castagneto Carducci.
Tel: 0565.766.092, GPS coordinates: lat: 43°20'78.35" long: 10°61'20.66",
www.lemacchiole.it.

Tua Rita, ★★★
Località Notri 81, Suvereto.
Tel: 0565.829,237,
www.tuarita.it.

Michele Satta, ★★★
Località Vigna al Cavaliere 61, Castagneto Carducci. Tel: 0565.773.041,
www.michelesatta.com.
The cellar is open from mid-April to late October, 4:00 p.m.-6:30 p.m. Tours need to be booked in advance at this cell number: 347.173.4573.

Mulini Di Segalari, ★★★★
Località Felciaino 115, Castagneto Carducci. Tel: 0565.765.202,
Cell: 327.989.2232,
www.mulinidisegalari.it.

Enoteca Tognoni, ★★★
Via Lauretta 5, Bolgheri
Tel: 0565.762.001,
www.enotecatognoni.it.
Open November-March, Thursday-Tuesday, 10:00 a.m.-11:00 p.m., closed Wednesday; April-late October, open daily, 9:00 a.m.-11:00 p.m.

🏃 | 95 | **Taste Fine Organic Wines** and Enjoy a Lovely Meal right on the Beach

If you've already visited Bolgheri and tasted the super Tuscans (highly recommended—see tips 92 and 93), or if you are simply looking for an alternative way to Enjoy the Etruscan coast, then this tip is for you.

Start your day at the tiny town of **Montescudaio**, which sits at the heart of the scenic Val di Cornia (Cornia Valley), just 30 minutes from Bolgheri. The town of Montescudaio itself is only modestly interesting and can be skipped in favor of the real draw here—the wine! Of the many wineries in the area, **Fontemorsi** is the one you don't want to miss. Small and rustic, this family-run agriturismo and winery offers an enjoyable alternative to the large and famous Bolgheri wineries, as well as an interesting selection of all-organic, delicious reds. You can taste and buy their wines directly at their shop on Montescudaio's main street, but it's far better to book a tour of the winery in advance, which includes a guided tasting.

Next, make another pit stop, at **Castello Ginori di Querceto**. This ancient ivy-covered castle sits on the slopes of Mount Aneo and has been in the hands of the Ginori Lisci family for centuries. Their wines are very good, though a little overpriced, in our opinion. Tours of their cellar can be organized, but it's actually better to simply stop by, buy a glass of wine and a platter of prosciutto and cheeses, take it out to their terrace, and enjoy the view.

It's worth noting that in season, the Montescudaio Winery Association organizes an activity called *Tramonti in Vigna*, meaning that guests can book a **sunset aperitivo right in the vineyards.** The program and list of participating wineries changes annually, and can be viewed on their website (in Italian only, sadly): www.consorziovinomontescudaiodoc.it.

Then, for a complete change of pace, drive from the valley to the seaside. **Marina di Castagneto Carduci** is where all the locals go, and the beaches here are a very different in style and atmosphere than those meticulous and fashionable hotspots in Pietrasanta and Viareggio. In fact, this entire area is half beach and half nature reserve, so expect to find merry locals bathing and fishing in the most unlikely places. The ambiance is calm and welcoming, and there are several free beaches to choose from. For a romantic dinner right by the water, try **Ristorante dell'Hotel I Ginepri.** Perfectly positioned (practically on the water) and welcoming, the restaurant offers a contemporary take on local seafood dishes. Booking a table in advance is highly recommended, as they are always full in high season.

Fontemorsi Organic Winery, ★★★
Via delle Colline, Montescudaio.
Tel: 0583.349025, cell: 328.5944117,
www.fontemorsi.it.

Ginori Lisci Castle and Winery, ★★★
Localita' Querceto, Ponteginori (PI).
Tel: 055.282.433, Cell: 335.540.5006.
The cellar can be toured by appointment only, call: 0588.37472 / 345.323.4042.
The castle's wine shop (no reservations required) is open April–October, Wednesday–Monday, 11:00 a.m.–1:00 p.m. & 4:00 p.m.–8:00 p.m.; closed Tuesday. Hours may change off season, call in advance.

Ristorante Hotel I Ginepri, ★★★
Viale Italia 13, Marina di Castagneto Carducci Tel: 0565.744029,
www.hoteliginepri.it

🏃 |96| **Immerse yourself in the Medieval** Charm
of Massa Marittima and Suvereto

Just 20 minutes from each other, the towns of Massa Marittima and Suvereto are two of the Etruscan coast's finest jewels. A day here, combined with a visit to one of the many wineries in the area, will guarantee a blissful and delicious experience for all.

Massa Marittima is a beautiful medieval town, famous for the lively Balestro del Girifalco medieval festival that takes place here twice a year (see tip 127). Park your car in Piazza Garibaldi (the town's main lot), and make your way on foot to the historic center and the main piazza, Piazza Duomo. Massa Marittima's **main cathedral** (**Duomo**), a true Romanesque masterpiece, is dedicated to Saint Cerbonius, who was the bishop of Populonia during the Barbarian Invasions. Inside you will find artwork by Duccio Buoninsegna and Segna di Buonaventura, as well as a wooden crucifix by the great Giovanni Pisano and the

beautifully carved sarcophagus of Saint Cerbonius himself. On the same piazza you will also find Massa Marittima's small **archeological museum,** displaying local finds from prehistoric to Etruscan times. For families, there is a fun little **mining museum** in the vicinity (Museo della Miniera di Massa Marittima—www.museidimaremma.it), and for shopping enthusiasts there are a few interesting boutiques that are worth visiting, especially **La Soffitta di Iris** (for stunning antiques and homeware), **Lo Scarabeo** (a little treasure trove for European and Asian décor) and the shops along Via della Libertà.

For lunch or dinner, our favorite eatery in town is the minuscule **La Tana dei Brilli** (see tip 73 for our full recommendation). As you leave Massa Marittima, it's worth noting that two excellent stops for foodies await right outside the town center—the famous **Saba farm** (see tip 73 for our detailed recommendation) is THE place to buy top-quality pecorino cheese that simply melts in your mouth, and **Frantoio Stanghellini** is where we often buy flavorful olive oil that adds a little something extra to any salad.

Next, drive down south to the beautiful town of **Suvereto**. Of the many medieval *borghi* in this area, this is our favorite stop to make, and we dare say it will become your favorite, too. Tour the cobbled streets that look as if they were taken straight out of some medieval fairy-tale, and make your up way to Piazza Gramsci and then the ruins of the 10th century **Rocca Aldobrandesca castle.** If you have some extra time, visit the tiny sacred art museum and the even tinier vintage doll museum, or the former **monastery of San Francesco.** For lunch, book a table at the best restaurant in town, **l'Ciocio.** In the evening, especially, this spot is quite romantic. On the menu you will find local specialties, mostly—on our last visit, for example, we tried the pasta with the day's catch from Follonica bay, seven versions of Tuscan ham served with slow-baked beans, and delicate *crespelle* (a sort of savory crepe) filled with goat cheese and grilled vegetables. Naturally, anything made with cinghiale (boar), a hugely popular dish in this area, will be very good, too.

The best time to visit Suvereto is when one of the many town festivities takes place—in June they have a festival dedicated to the local Vermentino wine; in July there's a fun medieval festival known as Serate Medievali; in August they host "Guest Night," featuring a lively dinner at the San Francesco cloister; at the end of November (or early December) they celebrate the best festival of cooked boar in Tuscany (La Sagra del Cinghiale). Additionally, three

times a year the people of Suvereto hold a Palio (race): the Palio Santa Croce takes place in May, the Palio della corsa a cavallo (horse race) in August, and the Palio alla corsa delle Botti (locals compete by rolling heavy barrels up the alleys of the borgo) in the autumn. Find out more here: www.suvereto.net.

Massa Marittima Duomo, ★★★★
Piazza Duomo.
Open daily, 8:00 a.m.-12:00 p.m. & 3:00 p.m.-7:00 p.m. (off season closes an hour earlier).

La Soffitta di Iris, ★★★
Via della Liberta 16, Massa Marittima.
Open 10:00 a.m.–1:00 p.m. & 4:30 p.m.–7:30 p.m.

Fattoria Frantoio Stanghellini (Olive Oil Shop), ★★★
Via della cava 24, Loc. Valpiana, Massa Marittima.
Tel: 0566.919.019, www.frantoiostanghellini.it.
Open Monday–Saturday, 9:30 a.m.–1:00 p.m. & 3:30 p.m.–7:00 p.m. (hours may vary).

Osteria l'Ciocio, ★★★
Piazza dei Giudici 1, Suvereto.
Tel: 0565.829947, www.osteriadisuvereto.it.

🛏 97 | **Book Your Stay** at the Incredible Castello di Magona

At around €25,000 a week during high season, **Castello di Magona** is "just a little" out of reach for most people. But it's always possible to dream, and there is no denying that this castle is one of the most luxurious destinations in Tuscany.

Castello di Magona is a Renaissance fantasy. Perfectly situated and set in rolling vineyards, the castle was built in the 16th century to house Leopold II, Grand Duke of Tuscany. Today visitors can indulge in fantasies of nobility on the sprawling, meticulously restored estate, which boasts a pool, Jacuzzi, beautiful gardens, and 10 air-conditioned rooms that can host up to 20 people. If you are feeling extra-royal, Castello di Magona also offers a full staff, including chambermaids, a chef, and a private concierge. The castle is rented out in the summer months on a weekly basis.

Castello di Magona, ★★★★★
Via Venturina 27, Campiglia Marittima.
Tel: 0565.851.235,
www.castellodimagona.it.

Pisa and the Arno Valley

🏃 98 | **Discover the Best of Pisa:** From the Tastiest Pizza and Gelato to the Finest Views and Shops

Pisa is our home town, and one of our favorite things to do here is go on the hunt for unique little surprises that often remain hidden from most tourists' gaze. Much has been written about the Leaning Tower of Pisa, which is, together with the rest of Piazza dei Miracoli, one of the most beautiful architectural achievements in all of Italy. But there is much more to Pisa than just the tower, and even a relatively short tour of the city's historic center can provide a thoroughly pleasing experience.

Start your day with a stop at the **De' Coltelli** gelateria, arguably the best ice cream shop in town. In this narrow, simply designed yet inviting space, the ice cream is prepared with the finest ingredients. This gelateria focuses on quality, not quantity, which means you may not find 25 flavors like in the uber-popular ice cream parlor in Piazza Garibaldi, but you will find genuine tastes, made with the season's fruit, and without any additives or artificial colorings. De' Coltelli also prepares some excellent granitas; the strawberry granita with whipped cream is especially wonderful.

To walk all this tastiness off, take a stroll along the Arno River to soak up some of the city's indisputable beauty. Of the many Tuscan towns we have visited, Pisa has one of the best views of the river, thanks to the numerous colorful medieval and historic buildings that line its banks. Contrary to typical tourist wisdom, the best place in town to enjoy the view isn't Ponte di Mezzo, but the next bridge along—the view from **Ponte della Fortezza**, near the Giardino Scotto (Pisa's charming public gardens), is actually even prettier than the similar river view that Florence has to offer. Set against the clear blue Italian sky on a hot summer's day, it's a sight that you won't want to miss.

Next on the list, it is time to hit Pisa's two main shopping streets, which provide great opportunities for splurging. Shopaholics will be in heaven hopping from store to store along Corso Italia, the main road leading from the train station to Piazza Garibaldi, and Borgo Stretto, the boutique-filled street that leads from Piazza Garibaldi to the Leaning Tower.

Corso Italia hosts some of the most popular mid-range fashion brands in Italy, including Zara, Motivi, and Twin-Set, as well as a number of cute shoe and jewelry shops. In among the tall buildings that stretch along on either side you will find many options for every taste, from fashion-loving teenagers (try Pimkie and Bijoux Bijoux) to older, more sophisticated buyers (check Furla, Max Mara, Marina Rinaldi, and Fiorella Rubino). Aside from the shops, there's also a bunch of little coffee shops and eateries where you can leave any uninterested parties for a few hours while you shop in peace!

Alternatively (or in addition), hit **Borgo Stretto**, the more high-end option of the two streets. Along the colonnaded pavements you'll find expensive and exclusive boutiques, such as Valenti, Pinko, Borbonese, and Versace. One of our favorite shops is, without a doubt, **Bottega Etrusca**, located right at the beginning of the street, two steps from Piazza Garibaldi. This jewelry shop stocks beautiful, handmade, one-of-a-kind pieces that you really won't find anywhere else. The shop is divided into two spaces, sitting across the street from each other; one mostly houses the jewelry collection while the other displays a very high-end assortment of home décor items, including serving sets by Hermès.

As you continue down Borgo Stretto you will find more shops as well as Pisa's most famous caffè–**Pasticceria Salza**, which first opened its doors in 1898, and today, more than a century later, still retains its old-world charm, serving excellent coffee and tempting sweets. The long counter stretches around the room, displaying a tremendous array of *gelato*, chocolates, and cakes. There is also a pleasant outdoor sitting area where you can watch the world go by over an authentic Italian espresso. If you are lucky enough to visit on a day when they sell *tartufo*, a sinfully creamy, chocolaty treat, be sure to try it!

For the best pizza in town, try one of these favorite spots: **Il Montino** is a hole-in-the-wall establishment that has been serving piping hot slices of pizza and cecina (a chickpea flour pancake—Montino's is extra good!) for over 50 years. There's always a queue, and you'll have to fight for your spot against the famished students who flock here daily, but the line moves quickly, and the food is definitely worth the wait. The convenient location on Borgo Stretto, and the fact that they are open for lunch, too, means that you can come here before or after your visit to the Leaning Tower.

Alternatively, try the top-notch pizza at **Gusto Pizza 129**. This pizzeria is only open in the evening, and the clientele is almost exclusively local. They specialize in rich tasting, thick crust bases, and a variety of high-quality toppings. Seating is limited, so try to come early.

For a calmer experience, book a table at **Osteria Il Fantasma dell'Opera**. This popular eatery is just two doors down from Pisa's theater (Teatro Verdi), and there's a lovely garden out back, where you can enjoy one of their delicious pizzas out in the open, under the stars.

Lastly, if you plan on staying for dinner in town, don't miss a romantic post-dinner stroll and visit to the Leaning Tower. In the darkness, without any tourists around, the white stones glow softly and the pervading silence allows you the space to take it all in.

De' Coltelli, ★★★★★
Lungarno Pacinotti 23,
Cell: 345.481.1903,
www.decoltelli.it,
Open mid-March-late October, daily,
noon-9:00 p.m. Closed from November to
mid-March.

Bottega Etrusca, ★★★★
Via Borgo Stretto 2 & 5. Tel: 050.578.294
/ 050.544.500. Open Tuesday–Saturday,
9:30 a.m.–1:00 p.m. & 3:00 p.m.–7:30 p.m.

Pasticceria Salza, ★★★
Borgo Stretto 46. Tel: 050.580.144. Open
Tuesday-Sunday, 7:45 a.m.-8:00 p.m.
(may close earlier off-season. May also be
closed on Sunday).

Il Montino Pizzeria, ★★★
Via Monte 1 (off Borgo Stretto)
Tel: 050.598695.
Open Monday–Saturday,
11:30 a.m.–3:00 p.m. & 5:30 p.m.–10:30
p.m.; closed Sunday.

GustaPizza 129, ★★★
Via Santa Bibbiana 10
(Behind Piazza Mazzini).
Tel: 050.620.3117, www.gustoal129.it,
Open Monday–Saturday, 6:30 p.m.–11:00
p.m.; closed Sunday.

Osteria Il Fantasma dell'Opera,
★★★
Via Palestro 20, Pisa.
Tel: 050.542402, www.
osteriailfantasmadellopera.com. Open
daily for lunch and dinner.

99 Savor a Meal at One of the Two Best Restaurants in Pisa

Many visitors to the Leaning Tower in Pisa hope to enjoy a good meal after their tour, but most of the restaurants surrounding the tower offer an incredibly mediocre culinary experience, at best. Luckily, there are two excellent restaurants that are located just 10 minutes away. **Il Campano** is set in a delightful medieval building, right off Pisa's vegetable market, in Piazza delle Vettovaglie. This restaurant is low-key, reasonably priced, family-run and completely unpretentious. And the food, of course, is excellent. We are always impressed with their seasonal menu and use of high-quality produce, but do pick your dishes wisely, and ask about the week's specials. Particularly recommended are the *affettati* (cold cuts and salami) and cheeses, the lovely tuna tartar, the grilled octopus with arugula, the excellent and slightly spicy *pici* with *baccalà* sauce, the *maltagliati* (fresh homemade pasta) with white ragù, and anything with truffles (the restaurant's speciality). If you are not sure what you might like, try the *antipasto del re*, a tempting selection of various *antipasti* dishes served on a large wooden platter— a dish that is ideally shared with someone with a serious appetite! The food menu is complemented by a tempting wine list. You may not find the most expensive brands here, but you will discover many popular local bottles that most Italians enjoy drinking on a regular basis.

Alternatively, head to **La Stanzina**, another personal favorite and the best Southern Italian restaurant in town. It is small, simply decorated and very inviting, and the food is fantastic. The pasta dishes (especially any pasta with seafood-based sauces and condiments) and the *antipasti* are the restaurant's *forte*, but the meat isn't bad at all. Don't miss La Stanzina's mozzarella, which is imported daily from Puglia, and is one of the best we've tried in Tuscany. For dinner, they also sell an enormous *burrata* (cream-filled mozzarella) that can easily serve as a satisfying *antipasto* for two hungry diners. The restaurant's famous dessert, a real Sicilian cannolo, is absolutely delicious, and together with a good espresso will be the perfect ending to your meal.

Il Campano, ★★★★
Via Cavalca 19, Pisa. Tel: 050.580.585, www.ilcampano.com.
Open Monday, Tuesday, Friday-Sunday, 12:30 p.m.-2.45 p.m. & 7:30-10.45 p.m.; Thursday, open for dinner only. Closed Wednesday.

La Stanzina, ★★★★
Via Curtatone e Montanara 7/9, Pisa. Tel: 050.991.1925. Open Tuesday-Sunday, 12:30 p.m.-3:00 p.m. & 7:30 p.m.-11:00 p.m. Closed Monday.

🏃 100 | Visit One of Italy's Best Food Markets–and Hunt for Truffles Yourself!

Every year, more than 100,000 visitors descend on San Miniato for the annual *Mostra Mercato Nazionale del Tartufo Bianco di San Miniato* (the International White Truffle exhibition in San Miniato). This market and exhibition is spread over the last three weekends in November, and is a pure delight for the senses. Since 1969, San Miniato, which is known as the second most important truffle producing town in Italy (after Alba, in Piemonte), has become packed with stands offering fresh, high-quality truffles, all adding to the intoxicating and wonderful aromas that fill the air. Apart from the truffles, all kinds of gastronomic and cultural events take place, and there is also an opportunity to taste a whole range of traditional Tuscan cuisine. The highlight, though, must be the tent that is set up in the town's Piazza del Duomo. It is here that you will find some of the best-quality fresh truffles that San Miniato has to offer.

To complete your experience, consider booking in advance a truffle hunting expedition. The truth is, although truffle hunting is a serious and skilled business, it can also be a lot of fun. There is no better way to discover this ancient art than to join a real, experienced truffle hunter and his dog in their daily explorations. For such an activity, we would highly recommend the tours led by **Truffle in Tuscany**. Unlike in other countries, pigs aren't as a rule used to search for truffles in Italy, as they often eat the truffles and dig the soil with such violence that they damage it and prevent future spores from growing there. Dogs, on the other hand, specifically Lagotto Romagnolo, are trained from a very young age and accompany the truffle hunters. In terms of tours, a number of options are available, including accompanying the chef, hunter, and dog on a search for truffles, followed by a cooking class, lunch, or wine tasting. Find out more on their website.

Another fun choice is the tours offered by **Savitar**. This company not only sells some of the best truffle products in the area (their truffle butter and the truffled porcini mushroom sauce are two of our favorites!), but they also offer visitors a chance to go truffle hunting with their trained guides and dogs. The hunt takes place along the trails of the beautiful Tenuta Camugliano, a historic 17th-century Tuscan estate. Guided tastings and light truffle-based lunches are also available, and all activities must be booked in advance. Naturally, you can also skip the hunt and simply stop by their shop and purchase some of their products. Don't let the (extremely) uninspiring setting in which the shop is located deter you—the quality here is excellent!

Truffle in Tuscany, ★★★★
Cell: 3479030371,
www.truffleintuscany.it.

Savitar, ★★★★
Via Luigi Capuana 4, San Miniato Basso.
Tel: 0571.42710,
www.savitar.it.

🏃 101 Try some of Tuscany's Finest Biodynamic Wines, and Get to Know San Miniato for Foodies

San Miniato's historical center is quaint, but lacks that spark you find in other Tuscan hill-towns and villages. In fact, it isn't the local Duomo or the medieval center that draws visitors here—it's the food. And rightly so! San Miniato is famous not only for its white truffles—the Tuber magnatum Pico, the most prized of all edible truffles—but for its centuries-old tradition of *norcineria* (charcuterie). In fact, many restaurants across Tuscany make a point of offering San Miniato *salumi* and cured meats. And, the fact that so many small outlets can be found in the surroundings, makes this a destination that not only foodies but any fashionable tourist will want to get to know.

Located halfway between Florence and Pisa, San Miniato is also very easy to reach. The town is divided into two parts: San Miniato Alto, the historic old town, is located high up

on the hill, and San Miniato Basso, the more modern part, is located at the bottom of the hill.

A foodie's tour of San Miniato will focus on San Miniato Alto, and will include a few obligatory stops. First on the list is **Macelleria Sergio Falaschi**, which is considered one of the best butcher shops in Tuscany. Just a minute from the tourist office, it is easily reachable and well-stocked. The shop is currently run by Sergio, a fourth-generation butcher, who speaks with passion and deep understanding about his products. Here you will find fresh meat (half a veal was hanging from the ceiling when we came in last time, though none of the customers seemed to mind), cuts ready to make *bollito misto* and *ossobuco*, steaks, and a vast selection of *salumi* (cured cold cuts). Some of the best choices here are their Tuscan prosciutto, which has a soft and delicate flavor, the *spalla* and *capocollo*, and the *salame di cinta senese* (made from locally-grown Cinta Senese pigs). From November to January you can buy real truffles in the shop (though it's better to call in advance if you are interested), and throughout the year you can find products from neighboring farms, such as saffron, salt, butter, olive oil, and local wine.

Just across the street from the Macelleria awaits **Cosi è se vi Piace**, the best grocery shop in town, which stocks everything from artisanal dried pasta to traditional biscuits, cheeses and wines, to chocolates to liqueurs. In short, the makings of what some may call a decadent (and we would call a decent) picnic basket. If you are shopping for products to take home with you, check out the truffle pasta and the truffle-infused oils, which give a wonderfully intoxicating aroma to any dish.

Staying for lunch in town is recommended and, of the many restaurants that fight for the tourist's attention, we particularly like two. **Ristorante Pepenero** is an elegant restaurant with some very good truffle-based dishes on offer (during truffle season, naturally). The tagliatelle with fresh truffles is our personal favorite, but the meat dishes are quite good, too. Book a place out on the terrace to enjoy the impressive vista. Another good option is **Papaveri e Papere**, which is located outside the historical center. Run by Paolo Fiaschi (formerly chef of Pepenero), this simple but delicious little eatery offers a modern version of local traditional recipes. Their pasta dishes are highly recommended, as are the desserts (such as the cannolo with almonds), and the €45 fixed tasting menu is a good way to discover some of the best dishes on offer.

Next, it's time to drink. Up in the hills behind San Miniato sits one of the best biodynamic wineries in the region. **Cosimo Maria Masini** is an all-natural, biodynamic and organic winery, which offers wonderful wines and an even finer setting; a tour of the beautiful grounds, the cellar and the tasting room is, in our opinion, a pleasurable must.

The estate was bought by the Masini family in 2000 and extends over 40 hectares of vineyards, olive groves, fields and woods. At the heart of the estate stands Villa la Selva, a noble mansion that once belonged to the Buonaparte family and later on to the Marquis Cosimo Ridolfi, an agricultural pioneer. It was here that the Marquis began experimenting and applying his innovative techniques to improve the vineyards.

Today the family follows the biodynamic teachings of Rudolf Steiner when working their land, thus completely excluding the use of synthetic chemical fertilizers. The wines themselves are lovely, especially when enjoyed on the terrace, overlooking the hills. Specifically, try their Biodynamic Mathilde IGT and Daphne IGT, and the crisp and fragrant Annick IGT, which is made with 85% Sauvignon Blanc grapes, and 15% Vermentino grapes. Those who prefer red wines, will appreciate the complexity of the Cosimo IGT, a biodynamic red made mostly with Sangiovese grapes.

Macelleria Sergio Falaschi, ★★★

Via Augusto Conti 18/20, San Miniato Alto. Tel: 0571.431.90, www.sergiofalaschi.it. Open Monday-Tuesday and Thursday-Saturday, 8:00 a.m.-1:00 p.m. & 4:00 p.m.-8:00 p.m. Sunday, 8:00 a.m.-1:00 p.m. (though the shop does sometimes close on Sunday, better to call first). Closed Wednesday.

Ristorante Pepenero, ★★★

Via 4 Novembre 13, San Miniato. Tel: 0571.419.523, www.pepenerocucina.it. Open Sunday-Monday, Wednesday-Friday, 12:00 p.m.-2:30 p.m. & 7:00 p.m.-10:30 p.m.; Saturday, 7:00 p.m.-10:30 p.m. Closed Tuesday. Hours may vary off-season.

Papaveri e Papere, ★★★★

Via Dalmazia 159/D, San Miniato. Tel: 0571.409.422, Cell: 346 7490241 www.papaveriepaolo.com. Open Thursday-Tuesday for dinner only, 7:30 p.m.-10:30 p.m. Open Sunday for lunch, too. Closed Wednesday. Check their website for directions on how to reach the restaurant.

Tenuta di Poggio-Cosimo Maria Masini Farm, ★★★★★

Via Poggio al Pino 16, San Miniato. Tel: 0571.465032. Visits must be booked in advance via email: hospitality@cosimomariamasini.it

San Gimignano

🏃 102 Book a Vespa Tour of Magical San Gimignano or the Chianti Hills

The Vespa has to be the quintessential Italian means of transport. So what better way to tour one of Italy's most "Italian" towns than on one of these wonderful scooters? **Fun in Tuscany** is a well-known tour operator offering a number of organized tours, including regional wine tours, cooking classes, and quads. They also offer fun Vespa tours through the scenic roads and trails in the Chianti region. They usually cater to a younger crowd (largely students), but honestly, you can ride a Vespa at any age!

The tour takes you into the heart of Tuscany, where some of the most famous Chianti wines are produced. For lunch, the tour stops at a local winery for some fantastic Tuscan grub. The only problem you will have then is getting back on your scooter...

Another good option for Vespa tours is **Florence Town**. These tours leave from Florence, and participants are transported by minivan to Chianti, where the actual tour begins. The

tour includes a visit to a winery and lunch (or dinner, depending on the hour). We recommend checking both websites to make an informed decision. If you feel like going your own way, check out **Tuscany Scooter Rental**, a Vespa rental service (not an organized tour), which operates in collaboration with the Gaiole in Chianti tourism office.

Fun In Tuscany, ★★★★
Via Bernardo Cennini 6, Florence,
Cell: 338.592.2682 or 392.633.9101,
www.funintuscany.com.
Note: You need a driver's license to participate (not necessarily a motorcycle license). Book at least a week in advance.

Florence Town, ★★★★
Via de' Lamberti 1, Florence,
Tel: 055.281103. Number for emergencies: 346.152.5515.
www.florencetown.com.

Tuscany Scooter Rental, ★★★
Via Bettino Ricasoli 50, Gaiole in Chianti,
Tel: 055.941.747, Cell: 338.979.6038,
www.tuscanyscooterrental.com.

103 | See Tuscany from a Unique Perspective–a Hot Air Balloon!

Tuscany is renowned as one of the most photogenic parts of Europe, if not the world. It goes without saying that the views on offer are memorable, but for an unforgettable experience, why not appreciate the view from the unique perspective of a hot air balloon? And how better to commemorate a romantic getaway or a special occasion than with a hot air balloon ride over the Tuscan fields, vineyards, and hill towns, looking down over San Gimignano, the Val d'Orcia and the Chianti region?

One recommended company for rides is **Banda Balloons**, which offers outstanding, although expensive trips. They also offer photography classes from the air, while you are in the balloon; this means you'll have souvenirs to remember your ride long after it's over. Their balloons leave from Montaione, 25 minutes north of San Gimignano. Flights last 50 to 70 minutes and usually leave early in the morning or late in the afternoon. Prices start from €500. Book at least a week in advance.

Another good option is **Balloon Team Italia.** Prices are similar, though you can also book a ride with other participants, so the price goes down to the more affordable level of about €250 per person. They also offer a number of different launch sites, giving you the choice between an aerial view of Siena, Lucca, Florence, Chianti, and more. When you land they'll also hand you a celebratory glass of champagne—now that's service!

Banda Balloons, ★★★★
Cell: 320.853.8998 (Nicola - Italian), or 335.765.6200 (Massi - English).
www.bandaballoons.com.

Balloon Team Italia, ★★★★
Cell: 348.404.4117,
www.mongolfiereitalia.net.

104 Revel in a Spectacular Meal at One of the Best Restaurants in Tuscany–Cum Quibus

San Gimignano, one of Tuscany's best-known and loved hill towns (perhaps too loved, judging by the number of tourists who roam the streets in high season), is a must-see destination. Famous for its stunning Duomo and its medieval "skyscrapers"—the impressive towers built by local noble families competing for fame and glory—San Gimignano bursts with medieval charm, and its well-preserved streets are a joy to explore.

When the time comes to enjoy a memorable meal in this delightful town, there is only one place to go: **Cum Quibus**. This is a hugely popular establishment, but we put off dining here for quite a while, since we were, to be honest, intimidated by the number of reviews posted on online websites like TripAdvisor. Any restaurant with so many reviews, located in the heart of one of the most touristy town in Tuscany must be a tourist trap, right? Well, not in this case. And while it is true that many restaurants in San Gimignano do offer simple or limited menus, in the case of Cum Quibus, this couldn't be further from the truth.

Their menu is seasonal, so depending on what time of year you visit you'll enjoy something different, but generally speaking, every single dish we have tried in this restaurant was either very good or excellent. Some of our favorites were the delicate fondue of pecorino cheese, topped with a lightly cooked egg and a generous grating of black truffles; the restaurant's creamy forest mushroom risotto;

the *pici* with ragù, the foie gras with sardines and a tangy orange sauce; the braised veal in a delicious Amarone wine sauce; and, of course, the delectable desserts. As expected, booking a table in advance is essential, especially during high season. Oh, and did we mention that they just recently received their first Michelin star?

Cum Quibus, ★★★★★
Via San Martino 17, San Gimignano.
Tel: 0577.943.199,
www.cumquibus.it.
Open Wednesday-Monday, 12:30 p.m.–2:30 p.m. & 7:00 p.m.–10:00 p.m. Closed Tuesday. The restaurant usually closes for a winter break, call in advance.

Y | 105 | **Taste San Gimignano's Delectable** Vernaccia Wine

Vernaccia is undoubtedly one of our favorite choices for a summer lunch or *aperitivo*. Made with Vernaccia grapes from the area around San Gimignano, this crisp-tasting white wine immediately brings to mind scenes of open hills and gorgeous Tuscan mornings. Though not as venerated as Brunello, Nobile di Montepulciano or the Super-Tuscans, it is one of Tuscany's best-loved whites, and has been produced since the early 13th century. Popular among noble families and clergy, Vernaccia was even the thirst quencher of choice for famous gluttons like Pope Martino IV, who was, according to Dante Alighieri, especially fond of a nice plate of Bolsena eels pickled in Vernaccia wine. A number of vineyards on the way to San Gimignano offer tastings and the chance to buy bottles to go. Here are some of our favorites:

Azienda Agricola Fontaleoni is an elite producer whose fresh, crisp-tasting Vernaccia has won numerous awards and is among the best in the area. They also have a B&B with a restaurant and wine bar on-site if you are interested in spending more time here.

La Mormoraia is another excellent choice, and is the producer of award-winning wines. The location of their estate, which is also an *agriturismo* with a small spa, is lovely—charming views of San Gimignano in the distance, tiny but lush green gardens, and a homey rustic building of brick and stone make this a perfect stop to make. Though the standard tours are meant for groups of six or more people, personal tours can be organized and tailored according to your preferences.

Next, **Sovestro in Poggio**, is a charming place that offers guests a beautiful vista, making this tasting experience all the more sumptuous.

If you don't have the time (or the will) to venture out of town and visit one of these wineries, a perfectly enjoyable alternative is to visit one of San Gimignano's many well-stocked *enoteche*.
For a friendly and professional experience, try **D!Vineria**. With a large selection of Tuscan wines, and a knowledgeable staff, this is a good place to start off any exploration of the region's products.

Azienda Agricola Fontaleoni, ★★★★

Loc. Santa Maria 39/A, San Gimignano.
Tel: 0577.950.193,
www.fontaleoni.com.
Note: Tours and tastings can be organized, book a week in advance.

La Mormoraia, ★★★★

Loc. Sant' Andrea, San Gimignano.
Tel: 0577.940.096, Coordinate GPS: Lat: 43°50'16.94", Long: 11°05'29.56".
www.mormoraia.it.

Sovestro in Poggio, ★★★

Loc. Sovestro, San Gimignano. GPS coordinates: 11.0585 E (11° 3' 31" E), Lat: 43.46 N (43° 27' 36" N).
Tel: 0577.907.209, Cell: 335.482.192,
www.sovestroinpoggio.it.

D!Vineria, ★★★

Piazza delle Erbe 1, San Gimignano.
Tel: 0577.943.041,
www.divineria.it.
Open daily, 10:00 a.m.–9:00 p.m. (off season opening days and hours may change).

106 | **Book a Romantic Stay** at Agriturismo Guardastelle in San Gimignano

The combination of magical views, friendly and attentive service, and a charming atmosphere makes **Agriturismo Guardastelle** a great choice for a weekend in San Gimignano. The style and décor here are romantic, with a sense of old-world charm—wooden furniture and iron cast beds, rich colors, and beautiful linens. Outside you will find a manicured lawn, rose bushes and flower beds, and a pool, perfect for a morning or afternoon dip to escape the heat.

Prices here are reasonable, and you can choose between rooms or self-catering apartments. The *agriturismo* is surrounded by vineyards and olive groves, which belong to Fausto and Susanna, the owners, who produce their own excellent oil and wine (pick up a bottle when you leave). The views of the valley are picturesque, and at night the *agriturismo* justifies its name; *"guardastelle"* literally

means "look at the stars." You can sit outside on a hot summer night, look at the sky, and feel happy about making the decision to stay in this wonderful little corner of the world. The *agriturismo* is conveniently located a short walking distance from the town itself, so take advantage of the proximity and enjoy a pleasant evening walk into town for dinner. As this is one of the most popular accommodation choices in the area, we recommend booking a room well in advance.

Agriturismo Guardastelle, ★★★★★
Loc. Sovestro, San Gimignano. GPS Coordinates: 11.0585 E (11° 3' 31" E), 43.46 N (43° 27' 36" N). Tel: 0577.907.209, www.guardastelle.com.

Volterra and the Elsa Valley

107 Book a Gourmet Dinner in Jail!

If there's one experience we are sure very few people will be able to top, it's this one: Enjoy a dinner in jail, cooked by the prisoners and the chef of a leading Tuscan restaurant. Wait, it gets better...

The restaurant is in the prison, which is housed in an impressive Medici fortress in the town of Volterra. It was built in the 15th century as a symbol of the Medici family's control over the town they had conquered, and has been used as a political prison since its inception. Today, it is one of Italy's most secure prisons, even holding a number of high-ranking mafia members. However, once a month, the prison comes to life thanks to a relatively new initiative designed to aid inmate rehabilitation: a dinner is cooked and served to a few dozen lucky guests who booked well in advance.

Fresh ingredients are donated by the Coop supermarket chain and the wine is provided by Fisar, a local company. Prisoners are paid for their work and encouraged to learn a new trade, and this successful project enjoys the support of the Ministry of Justice. The food, not surprisingly, is served on paper plates with plastic cutlery. Music is even provided— Bruno, a convicted murderer, plays the piano beautifully!

The dinners take place once a month, from November to June. The prisoners cook under the guidance of some of the leading chefs in Tuscany, from restaurants such as Il Santo Graal in Florence and Oasi Bagno in Follonica. Reservations are handled by **Argonauta Viaggi Travel Agency**; book well ahead, as each visitor has to complete an advance security clearance. We recommend booking at least three months prior to your visit. For foreign nationals, special documentation is required to enter the prison, and to get clearance. Contact the travel agency to find out more.

Argonauta Viaggi Travel Agency,
★★★★★
Tel: 055.234.5040,
www.cenegaleotte.it.

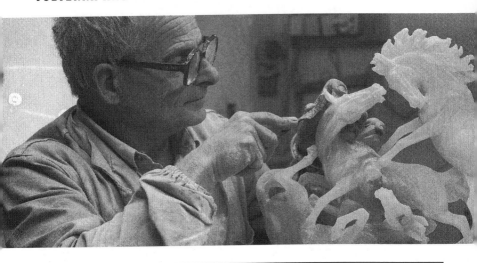

108 Buy Some Beautiful Alabaster Artifacts in Volterra

Alabaster craftsmanship has been woven into the fabric of life in Volterra for hundreds of years. Generations of families have honed the skill of sculpting with this elegant stone, and many of today's master alabaster artisans still use traditional, centuries-old techniques. The items they create are some of the best souvenirs you will find in Tuscany.

There is a wide selection of alabaster workshops in Volterra, catering to different budgets. If you are looking for something special, skip the run-of-the-mill items in the touristy shops, and head to **Artieri**, a large store with an impressive and varied collection of alabaster and agate items, all made by the 33 artists who own the cooperative. Another recommendation for artisanal items is the Alabastri Lavorati Italiani shop, better known simply as **Ali**, situated right next to Piazza Martiri della Libertà.

A smaller, more specialized store is **Romano Bianchi**. This shop is renowned for its intricate chess sets, as well as its elegant statues.

Alternatively, to get a closer look behind the scenes, try visiting **Alabarte**, a workshop and store that offers a peek into the processes and techniques used by the artists. Alabarte, as well as most other shops in Volterra, can also personalize orders and will ship around the world.

Artieri Alabastro, ★★★★★
Via Provinciale Pisana 28, Volterra.
Tel: 0588.86135,
www.artierialabastro.it.
(They also have a much smaller shop in Pisa, near the Leaning Tower, at Via Santa Maria 12). Open September-June, daily, 10:00 a.m.-1:00 p.m. & 3:00 p.m.-7:00 p.m.; August, open daily 10:00 a.m.-8:00 p.m.

Ali, ★★★★
Piazza Martiri della Libertà 5/9, Volterra.
Tel: 0588.86078,
www.alialabastro.it.
Open daily, 10:00 a.m.-7:00 p.m.

Romano Bianchi, ★★★
SR 68, Km. 37,200 (right outside Volterra), Tel: 0588.87237,
www.romanobianchi.com.
Hours of operation tend to vary, especially off-season. The shop is usually open Monday-Friday, 10:00 a.m.-1:00 p.m. & 3:30 p.m. -6:30 p.m., but calling before coming here is always a good idea.

Alabarte, ★★★
Workshop: Via Orti di Sant'Agostino 28, Volterra. Shop: Via Don Minzoni, 18, Volterra. Tel: 0588.87968, Cell: 340 7187189 (Roberto), 340 9816908 (Giorgio)
www.alabarte.com.
Open Monday-Friday, 10:00 a.m.-12:30 p.m. & 3:00 p.m.-6:30 p.m. March-September, also open on Saturday. August, open on Sunday, too.

¶¶ 109 | **Enjoy a Delicious Meal** with a Stunning View in the Volterra Countryside

Volterra—or as we like to call it, San Gimignano's older, more sensible sister—is a wonderful place to visit. The streets are a joy to explore and are filled with historic *palazzi* and monuments, some of which date back to Etruscan times. There is even a historic 1,500-year-old Roman theater to tempt history lovers. Volterra is also world-famous for its alabaster industry; the town is brimming with workshops that sell beautiful handcrafted items made from this delicate stone (see previous tip).

But touring tends to awaken the appetite, and once you have explored the town itself, you will surely look for a good place to enjoy a delicious lunch. Volterra does offer a variety of fun little *trattorie*, but our favorite restaurant is actually located just outside the town itself, in **Agriturismo Villa Felice**.

As soon as you pull up to this *agriturismo*, it will become clear why the restaurant here is so popular (booking a table in advance, especially on the weekends, is essential). The villa enjoys a coveted and absolutely spectacular panoramic view that immediately sets it apart from the competition. Although the menu is simple, it is very well executed—the pasta is delicious, and the meat dishes are a point of pride for the owners, making this eatery a top choice for avid carnivores, too.

On our last visit, for example, we enjoyed a delicious plate of steaming gnocchi with mozzarella, basil and sun-kissed tomatoes, as well as a flavor-packed plate of

ravioli served in a butter and sage sauce. For dessert, skip the usual Tuscan fare and try the Seada, a typical Sardinian pastry (the owner of the villa is of Sardinian descent), made with flaky dough, filled with ricotta, deep fried and then coated with honey.

Agriturismo Villa Felice, ★★★★
Podere Monteterzino , Volterra.
Tel: 0588.39017, Cell: 345.0671.489,
www.villafelicevolterra.com.
The restaurant is normally open daily for lunch and dinner in high season, but opening hours may vary, so it is probably best to call in advance (and book a table). The agriturismo usually closes down off-season.

110 | **Try Some Excellent Artisanal Cheeses** from Farms around Volterra

The area around Volterra is filled with little farms, each offering its own individual interpretation of pecorino cheese. Of course, much of this cheese is very good, but at the same time, not every farm deserves a visit. A few producers rise above the others thanks to the quality of their products. **Fattoria Lischeto**, located six kilometers from Volterra, is one of these. The pecorino made by Giovanni Cannas on his incredibly positioned farm (the views around the *agriturismo* are beautiful!) really stands out from the competition. Their *forte*, in our opinion, is the more delicate pecorino cheeses, where the freshness and creaminess really come across. Try the *pecorino degli sposi*, made with pasteurized sheep's milk; it's a subtle, smooth pecorino that is aged for about a month and goes perfectly with a nice bottle of Vermentino or San Gimignano Vernaccia. For a stronger flavor, try the *pecorino balze volterrane*, aged for at least two months and made with

vegetable-based rennet (making it perfect for vegetarians). Their ricotta cheese, which is only produced when fresh sheep's milk is available, is another recommended choice. A soft delicacy, this cheese is excellent on its own or with a light drizzle of honey. This farm, which is also an active *agriturismo* with comfortable, inviting rooms and apartments for rent, also produces organic cosmetics, and a light yet full-bodied olive oil. The fact that the farm is so close to the stunning **Teatro del Silenzio** (see tip 129) is an added reason to stop here.

Fattoria Lischeto, ★★★
Strada Provinciale del Monte Volterrano, Volterra (check the detailed explanations and map on their website), GPS coordinates: 43.420385, 10.813465. Tel: 0588.30414, Cell: 348.3327570 / 393.9036970, www.agrilischeto.com. Open daily, 9:00 a.m.–5:30 p.m. Hours of operation may change off-season. In the summer, the agriturismo's shop is often open later than 6:00 p.m.

111 | Discover the Charms of Colle di Val d'Elsa and Buy Stunning Crystal Artifacts

Souvenirs can be a tricky business. What seems like a sane purchase when traveling becomes an unnecessary (and sometimes embarrassing) extravagance when you get back home. But thoughtfully purchased souvenirs can and do serve as happy reminders long after our travels are over.

With our past mistakes informing our future decisions, we have identified two rules for souvenir shopping. First, we only buy souvenirs we can actually use. Second, the items must represent the essence of the place we've visited rather than the Disneyesque version. A case in point is a set of six hand-made crystal wine glasses we bought a few years ago at a small shop called La Grotta del Cristallo, hidden in an alley in Colle val d'Elsa's historical center. Every time we sip wine from them, we are fondly transported back to that fresh winter morning we spent in town.

Despite its small size, the town of Colle val d'Elsa is responsible for over 95% of the authentic crystal production Italy, and even hosts a small (but surprisingly interesting) museum dedicated entirely to the history of crystal production. Colle Val d'Elsa may not be as lovely as nearby San Gimignano or Monteriggioni, but it has a special atmosphere and is worth a stop. If you plan on purchasing any housewares or other souvenirs, note that while there is a reasonable selection of shops to choose from inside the historical center, the best artisans are located outside the walls, in the industrial area about 10 minutes from town. Colle val d'Elsa's (tiny) local culinary scene is thriving, too; consider stopping in at the excellent Michelin-starred Arnolfo Restaurant, or at the lively Officina Popolare (see next tip) for a good meal.

Franco Cucini has been making quality crystal items for over 40 years. To get a better idea of his style and admire the delicate artifacts he produces, check his website before your tour of the town. **Cristallerie Mezzetti** is another good choice. We especially admire their Da Vinci collection, which mostly consists of bottles and carafes. **Duccio di Segna** has an interesting show room and some beautiful pieces worth exploring. **La Grotta del Cristallo** and **Cristalleria Moleria** both have beautiful collections and are located within Colle Val d'Elsa's historical center. We especially like La Grotta's glasses and Moleria's selection of gorgeous, masculine bottles and tableware.

Franco Cucini, ★★★★
Zona industriale Belvedere, Ingresso 5, number 36, int.8, Colle di Val d'Elsa. Tel: 0577.931.890, www.formesulcristallo.it. Open Monday-Friday 8:15 a.m.-1:00 p.m. & 3:00 p.m.-8:00 p.m.; Saturday, 8:15 a.m.-12:00 p.m.. Groups interested in guided visits should book about 4-5 days in advance.

Cristallerie Mezzetti, ★★★★
Via Guglielmo Oberdan 13, Colle di Val d'Elsa. Tel: 0577.920.395, www.cristalleriemezzetti.com. Open Monday 3:30 p.m.-7:30 p.m.; Tuesday-Saturday 9:00 a.m.-1:00 p.m. & 3:30 p.m.-7:30 p.m. Closed Sunday.

Duccio di Segna, ★★★★
Loc. Pian dell'Olmino 42, Colle di Val d'Elsa. Tel: 0577 929656, www.ducciodisegna.com. Open Monday-Friday, 9:00 a.m.-12:30 p.m. & 2:30 p.m.-7:30 p.m. Guided visits to the workshop should be booked in advance, and can be organized Monday-Saturday 9:00 a.m.-12:00 p.m.

La Grotta del Cristallo, ★★★★
Via del Murolungo 20, Colle di Val d'Elsa. Tel: 0577.924.676, www.lagrottadelcristallo.it. Open daily, 10:00 a.m.-7:00 p.m. (Off-season the shop closes down for a lunch break between 1:00 p.m. and 2:30 p.m.)

Cristalleria La Moleria ShowRoom/Outlet, ★★★★
Via delle Romite 26-28, Colle di Val d'Elsa. Tel: 0577.920.163, www.lamoleriagelli.com. Open Monday-Saturday 9:30 a.m.-12:30 p.m. & 2:00 p.m.-6:00 p.m.

112 Stay at a Delightful Eco-Lodge Outside Medieval Certaldo

Il Paluffo is one of the most charming B&B's we've come across in Tuscany. A sustainable eco-lodge which sits right outside of Certaldo, this 15th century olive mill-turned-B&B offers guests a unique and environmentally-friendly experience.

It took five years of meticulous work to renovate the manor and bring it to its current charming state. During that process, the owners decided to take things one step further, and turn their life project into the most environmentally friendly residence possible, by reducing the B&B's footprint to zero, relying on renewable energy for most of their needs, and using only local materials for the decor. Even the pool is a natural bio-pool, cleaned and maintained using aquatic plants.

The result is a warm and peaceful oasis. The rooms are decorated with family antiques, and some even feature frescoed walls. Since the B&B is an active farm, too, guests can enjoy the honey, olive oil and wine made by owners, and book a spot on one of the many (extra) activities organized here, such as cooking classes, guided wine tastings, truffle hunting, and even a pizza making lesson.

Il Paluffo, ★★★★
Via Citerna 144, Certaldo.
Cell: 335.8326653, Tel: 0571.664259,
www.ilpaluffo.com.

🏃 113 | **Visit Casole d'Elsa, Catch a Jazz Concert,** and Stop by Caseificio Carai, a Charming Artisanal Cheese Maker

Here's our idea of a perfect and alternative day: Spend the morning in Volterra, exploring its charming streets, the Duomo, the Etruscan Museum, the Roman Theater, and, of course, the town's wonderful array of alabaster shops (see tip number 107). Then, drive south to Casole d'Elsa (not to be confused with Colle Val d'Elsa) for some foodie adventures.

Leave Volterra and drive along the scenic SR68 towards Casole. After about 16 kilometers, turn right (still directed towards Casole) and get on the SP52. After about one kilometer, you will see **Caseificio Carai.** Watch out, as it's easy to miss, the only marker is a tiny sign on your right. Don't be put off by the (very) simple setting—the cheese here is mouth-watering, and has won several awards over the years. If you feel like you're in someone's back yard, you're not wrong; this is actually the

owner's house. The Carai family have produced multiple award-winning cheeses and the business dates back to the early 1900s in Sardinia. In the 1950s the family moved its herd and its home to Tuscany, and today the operation is headed by Giuseppe Carai, who is quite a *personaggio,* as one might say in Italian. The family has a small herd, no more than 1,200 sheep, which allows them to focus on quality rather than quantity, and produce some excellent cheeses. Strong emphasis is placed on organic ingredients. Be aware that as for most cheeses in Tuscany, the milk used is raw; nothing here is pasteurized or chemically altered, it's just pure and simple, naturally delicious cheese. Don't miss *Il Bandito,* a flavorsome, aged, sharp-tasting cheese, the *Cervellone,* which is more delicate but still rich and intense, the *Barricato,* aged in marc, and the fresh ricotta, when available.

From here, continue towards Casole itself. Located in the middle of the Elsa Valley, Casole d'Elsa may be a relatively unknown town, but it is also a tranquil little corner to escape to, and it offers some particularly spectacular views.

Park in the car park on your right as soon as you enter Casole and look up—you'll see two elevators attached to the back of the mountain that will bring you directly to the *centro storico* (you can of course walk up if you prefer). A tour of the town itself is fun, though the biggest attraction is actually walking along the fortified town wall (Casole occupied an important defensive position in Renaissance times) to enjoy the surrounding views.

Once you've finished your tour of the town, stop at **Caffè Casolani**, a unique little venue that oozes charisma. Located in a charming row of terraced red brick stores, Caffè Casolani has a wonderfully relaxed vibe and a novel way of serving its food. You pay beforehand for a set dinner menu of four courses without knowing what you are going to be served. Don't worry—you shouldn't be in for any nasty surprises, the food here is not only appetizing but also authentically Tuscan. A rotating wine list also ensures you can try different but equally palatable wines every time you visit. The owner is very knowledgeable about wine, and can recommend a bottle from his large collection to buy and take home with you. This place prides itself on quality, so you will find some of the top Tuscan names here—chocolate from *Amadei* in Pontedera, pasta from *Martelli* in Lari, Chianti from *Castello di Ama*, and much more. Jazz shows

and other events take place in the summer months, so if you are visiting around then, be sure to check their website before you go to see if there's something going on!

Formaggi (caseificio) Fratelli Carai, ★★★

Località Montemiccioli, Podere Rimini, Volterra. Tel: 0588.35006,
Cell: 339.5975830,
www.formaggicarai.it.
Open Monday-Saturday, 8:00 a.m.–1:00 p.m. & 3:30 p.m.–8:00 p.m.

Caffè Casolani, ★★★★

Via Casolani 41, Casole d'Elsa.
Tel: 0577.948.733,
www.caffecasolani.com.

Lucca and Its Surroundings

🍴 114 | **Enjoy a Perfect Meal** in the Heart of Lucca

Tourists come to dine in Lucca's many restaurants, but so do many locals, which means there are several interesting and authentic culinary options in town. When we are in the mood for a homey, simple meal, we like going to **Gigi Trattoria**. The food isn't exactly high cuisine, but it is hearty, tasty, and reasonably priced (book a table in advance, they are always full). It's hard to go wrong with any of the dishes here! Equally good is **Gli Orti di Via Elisa.** This beautifully decorated and modern venue is the perfect choice for an easy going dinner. The menu offers a tasty interpretation of the traditional Lucchese flavors. Try the tordelli lucchesi (a sort of ravioli, typical of Lucca), served with a beef ragu; the capretto al forno (oven baked goat, served with fresh spinach); and the rabbit, served with polenta. The wine list here is very good, too. Consult with your waiter to find the perfect local bottle to compliment your meal.

If you are just looking for a quick, light lunch on the go, Piazza San Michele, one of the prettiest town squares in Lucca, offers the perfect solution. Here you will find two places which are loved by the locals–**Pizzeria Pellegrini** and La Tana del Boia. Pizzeria Pellegrini offers tasty slices (as good as the slice at the hugely popular **Pizzeria San Felice**, in our opinion), and delicious cecina (a traditional Tuscan salty flat cake, made with chickpea flour and olive oil). **La Tana del Boia** offers the best sandwiches in town, prepared with top-quality ingredients such as truffled boar salami and aged pecorino cheese. Wash it all down with a glass of the house red.

For a serious culinary experience, we absolutely love **Da Pasquale** (also appears as *Da Pasqualino* on some websites). This smart restaurant is one of the most popular venues in town, so make sure you book a table at least a few days in advance. The menu here is seasonal, but many of the classic dishes can be found throughout the year. Try some of the chef's best delicacies, such as *risotto con porri e Champagne* (a creamy risotto, flavored with leeks and Champagne), the *ravioli con porcini e fonduta di pecorino e tartufi* (porcini-stuffed ravioli, served with a truffled pecorino cheese fondue), *filetto sul letto di patate e tartufo* (a delicious and tender beef steak, served on a bed of crispy potatoes and truffles), *coniglio di Pasqualino* (the restaurant's famous rabbit dish) and the *baccalà con purè di porri, pomodorini e capperi* (salt cod served with leek puree, fresh tomatoes, and capers). If you are unsure what to order, ask for your waiter's recommendation—they will be able to point out the day's specials, and suggest a good wine pairing, too.

End your meal with a romantic walk to discover the magic of Lucca by night. If you prefer a guided experience, book (in advance) a spot on the **Lucca sotto le stelle** (Lucca under the stars) tour, which is available through the Lucca tourist office. Tours leave June through September, on Thursdays and Saturdays, at 9:00 p.m. (these hours tend to vary, contact the office for more details: www.visitlucca.eu/lucca-tour-di-notte-passeggiando-sotto-le-stelle.

Alternatively, if you are visiting during the day, relax for a few hours at **Palazzo Pfanner** (Via degli Asili 33). The mansion's small but manicured gardens are delightful, and a perfect place to unwind in between sightseeing stops or after a good meal. Just don't fall asleep on one of the benches as we did...

Trattoria Gigi, ★★★
Piazza del Carmine 7, Lucca.
Tel: 0583.467.266,
www.gigitrattoria.it.
Open daily, 12:00 p.m.–2:30 p.m. & 7:30 p.m.–10:30 p.m. Booking in advance is highly recommended.

Gli Orti di Via Elisa, ★★★★
Via Elisa 17, Lucca.
Tel: 0583.491.241,
www.ristorantegliorti.it.
Open Friday-Tuesday, 12:00-2:30 p.m. & 7:30-11:00 p.m.; Thursday open for lunch only; Wednesday closed.

Pizzeria Pellegrini, ★★★
Piazza San Michele 25, Lucca.
Tel: 0583.467.891. Open Monday-Saturday, 12:30 a.m.–9:00 p.m.

La Tana del Boia, ★★★★
Piazza San Michele 36, Lucca. Open daily (usually), 12:00 p.m.–10:00 p.m.

Da Pasqualino, ★★★★★
Via del Moro 8, Lucca. Tel: 0583.496.506. Open Wednesday–Monday for dinner only, 7:15 p.m.-10:30 p.m. Closed Tuesday. Booking in advance is essential.

 # 115 | **Get Some Serious Shopping Done** in Lucca

Lucca is widely known as one of Tuscany's most delightful towns to visit, and quite rightfully so. It is easy to fall in love with its perfectly preserved, romantic streets and quaint *piazze*; and it is impossible not to enjoy a walk along its beautiful Renaissance ramparts, especially at sunset. However, what many visitors miss is the fact that Lucca is also a great place to get some shopping done. The town's main street, **Via Fillungo**, is a small shopper's paradise. Fun, compact and varied, Via Fillungo is lined with shop after shop of leading mid-range brands, from Sephora to Guess, from Patrizia Pepe to Motivi. This continues on the adjacent streets, too; the entire area, in fact, is perfect for visitors who are looking for some swanky Italian fashion, shoes, bags, or jewelry. And because the historical center is so small, it is actually easier to get some of your shopping done here than in Florence. In addition to the main street, there are many other, lesser-known corners of Lucca that offer

interesting finds, too. Here are some of our favorites:

The shops along **Via Buia** and **Via del Moro** offer many fantastic finds too. For beautiful handmade jewelry, try **Manidoro** and **Leoncini**. For leather bags and leather-bound journals, try a personal favorite— **L'Officina della Pelle**. For cool, chic eyeware, check the smart collection at **Ottica Talini,** a deceptively simple-looking shop that stocks many hard-to-find Fendi frames, along with other surprises.

When you feel your blood sugar dropping (or the shameless hedonism level rising), visit **Ladurèe**. This famous Parisian shop has recently opened a small branch in Lucca, and their macaroons are nothing short of wonderful. You will also find several high-end products, from fashionable bags to ambiance perfumes and even books.

Easy to miss but well worth a visit is **Barsanti**, in Via San Paolino (just off Piazza San Michele). This little neighborhood shop, serving mostly a local clientele, doesn't look like much from the outside, but they do have a great selection of copper serving dishes and other interesting cooking utensils in the back. If you are a fan of rustic country chic or if you like to collect special kitchenware during your travels, you'll want to stop here; sometimes you'll find nothing, but sometimes you'll hit the jackpot. For more modern kitchen utensils try **Cookit** and **Coin Casa**, which sit side by side on Via Cenami and will delight any aspiring chef. Naturally, visit **Vissidarte**, too, a shop that holds a stunning collection of handmade ceramics.

Antique lovers will find Lucca bubbling with interesting finds. Among our favorite shops is **Daniele Squaglia**, where you can find some beautiful antiques at reasonable prices, everything from 18th-century prints bronze Napoleonic statues. **Be' Mi' Tempi** is another shop worth stopping at, as is **Cose Vecchie di Lenzi & C.** Additionally, Via del Battistero, a small street connecting Lucca's Duomo with Piazza Napoleone, is filled with small and delightful antique shops and shouldn't be missed. Especially noteworthy boutiques on this street are **Galleria Kraag**, offering primarily Oriental art; **Manfredini Raffaella**, a tiny shop that focuses on antique globes and ancient prints; **Renata Frediani, Galleria Vannucci**, and **Antiqua**.

All that spending will surely build up a thirst—for wine, that is. Luckily, Lucca's graceful *piazze* and alleys are the perfect setting for a fun *aperitivo*. There are many options in town, but we just love **Il Baccanale**. Hiding in a small street off Via Fillungo, Il Baccanale is set in a converted shoemaker's shop and has a young

vibe. Cramming inside with the jovial locals is half the fun! If you don't particularly enjoy vivacious guests invading your personal space, choose **L'Enoteca Vanni**, instead. A centrally located, old-world *enoteca*, this is a fantastic place to relax with a glass of a good Tuscan Red (the selection here is one of the best in town, hands down). Note that if you are in a group of four or more people, you can book a guided tasting in the *enoteca's* picturesque cellar, which is located downstairs (booking in advance is required). To round off your tour, visit **Enoteca Marsili**, one of our favorite *enoteche*, located in Piazza San Michele. Their selection is excellent, with everything from a Poggio di Sotto Brunello to a nice Tignanello, and from Solaia and Guado al Tasso to Sassicaia and Peppoli wines.

Cookit & Coin Casa,
Via Cenami 6. Tel: 0583 48915 Open daily, 10:00 a.m.-1:00 p.m. & 2:30 p.m.-7:30 p.m.

Vissidarte,
Via Calderia 20,
Lucca (2 minutes from Via Fillungo).
Tel: 0583.48383, www.vissidarte.it. Open Monday-Saturday, 11:00 a.m.-7:30 p.m.; Saturday 10:00 a.m.-1:00 p.m. & 3:00 p.m.-7:30 p.m.; Sunday 11:00 p.m.-4:00 p.m.

Manidoro, ★★★
Via S. Giorgio 15, Lucca. Tel: 0583.955.984. Open Monday-Saturday, 10:30-1:00 p.m. & 3:30 p.m.-7:30 p.m.

Leoncini, ★★★
Via Mordini 12 (also marked on some maps as Già Via Nuova 12), Lucca. Tel: 0583.494.134, www.leonciniorafo.it. Open Tuesday-Saturday, 9:10 a.m.-12:50 & 3:40 p.m.-7:30 p.m.

L'Officina della Pelle, ★★★★
Via della Fratta 29, Lucca.
Tel: 0583.341.214, www.capuozzo.it. Open Monday-Saturday, 9:0 a.m.-7:00 p.m. Note that they have two more shops in town: A smaller shop on Via Fillungo 196, and a larger shop on Via San Paolino 12, which is also open on Sundays (usually).

Ottica Talini, ★★★★
Via Fillungo 50. Tel: 0583.494.946. Open Monday 3:30 p.m.-7:00 p.m.; Tuesday-Saturday, 10:00 a.m.-1:00 p.m. & 3:30 p.m.-7:00 p.m.

Ladurèe, ★★★
Piazza dei Mercanti, Lucca.
Tel: 0583.491.344. Open Monday-Friday, 10:00 a.m.-7:30 p.m.; Saturday, 10:00 a.m.-8:00 p.m.; Sunday 10:00 a.m.-1:00 p.m. & 3:30-8:00 p.m.

Barsanti, ★★★★
Via San Paolino, 88, Lucca.
Tel: 0583.55962. Open Monday-Saturday, 8:30 a.m.-12:30 p.m. & 3:00 p.m.-7:00 p.m.

Daniele Squaglia, ★★★★
Via Cenami 21, Lucca.
Tel: 0583.492.140,
www.danielesquaglia.it.
Open Tuesday-Saturday, 10:00 a.m.-1 p.m. & 3:30 p.m.-7:30 p.m.

Be' Mi' Tempi Antiques, ★★★★
Via del Gallo 24, Lucca.
Tel: 0583.462.575, Cell: 338.5067333 / 349.8515564, www.bemitempi.it. Open Tuesday-Saturday, 10:30 a.m.-7:00 p.m.

Cose Vecchie di Lenzi E C. S.N.C., ★★★★
Via della Cittadella 40, Lucca.
Tel: 0583.496.731,
www.antiquariolucca.it.

Galleria Kraag,
Via del Battistero 17,Lucca.
Tel: 0583.496.074. Open Tuesday-Saturday, 10:30 a.m.-7:00 p.m. Hours of operation may vary.

Il Baccanale, ★★★
Via Sant' Andrea 14, Lucca.
Tel: 0583.080743. Open Tuesday-Sunday, 11:30 a.m.-3:00 p.m. & 6:00 p.m.-midnight. Closed Monday.

L'Enoteca Vanni, ★★★★★
Piazza San Salvatore 7, Lucca.
Tel: 0583.491.902,
www.enotecavanni.com.
Open Monday 3:30 p.m.-9:00 p.m.; Tuesday-Saturday, 10:00 a.m.-1:00 p.m. & 3:30 p.m.-9:00 p.m.

Enoteca Marsili, ★★★★★
Piazza San Michele 38, Lucca.
Tel: 0583.491.751 ,Via del Moro, 22
Tel: 0583.496.184. Via dei Borghi, 103
Tel: 0583.493.017, enotecamarsili.it Open Monday-Saturday, 11:00 a.m.-7:30 p.m.

🏃 116 | **Visit the Stunning Gardens** of Villa Reale Near Lucca

Lucca's historical center is well-known and loved. But what few visitors realize is that the surrounding countryside offers a number of surprises, too. The hills around Lucca are dotted with several historic mansions and villas. Some of these estates are privately owned and therefore can't be toured, while others are open to the public, but don't offer very much to see or do. Villa Reale, on the other hand, is, in our opinion, a joy to explore, and makes for a perfectly relaxing afternoon stop, especially in the summer, when trying to escape both the heat and the multitude of tourists in the city.

Villa Reale sits just 10 minutes from Lucca's historic center. You can reach it by car, or even by bicycle. The villa was originally built as a medieval fortress by the Duke of Tuscia. Over the years it exchanged many (noble) hands, and in 1806 Elisa Baciocchi Bonaparte, Napoleon's sister, took over and expanded the estate and gardens further, making them fit for royalty.

Then began a long period of decay, which ended in 2015 when the estate was purchased by a young Swiss couple, who took upon themselves the hefty mission of bringing Villa Reale back to its former glory. This project is still ongoing—today (May 2017) the gardens can be toured, but the villa itself is still undergoing restoration work and is not yet open to the public. The entrance fee (9 euro) isn't low, but in our opinion it is justified given the beauty of the gardens and the amount of work that has been invested in this estate. As you walk along the camellia

walkway, enjoy the picturesque and placid lake, and visit the Spanish garden and the delightful grotto of pan, we are sure you will agree. It also worth noting that during the summer months, the villa hosts several concerts (mostly jazz) and other cultural events—consult their website to find out more.

If you are interested in learning more about the other historic mansions in the hills around Lucca, see: www.villeepalazzilucchesi.it.

Villa Reale, ★★★★
Via Fraga Alta 2, Marlia, Capannori (LU). Tel: 0583.10108, www.parcovillareale. it. Open March–October, daily, 10:00 a.m.–6:00 p.m. (last entrance 5:30 p.m.); Off season (November–February) open by appointment only.

🏃 117 | Catch a Puccini Concert in the Beautiful San Giovanni Church in Lucca

San Giovanni is, without a doubt, one of the most beautiful churches in Lucca. Though it doesn't have the crowd-gathering art of the Duomo (which hosts Tintoretto's *The Last Supper*), or of San Michele's church (which features Filippino Lippi's *Pala Magrini*), San Giovanni does boast two very special attractions.

The first is the underground tour. This ancient church which, until the 8th century served as Lucca's main cathedral and residence for the town's bishop, was actually built atop a Roman temple. Though most of the decorations of the church itself did not survive the Napoleonic invasion (except for the exquisite wooden ceiling—look up!), the Roman excavations, which include ancient mosaic floors and pre-Roman and Roman relics, remained intact and can still be visited.

The second attraction is the concert program. The church regularly hosts concerts and arias by Puccini, which means that if you love opera, and aren't visiting Tuscany during the annual Puccini festival, you can still enjoy a fun concert. The location for these concerts, by the way, is hardly incidental; this was the church where Giacomo Puccini (or, to be exact, Giacomo Antonio Domenico Michele Secondo Maria Puccini) was baptized. Find out the monthly program, and make a free booking for a very special night, on their website.

Chiesa di San Giovanni, ★★★★
Piazza San Giovanni, Lucca.
www.puccinielasualucca.com.
The church is open for visits daily, 10:00 a.m.–6:00 p.m.

118 Stay in One of the Best Hotels in Lucca

Choosing a place to stay in Lucca is easy. Depending on your tastes and preferences, there are some excellent options in town. For a homey and more easygoing countryside B&B experience, try **Villa Agnese**. Simple, tranquil, and romantic, this B&B has its fair share of fans. As soon as you walk up the white marble staircase and enter the 19th-century villa, you feel welcome. The décor is unpretentious yet elegant, the staff is friendly, and the free parking and the air conditioning in the rooms (not a given in many Italian B&Bs!) are added bonuses that more than make up for any disadvantages this B&B may have. The villa even offers guests free bikes to tour the historical center and ride along Lucca's famous ramparts.

Hotel San Luca Palace offers a more luxurious stay, and this perfectly positioned four-star hotel is definitely an option worth considering. The hotel is located within a 16th-century former hospital, which once sheltered the town's sick and weak, and has been beautifully restored. The rooms are elegant and spacious, the rich buffet breakfast is quite good, the staff is friendly and professional, and there is a small parking lot for guests (useful, since the hotel borders on the ZTL).

Finally, **Palazzo Rocchi** is one of our favorite choices in Lucca. A more traditional and classic hotel, Palazzo Rocchi is simply beautiful, especially the lobby, which resembles the drawing room of a noble family's town mansion. Many of the rooms, which are still filled with historical mementos and antiques, are impressive, too. The rooms facing the inner courtyard are much quieter (the rooms facing Piazza San Michele, one of Lucca's busiest *piazze*, are noisier); and if you prefer to do your own cooking, there is an apartment to rent on the top floor. Prices here can be relatively high in the summer months, but if you book in advance, there's a good chance you might come across an offer or two.

B&B Villa Agnese, ★★★★
Viale Agostino Marti 177, Lucca.
Cell: 348.731.2588,
www.bbvillaagneselucca.it.

Hotel San Lucca Palace, ★★★
Via San Paolino 103, Lucca.
Tel: 0583.317.446,
www.sanlucapalace.com.

Palazzo Rocchi, ★★★★
Piazza San Michele 30, Lucca.
Tel: 0583.467.479, Cell: 338.207.0261,
www.palazzorocchi.it.

Forte dei Marmi
and the Italian Riviera

🍴|119 | Revel in a Modern and Delicious Meal in Forte dei Marmi–one of Tuscany's Most Exclusive Beach Towns

Lux Lucis Restaurant, which is located within the five-star Principe Hotel, is currently one of the most interesting and promising restaurants in Forte dei Marmi, in our opinion. Run by an up-and-coming young chef—Valentino Cassanelli—Lux Lucis offers innovative five- or nine-course tasting menus that are well worth your time, and we suspect this restaurant will soon become one of the leading spots on the Italian Riviera and will earn the attention it deserves. Cassanelli's distinctive and delicious menu combines haute cuisine techniques that, quite frankly, are rarely found in Tuscan restaurants, with the freshest produce. Dishes such as ravioli filled with anchovies and served with chicory and burrata cheese, or sea bass covered with Mediterranean herbs, are especially delicious. Should you arrive early, you can always enjoy a tasty cocktail or glass of wine upstairs, at the Sky Bar Lounge—the hotel's exclusive rooftop bar.

Lux Lucis Restaurant-Hotel Principe Forte dei Marmi, ★★★★★
Viale Amm. Morin 67, Forte dei Marmi, Tel: 0584.783.636, www.principefortedeimarmi.it.
The hotel's roof top bar is open daily, after 6:00 p.m. Lux Lucis Restaurant is open daily during the summer months, 8:30 p.m.–10:00 p.m.; Off-season, Wednesday–Sunday, 8:00 p.m.–10:00 p.m. Closed Monday-Tuesday. Please note that there is a smart-casual dress code in this restaurant.

🏃 120 Book Tickets for the Puccini Festival in Torre del Lago and Visit the Composer's Graceful Villa

The **Giacomo Puccini Opera Festival** (also known as the 'Festival Pucciniano') is a veritable feast for opera lovers. One of Tuscany's best known events, it is the only festival in the world exclusively dedicated to the composer who wrote such beautiful works as *La Bohème, Madam Butterfly*, and *Turandot*; anyone, opera lover or not, can hum along to these perennial favorites. The location of the festival is quite charming, too, set in an open-air theater in Torre del Lago, a historic resort town, situated just 15 minutes from Lucca. Every year, the four or five full productions of Puccini's work draw tens of thousands of spectators to the town. The annual program can be found online, and if you are thinking about seeing one of the performances, be sure to book a ticket well in advance. Alternatively, if you haven't managed to book any tickets for

the Puccini festival, note that most summers the **Associazione Culturale Ville Borbone** hosts a series of **classical music concerts** held in various **historic mansions and villas** along the Tuscan coast. The concerts are a pleasure for the ears and the eyes, as they give you a chance to visit some stunning mansions that are normally closed to the public. To find out more, consult the association's website (sadly, in Italian only: www. associazionevilleversilia.com).

Naturally, don't miss a visit to **Puccini's villa**, a fascinating site not only for music lovers and fans of the composer's work but also for anyone with an interest in history. Sitting on the shore of Lake Massaciuccoli, this small but beautifully decorated historic mansion was Puccini's home for thirty years, from 1891 to 1921, until pollution from the lake forced him to move. Visitors can see various antiques and mementos, including Puccini's piano, an assortment of photos and paintings, original sheet music, and much more. After his death, his son, Antonio Puccini, turned the house into a museum and converted the drawing room into a mausoleum, where Puccini is buried. The villa can be toured with a guide only, and the tour, which is available in English, too, is interesting and detailed. In fact, we would recommend a visit here above Puccini's other home, in Lucca. Though that site has also recently been converted into a museum, it is far less interesting to explore.

Festival Puccini
(held in the Gran Teatro all'Aperto Giacomo Puccini), Via delle Torbiere, Torre del Lago. Tel: 0584.359.322, www.puccinifestival.it. Tickets: ticketoffice@puccinifestival.it.

Associazione Culturale Ville Borbone, ★★★★
Via Conca Di Sopra 166, Bargecchia, Massarosa. Cell: 328.2010585, www.associazionevilleversilia.com.

Villa Puccini, ★★★★★
Viale G. Puccini 266, Torre del Lago. Tel: 0584.341.445, www.giacomopuccini.it. The villa can be visited only with a guide. Tours leave Tuesday-Sunday, every 40 minutes. Closed Monday morning. November 30-January 31, tours leave at 10:00 a.m., 10:40 a.m., 11:20 a.m., 120 p.m., 2:00 p.m., 2:40 p.m., 3:20 p.m., 4:00 p.m., and 4:40 p.m.; February 1-March 31, tours leave at 10:00 a.m., 10:40 a.m., 11:20 a.m., 12:00 p.m., 2:30 p.m., 3:10 p.m., 3:50 p.m., 4:30 p.m., and 5:10 p.m.; April 1-November 1, tours leave at 10:00 a.m., 10:40 a.m., 11:20 a.m., 12:00 p.m., 3:00 p.m., 3:40 p.m., 4:20 p.m., 5:00 p.m., and 5:40 p.m.; July-August (during the Puccini Festival), tours leave at 10:00 a.m., 10:40 a.m., 11:20 a.m., 12:00 p.m., 4:00 p.m., 4:40 p.m., 5:20 p.m., 6:00 p.m., 6:40 p.m., 7:20 p.m., and 8:00 p.m.

121 | **Work on Your Tan** at Some of the Best Beaches in Forte dei Marmi

As we've already mentioned, Forte dei Marmi (and it's 'younger sister', Marina di Pietrasanta) have long been where Italy's well-heeled come during their summer vacation to enjoy some beach time in style. Here you will find a number of popular beaches that offer pristine and manicured grounds, attentive service, the chance to occasionally spot a Hollywood celebrity, and all in all—the perfect bathing experience. Note that wherever you go, you should book your beach chair or cabin well in advance (many Tuscans have standing orders, which means that there aren't that many available spots on the beach), and, as always, dress the part.

Twiga beach is a very popular option. Beach by day, lively club by night, this is one of the best loved venues in the area. **Bagno Piero**, just down the road from Twiga, is a historic beach, one that has been serving locals and foreigners for over 70 years and is still considered a top choice. **Bagno Alaide** is another fun option, and suitable for families, too (though the best family-friendly beaches aren't here, but farther south, in Viareggio and Lido di Camaiore). Lastly, we have always enjoyed coming to **Bagno La Perla**, a well located and very inviting beach in Marina di Pietrasanta.

Twiga Beach, ★★★★
Viale Roma 2, Marina di Pietrasanta. Tel: 0584.21518,
www.twigabeachclub.com.

Bagno Piero, ★★★★
Via Arenile 1, Forte dei Marmi. Tel: 0584-1848640,
www.bagnopiero.it.

Bagno Alaide, ★★★★
Viale Achille Franceschi 25, Forte dei Marmi. Tel: 0584.89100.

Bagno La Perla, ★★★★
Via Lungomare Roma 34, Pietrasanta. Tel: 0584.20384,
www.bagnolaperla.com.

¶|122 | Savor the High Cuisine at Ristorante Lorenzo, One of Tuscany's Best Seafood Restaurants

A Tuscan institution and symbol, Lorenzo is a restaurant equaled by very few. Its critics claim that it has lost some of its charm in recent years, but even the strictest guests cannot deny that this is still one of Tuscany's leading venues. Stylish, smart, expensive and always tasty, this Michelin-starred restaurant is somewhat of a local sea-food Mecca. The menu is seasonal, so ask for your waiter's recommendation. We greatly enjoyed dishes such as delicious royal red prawns cooked in vegetable stock and flavored with a dash of dry vermouth, ravioli-stuffed with whitefish, pan-roasted scallops, and creamy, rich champagne-spiced risotto dotted with shellfish. Those who do not shy away from raw delicacies will surely enjoy the *antipasto crudo*. The wine list is incredible, and there is a very good selection of both Italian and foreign bottles (though prices tend to be very high). If you play your cards right, you may be invited to visit the cellar.

Ristorante Lorenzo, ★★★★★
Via Giosuè Carducci 61, Forte dei Marmi.
Tel: 0584 874030,
www.ristorantelorenzo.com.
The restaurant's hours of operation change by season: September 16-December 15, and March 1-June 15, open Wednesday-Sunday, 12:30 p.m.-2:30 p.m. & 8:00 p.m.-10:00 p.m. Closed Monday. Tuesday open for dinner only; June 15-September 15, open for dinner only. December 15-February 1, closed for winter break.

Pistoia and
Montecatini Terme

🏃 |123| Indulge your Senses with an Exclusive Dip in the Monsummano Terme Thermal Pool and Caves

At first glance, the Grotta Giusti Resort seems like your average Tuscan 4-star hotel; golf course, spa, and elegantly converted rooms overlooking the town of Monsummano Terme. But look (quite literally) a little deeper and it becomes clear that Giusti has some secrets. Below the hotel and set deep into the Tuscan hills is an enchanting grotto spa—the labyrinthine cave system, which experiences 100% humidity and temperatures between 31°C and 34°C, has been converted into a full-service thermal spa. Stalactites loom overhead across three steamy zones delectably named Paradise, Purgatory, and Hell, each of which offers luxurious treatments and therapies, including mud packs and chocolate treatments, for the ultimate in pampering and relaxation.

Diving excursions through the depths of the cave system can be

organized for the more adventurous. Alternatively, the view of the Tuscan countryside from the thermal swimming pool is the perfect way to relax, and a cocktail will surely contribute to your overall condition.

After your visit to Giusti, you might want to end on a sweet note and stop by **Slitti,** a renowned local chocolatier, in the nearby town of Monsummano Terme. This little place was World Champion in a chocolate competition held in London in 2012. Try the excellent espresso-flavored chocolates (for a start).

Then, visit the town of **Montecatini Terme** itself. Beautiful, historic and an absolute delight to walk around, Montecatini still retains so much of the charm that made it a favorite vacation destination for Europe's noble families. Shops line the main street, a historic cable car (*funicular*) will take you up the mountain to a panoramic viewpoint, there are a number of beautiful parks to relax in, and cultural events are held here year-round. Most important of all, this is where you will find Tuscany's most famous historic thermal spa—**Terme Tettucio**, a marble extravaganza that dates back to the 17th century and will immediately conquer your heart. Though it is no longer operational (they only sell bottles of their thermal water), Tettucio Thermal Spa can be visited as a highly recommended tourist attraction. Tours can be done privately, or on a guided visit (available for groups, must be booked in advance).

Grotta Giusti Resort, ★★★★★
Golf & Spa, Via Grottagiusti 1411, Monsummano Terme. Tel: 0572.907.71, www.grottagiustispa.com.

Slitti, ★★★
Via Francesca Sud 1268, Monsummano Terme. Tel: 0572.640.240, www.slitti.it.
Open Monday-Saturday, 7:00 a.m.-1:00 p.m. & 3:00 p.m.-8:00 p.m. The shop is closed in August.

Terme Tettucio, ★★★★★
Viale Verdi 71. Tel: 0572.778543, www.termemontecatini.it.
Water Drinking Therapy & tours are available in high season only, 9:00 a.m.-1:00 p.m. & 3:00 p.m.-6:00 p.m. Visits cost €5. Find out more about the historic terme and book various treatments at other hotels in Montecatini through the local tourist office, which is located at Viale Verdi 41. Tel: 0572.7781. Open Monday-Saturday, 8.30 a.m.-1:00 p.m. & 3.30 p.m.-6.30 p.m. Sunday, open in the morning only. Off season hours may vary.

🏃 124 Book a Fun and Delicious Wine Tasting and Cooking Class at the Capezzana Estate

When it comes to historic Italian wine estates, **Tenuta di Capezzana** in Carmignano stands out. The earliest written document noting wine production at Capezzana dates back to 804, and in 1716 the Medici family designated the area a top-class wine producer. The current owners, the Bonacossi family, purchased the estate in the 1920s and opened the doors of this magnificent estate to the public in the 1980s.

The 100-hectare farm produces Carmignano DOC wine and olive oil. At 100 to 200 meters above sea level, the estate has fresh night breezes and warm days, a delicious climate if you decide to stay some nights here. A visit to the estate can include a tour of the wine cellar, tastings, and cooking classes. The cookery classes are taught by the friendly and exuberant Chef Patrick and are available Monday to Friday. Each participant receives a bottle of olive oil and a bottle of wine from the estate plus an apron.

For us this is a country estate at its best—historic and of high quality, yet still rustic, authentic, and familial. The area around Capezzana is quite different from the typical hills of Chianti and the Val d'Orcia. This is a more rural, hilly, remote area that goes about life at its own pace. Naturally, don't leave without tasting a bottle of this famous producer's Carmignano wine. The Barco Reale and the Trebbiano are quite good, too.

Tenuta di Capezzana, ★★★★★
Via Capezzana 100, Carmignano.
Tel: 055.870.6005,
www.capezzana.it.
All tours and cooking lessons must be booked in advance. Please note that no cooking lessons are held in August.

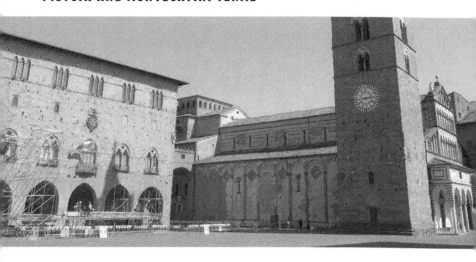

🏃 125 | Discover Pistoia for Art Lovers and Foodies

Pistoia is the perfect destination for half a day spent idly roaming old streets and dipping into lovely little eateries, ancient churches and boutiques. A well-off town about thirty minutes from Florence, Pistoia is often skipped by tourists. And to be perfectly honest, it's their loss. Pistoia may lack monuments on the scale of Pisa or Lucca, but that is precisely the town's main advantage, as it offers a break from tightly packed sightseeing schedules. If you are looking for a bit of a change of pace and a place to relax for the afternoon, Pistoia is a good choice. And once you've toured the town's delightful monuments, you can use the recommendations in this tip to buy the best Tuscan delicacies in town, return to your rented villa or apartment, and prepare a meal to remember.

Start your tour at **Piazza del Duomo,** to admire both the incredibly elegant Cathedral itself and the adjacent bell tower (campanile)

which you can climb up to enjoy an impressive view. The best time to come here is on July 25, when the city celebrates *La Giostra dell'Orso* (the bear joust) and colorful parades, jousting matches and medieval themed processions fill the streets.

Then, make your way to **Ospedale del Ceppo.** Once an important hospital built to treat the poor souls afflicted by the black plague, today the hospital stands empty, but you can still admire the stunning 16th century loggia, which is decorated with colorful glazed terracotta sculptures. In our opinion, for art lovers this unique façade alone justifies the drive from Florence to Pistoia. To make the most of your visit, book in advance an underground tour known as **Pistoia Sotteranea.** These tours will take you on a fun exploration of the medieval tunnels and secret paths that hide underneath the hospital. This is a relatively new attraction, and while the organizers do still

need to work out a few technical difficulties, we enjoyed the visit and found it to be both entertaining and informative. The chance to explore such ancient paths that reveal the city's past is certainly an experience. To find out more, call 0573-368023 or email pistoiasotterranea@irsapt.it.

If you have the time, make one last stop, at the **Museuo Marino Marini,** dedicated entirely to the Tuscan-born and internationally acclaimed sculptor and artist. This is a small museum, in the best sense of the word—its size creates a sense of intimacy and invites visitors to reflect. Next to the Marini section stands the small but beautifully decorated Tau gallery, which is also very much worth a quick visit.

Then, begin the culinary part of your adventure. Make **Il Raviolo Pistoia,** just a couple of minutes away from the Duomo, your first stop. Here, in a tiny non-descript pasta shop, located on Piazza Da Vinci, hides the best fresh pasta of any shop we've tried in Tuscany. This may be a dramatic statement, but we stand by it. Once you try their potato ravioli, or salmon gnudi, or the fantastic *treccia mozzarella,* a

mouth-watering mozzarella in the form of a braid, we know you will agree. Gabriele and Giulio, the team that runs Il Raviolo, have a magic touch. When you leave Il Raviolo, turn right onto Via Carratica and walk toward the town center. **Da Romolo,** perhaps the most famous butcher in Pistoia, will soon come into view on your left. Fans of rustic traditional Tuscan charcuterie will find a wide selection of salamis, a very good *finocchiona* and much more. English isn't their strong suit, but with short sentences and a lot of pointing, everything should go smoothly enough. Next, don't miss **Fiordilatte**, a traditional caseificio (cheese producer) run by Fabrizio Nerucci. Their oven-baked ricotta is excellent, as is their fresh mozzarella filled with ricotta or gorgonzola, and the burrata, a mozzarella filled with cream. You will also find homemade butter, perfect for making butter and sage sauce to go along with fresh pasta from Il Raviolo. Then, don't forget to visit the many shops in **Piazza della Sala,** as well as the charming produce market set up daily at the center of the piazza. This is the perfect places to pick up some more cheeses, bread, roasted meats, wine, wonderfully fresh vegetables and fruit, and other delicacies. It's also the best in town to sit down for a pre-dinner *aperitivo*, surrounded by the locals.

For a proper lunch or dinner, try the **Locanda del Capitano del Popolo** (50 meters from Piazza della Sala). The clientele is almost exclusively Italian, and at any given moment the restaurant is nearly full (on our last visit we actually had to negotiate with the owners to get a table; the delicious and hearty food helped us forget that rocky start). The menu is very traditional in style, and as you might expect, pasta and meat are the real stars here. Be prepared for somewhat heavier sauces and flavors—the Locanda ideally caters to those with a serious appetite!

Lastly, Pistoia offers the ardent shopper quite a few treats. The entire historical center is filled with interesting shops and boutiques. Via Porta Carratica, **Via degli Orafi, Via dei Fabbri** and the entire area around the **Duomo** are all worth Exploring, as are the fashion boutiques along **Via Mazzini** and **Corso Gramsci**.

Ospedale del Ceppo & Pistoia Sotteranea Tour ★★★

Piazza Giovanni XXIII, Pistoia.
Tel: 0573.368.023
www.irsapt.it.

Fondazione Marino Marini Museum ★★★

Corso Silvano Fedi 30, Pistoia.
Tel: 0573.30285,
www.fondazionemarinomarini.it
Open Tuesday–Saturday, 10:00 a.m.–6:00 p.m.; Sunday open 2:30 p.m.–7:30 p.m.; Monday closed. Off-season (September to April) opening hours vary–call first.

Il Raviolo Pistoia, ★★★★★

Piazza Leonardo Da Vinci 6, Pistoia.
Tel: 0573.24738,
www.ilraviolopistoia.com.
Open Tuesday-Sunday, 8:00 a.m.-1:00 p.m. & 4:30 p.m.-7:30 p.m. Wednesday and Sunday closed in the afternoon. Closed Monday.

Da Romolo, ★★★★

Via Porta Carratica 84, Pistoia.
Tel: 0573.21397. Open Monday-Saturday, 9:00 a.m.-1:00 p.m. & 4:30 p.m.-7:30 p.m.

Fiordilatte, ★★★★

Via Orafi 35, Pistoia. Tel: 0573.452.216 (the production facility itself is located outside Pistoia, in Via Sestini 40, Frazione Pontenuovo, Pistoia. Tel: 0573.452216). Open Monday-Saturday, 9:00 a.m.-1:00 p.m. & 4:30-7:30 p.m.

Locanda del Capitano del Popolo, ★★★★

Via di Stracceria 5, Pistoia.
Tel: 0573.24785. Reservations are recommended. Open Wednesday-Sunday, 12:00 p.m.–2:30 p.m. & 7:30 p.m.–11:45 p.m.; Tuesday open for dinner only; Monday closed.

The Garfagnana and Northern Tuscany

126   **Embark On a Wild Adventure**-Discover Michelangelo's Marble Quarries on an Exciting Jeep Tour, and Taste the Delicious Lardo di Colonnata

The Garfagnana, a stunning and magical area in Northwest Tuscany, is often overlooked by tourists who are more interested in the picture postcard views of the Chianti region, Florence, and Siena. But if you are hoping to get away from the crowds, this area offers some real surprises.

Backed by the Apuan Alps and dominated by forests of chestnut trees that were once the main source of income for poor local farmers, the Garfagnana still maintains a very rural life style. The Garfagnana is also a dream for nature lovers: Beautiful hiking trails crisscross the entire region, and biking, canoeing, quad riding, canyoneering, and cave exploration are all popular sports here (find out more at the local tourist offices, and on tip 127). But culture lovers will find their fair share of attractions, too.

The **Marble Quarry** (or perhaps quarries, plural, as there are several in the mountains towering above Carrara) supplied one of the greatest artists in human history: Michelangelo, who used this famous stone to create the *David*. For many centuries, and to this very day, actually, Carrara marble can be found in the homes of noble families, the rich and stylish.

Today, the only way to visit the quarry is on a tour. The **Marmo Tour**, which is the most basic option, is interesting. It allows you full access and lasts for 30 minutes, leading you deep into the mountain and into huge, cavernous rooms. It's fascinating to learn about the marble's full extraction process. However, if you are serious about experiencing the quarries and the local scenery, we recommend the **Cave di Marmo Tours**, which is far more comprehensive (and exciting!)

and includes a jeep ride up into the mountains and into the quarries. The guide and driver take you to some beautiful panoramic points, 900 meters high, with gorgeous views of the marble mountains and exclusive entry right into the paths used by the workers themselves. You also make a stop at the nearby village of Colonnata, to pick up the world-famous *lardo di Colonnata* (a northern Tuscan delicacy—lard aged in marble boxes). Ideally, you should book this tour on a weekday, so that a visit to a working quarry can be included in your tour, to see how the experts cut the marble.

For foodies, a visit to the Garfagnana area isn't complete without a stop in **Colonnata**, the town famous all over Italy (and abroad) for its *lardo di Colonnata*—seasoned lard, prepared with salt and a mix of ground herbs, and aged in marble boxes to give it a distinct, rich taste and aroma. In Tuscany, they love spreading it on toast as antipasti, or adding it to bean dishes or even to pasta to enrich the flavor. The base of the spices is ground black pepper, rosemary, salt, and garlic; but

depending on the family and their traditional recipe of choice, other herbs may be added. This delicacy is only prepared from September to May, as in ancient times. Today *lardo di Colonnata* is marked with a symbol of quality—IGP, which indicates that the product came from a certified geographic location in Italy.

Just about every bar and restaurant in the tiny village of Colonnata, up in the Apuan Alps above Massa-Carrara, has a sign saying "We sell Colonnata." If you've come all the way up here, one of the best place to taste it is **Ristorante Venanzio**, conveniently located in the town's main piazza. They serve the creamy *lardo* on just about anything, and if you are lucky enough to be visiting during truffle season (late autumn–early winter) you can try some very tasty dishes with fragrant truffles, too.

Carrara Marble Quarry and Marmo Tour, ★★★
Piazzale Fantiscritti 84, Miseglia (near Carrara). Cell: 339.765.7470,
www.marmotour.com.
Tours take place April 12-November 2, daily, 11:00 a.m.-5:00 p.m. (until 6:30 p.m. on weekends and holidays); May-August, daily, 11:00 a.m.-6:30 p.m.

Cave di Marmo Tours, ★★★★★
Tel: 0585.857.288, Cell: 328 4156084/ 328 7494324,
www.cavedimarmotours.com.

Ristorante Venanzio, ★★★★
Piazza Palestro 3, Colonnata. GPS coordinates: 44.086189, 10.155794. Tel: 0585.758.033.
www.ristorantevenanzio.com.
Open Monday-Wednesday and Friday-Saturday, 12:00 p.m.-3:00 p.m. & 7:00 p.m.-10:30 p.m.; Sunday, 12:00 p.m.-3:00 p.m. Closed Thursday.

127 Visit the historic town of Bagni di Lucca, Tour a Mysterious Castle, and relax by the shores of a hidden Lake

The Garfagnana and Lunigiana regions in northern Tuscany are incredibly scenic, though not in the traditional Tuscan sense—instead of soft rolling hills and endless vineyards, this area is characterized by dramatic cliffs, chestnut forests, and strong rural charm. Those who are hoping to spend a day out in the open, exploring historic monuments that are off the beaten path will surely enjoy coming here.

Start your day in Bagni di Lucca, a commune of villages 30 minutes north of Lucca, at the entryway to the Garfagnana region. About three kilometers before you enter the town itself, you will come upon the famous **Ponte della Maddalena,** also known as Ponte del Diavolo (the devil's bridge) in the minuscule town of Borgo a Mozzano. This 1000-year-old, three-arch stone bridge was built over the Serchio River for the sake of the many pilgrims and merchants on their way to Rome, along the historic Francigena route. If you have the time, enter Bagni di Lucca's historical center. In the 19th century, Europe's elite (including Napoleon's sister, Elisa Baciocchi) turned Bagni di Lucca into a favorite vacation spot, spending their days dipping in the therapeutic spring waters and their nights dancing and gambling in the local casino. Today those decadent days are just a memory, but those who still want to try the hot springs can do so in the little spa in town (www.bagnidiluccaterme.info).

There isn't much to see or do here today, but on crisp summer mornings it's a real pleasure to walk down the Elizabeth Barrett and Robert Browning promenade, which winds along the river and is named after the two poets who spent a number of romantic summers here. An even simpler and shorter walk, from Piazza Ponte a Serraglio to the Villa Fiori park, affords beautiful views, too.

From Bagni di Lucca, make a beeline to the tiny town of **Verrucole** (near San Romano in Garfagnana). As soon as you enter the town you will see the signs indicating the way to the impressive **Verrucole Fortress**. This large medieval structure was built by the Gherardini family between the 10th and 13th centuries as a strategic stronghold for surveilling the territory. Today it stands in solitude, but in medieval times, it was one of many such fortresses; in fact, this area was known as the land of castles, with more than 150 castelli and fortezze (fortresses) dotting the landscape.

In the summer months the Verrucole Fortress comes to life with organized tours (mostly in Italian) led by guides wearing traditional medieval dress. Don't leave Verrucole without buying some artisanal cheese (for your picnic—see later in the itinerary). **Caseifcio Marovelli Mauro** sits at a privileged point right above the fortress, and offers visitors not only deliciously creamy pecorino cheeses, but also some stunning views (actually, these alone justify the drive). Complete your picnic basket by driving back down to San Romano and buying some bread, cold cuts, fresh fruit and a bottle of local wine at Minimarket Alimentari Donati, which sits on San Romano's (only) main road. Then, drive along scenic SR45 for about 35 minutes, until you reach Lago di Gramolazzo (marked as Lake Gramolazzo on both Google Maps and Waze).

Lago di Gramolazzo is a stunning hidden lake, and the perfect place to relax while enjoying a decadent picnic. If you don't feel like having a picnic, know that there are a few restaurants in this area, but only one is worth trying: **Trattoria Morena**, on the other side of the lake. This small family-run diner doesn't exactly have a menu, but Morena is a passionate cook, and comes up with something homey and tasty daily. The best times to come here are on Saturday and Sunday, when Morena and her daughter-in-law cook up an extra-special lunch, Italian style!

If you somehow have any energy left, drive farther up north to the fortified Romanesque village of Filetto (also marked on some maps as: Borgo di Filetto). Tiny but absolutely lovely, this ancient village is especially worth visiting in August, when the local tourist office organizes a fun medieval feast, complete with archery competitions, jousters and live music. For dinner, the best place in town is **Alla Piazza di Sopra**, a wonderful restaurant that sits right in the heart of Filetto.

Verrucole Fortress, ★★★★
Verrucole, San Romano in Garfagnana. Open May–October, Friday–Sunday, 10:00 a.m.–7:00 p.m. (closed Monday–Thursday); June & September, Thursday–Sunday, 10:00 a.m.–7:00p.m. (closed Monday–Wednesday); July–August, open daily: Tuesday–Thursday, 10:00a.m.–7:00 p.m., Friday–Sunday 10:00 a.m.–9:00 p.m.

Caseificio Marovelli Mauro-Artisanal Cheese, ★★★
Via dell'Orecchiella 1, Vibbiana, San Romano in Garfagnana. Tel: 0583.613212, Cell: 329.1920.973, www.caseificiomarovelli.com.

Trattoria Morena, ★★★
Localita' la Piana 6, Gorfigliano (near Lake Gramolazzo). Tel: 0583.610.098. Open daily for lunch, in season only. Call in advance to make sure they are open.

Ristornate Alla Piazza di Sopra, ★★★★
Piazza Immacolata 11, Filetto, Villafranca in Lunigiana. Tel: 0187.493796, cell: 349.878.3364, www.allapiazzadisopra.it. Open Wednesday–Saturday, 12:00 p.m.–2:00 p.m. & 7:00 p.m.–9:00 p.m. Hours may vary off season. Sunday–Tuesday, open for groups only, by appointment.

128 Visit Isola Santa, Tuscany's Most Beautiful Lake

There are a number of charming hidden lakes in Tuscany, but none can rival the beauty of **Isola Santa**—a tiny *borgo* made of stone that sits on a turquoise lake, surrounded by endless forests. A visit to this splendid area in the fall is nothing short of magical, but it is lovely in the summertime, too. Reaching Isola Santa does require some driving along winding mountain roads, but in our opinion, it is well worth the effort. And if you walk down the fairy-tale cobbled streets of the *borgo* and reach the lake itself, we are sure you will agree with us that this is one stop that is definitely worth making. Note that this destination is a bit of a secret that the locals like to keep to themselves, so it is not set up for large numbers of tourists (to say the least...), which means that parking here can be challenging; try to come on weekdays, when the area is relatively visitor-free, and you will have a better chance of having

it all to yourselves. To complete your visit of the area consider stopping for lunch at **Castelnuovo di Garfagnana**, where you will enjoy a delicious and inviting meal at **Il Vecchio Mulino**, a tiny but excellent and authentic eatery. Try their €18 lunch tasting platter, which will allow you to enjoy a tempting selection of their specialties.

Isola Santa, ★★★★★
Careggine. The easiest way to reach Isola Santa is with Google maps (the lake is located about 40 minutes from Forte dei Marmi).

Il Vecchio Mulino, ★★★★
Via Vittorio Emanuele 12, Castelnuovo di Garfagnana. Tel: 0583.62192, www.vecchiomulino.info.
Opening hours may vary, call before making your way here.

Throughout Tuscany

🏃 | 129 | **Visit One of the Top Ten Festivals** in Tuscany

A complete list of all the concerts, farmer's markets, exhibitions, competitions, food events, opera performances, and medieval festivals on offer in Tuscany would be almost inconceivably varied and numerous. Many fantastic events have already been listed but there are several others to enjoy, and, in truth, these events would require a guide of their own to fully do them justice. Until we get around to writing such a guide, we have done our best to highlight some exceptional ones in this publication—ten top events you shouldn't miss if you happen to be visiting when they are on; information on others can be found online. Regardless, we always recommend checking with the local tourist office to see if any interesting events are taking place while you are visiting the region. The busiest time of year, naturally, is during the summer months, and from May to October.

1. The **Palio di San Paolino**, also known as Palio della Balestra, is a lively medieval feast in Lucca that has taken place since the 15th century. Replete with fantastic Renaissance outfits and age-old contests, this event is dedicated to the ancient art of crossbow shooting. Enjoy the banquet, accompanied by medieval processions and music, on July 12 at Piazza San Martino. For more information, go to www.Luccaturismo.it.

2. If you are in Tuscany toward the end of August, don't miss **Volterra A.D. 1398.** Medieval Volterra comes to life, with the whole town dressed as fearless knights, noblemen and ladies, artisans, merchants, peasants, flag-wavers, crossbowmen, musicians, and jesters from the year 1398. Reenactments take place to transport people back to how life was lived more than 600 years ago. Each year's event revolves around a different theme, which ensures that the festivals are not the same. The celebration kicks off around the *centro storico* on the third and fourth Sundays of every August. Find out more here: www.volterra1398.it.

3. It is worth the drive out to the lovely *borgo* of **Monteriggioni**, just 15 minutes south of Siena, for this town's medieval festival, which takes place every July. Artists, vendors, and performers fill the main piazza while stalls sell medieval wares. Processions of men and women in costume dance through the streets to the music of the time to create a fun and festive atmosphere. The main events usually take place during the first two weekends of July. Find out more and check for the exact dates each year at www.monteriggionimedievale.com.

4. **The Luminara** lights up Pisa on June 16. In Piazza Garibaldi and on the streets that stretch along the river, also called "Lungarni di Pisa," an incredible 70,000 candles are lit, filling the town with a yellow and orange glow. A vibrant atmosphere takes over the city as the streets fill with locals, tourists, and vendors enjoying the many concerts and cultural events organized for the night. In recent years the festival has become somewhat more hectic, and unbearably crowded (after 11:00 p.m. avoid the area around Piazza Garibaldi and find a spot on one of the bridges instead, to enjoy the fireworks), but it is still worth a visit, if you are in the area. Alternatively, visit Pisa during the **Gioco del Ponte**—a wonderfully colorful and lively medieval procession goes through the town, accompanied by music, horses, and people dressed in period attire. The *Gioco del Ponte*, or Battle on the Bridge, then takes place as groups of men from various neighborhoods in Pisa have a faux battle dressed in elaborate 16th-century costumes for the glory of their district. Find out more here: www.giugnopisano.com.

5. **La Giostra del Saracino** is a festival that dates back to the 13th century. It is based on the historic jousting matches that took place during medieval and Renaissance times and is Arezzo's most renowned event. Jousts are held twice a year, one in June and one in September. The whole town comes to life with colorful processions and men and women in medieval clothes descending on the town's Piazza Grande. Other colorful events are usually organized during the week preceding the giostra, too. For more information, visit the website: www.giostradelsaracino.arezzo.it. Equally impressive is the **Giostra di Simone**, in the delightful village of Montisi in southern Tuscany. Read more here: www.giostradisimone.it.

6. The **Palio** is probably the most famous horse race in Italy. Held in Siena twice a year, on July 2 and August 16, this is a huge event that draws a crowd of hundreds of thousands of people. The race takes place on Piazza del Campo, and sees 10 jockeys, each representing a Sienese *contrada* (neighborhood) racing wildly along the track. Aside from the horse race itself, many other colorful events take place on the day of the Palio, including medieval-themed pageants and colorful processions. To see the race itself you must buy (expensive!) tickets in advance. Find out more here: www.ilpalio.org.

7. A pleasant destination on its own, the town of Massa Marittima is especially popular for the duration of the **Balestro del Girifalco**, one of the greatest medieval festivals in Tuscany. The town becomes awash with medieval processions, colorful flags, and wonderful decorations. The highlight of the entire festival has to be the archery contest between the ancient quarters of the town, during which arrows are spectacularly shot from a huge wooden crossbow. The Balestro del Girifalco is celebrated twice a year: on the fourth Sunday of May and the second Sunday of August. The events take place in the piazza in front of the Duomo. Find out more here: www.massamarittima.info/folklore/balestro.htm.

8. The **Bravio delle Botti** is Montepulciano's main summer event. A slightly insane contest between the *contrada* (neighborhoods) of the town, the aim of this competition is

to see who can roll an 80-kg barrel fastest two kilometers uphill. The event, which dates back to 1373, was once celebrated to honor the town's patron, Saint John the Baptist. How exactly such a challenge commemorates the saint is anyone's guess. This is another ideal day out for kids, as a medieval court complete with decorations, music, and flags accompanies the event. The Bravio delle Botti takes place on the last Sunday of August; arrive early to catch a place near Piazza delle Erbe or Piazza Grande or along the Corso. Find out more at www.braviodellebotti.com.

9. A real treat for music lovers, the annual **Pistoia Blues Festival** attracts artists of a high caliber, along with many international names. One of the main music festivals in Tuscany, Pistoia Blues sees a large stage erected in a fabulous *piazza* in the heart of the lovely town of Pistoia, creating a beautiful temporary venue to accommodate some great music. The yearly program and ticket prices can be viewed here: www.pistoiablues.com.

10. The **Lucca Summer Festival** is the best rock show in town, a month filled with concerts by world-famous artists, from Alicia Keys and Elton John to Lenny Kravitz and Leonard Cohen, in the town's Piazza Napoleone. Every year since 1998, this festival has provided a special experience for music lovers. As long as you don't mind the crowds and having to stand outside in the heat, as there is no seating available, then these concerts and the atmosphere around the town are great. Find out more here: www.summer-festival.com.

🏃 130 | Book a Hike in the Beautiful Tuscan Countryside, Led by a Professional Guide

Think about exploring the hills of Chianti on foot, following the hidden trails of the Val d'Orcia, or wandering along the ancient roads traveled by pilgrims on the way to Rome. Imagine discovering the Maremma on unknown paths once controlled by the Etruscan population. Or think about a more adventurous trek into the heart of the Orrido di Botri Canyon in Northern Tuscany. Can there be a better, more intimate way to discover the beauty of the land? To learn its secrets, to take in the smells, the sounds and the wonderful sights Tuscany has to offer?

Tuscany may not be the first place that comes to mind when thinking about hiking and trekking, but the region actually has a wonderful variety of walks. Approaching maps and navigation can be intimidating, but don't let your sense of direction (or lack thereof) deter you from discovering the charm of the countryside. There are several tour companies and professional guides who will build a custom-made hike, based on your interests, time, budget, and physical abilities. Everything from a light, two-hour walk in a reserve to a challenging Alpine hike can be arranged.

Terre di Mare is a group of licensed guides that offers several tours into hidden, charming corners of Tuscany, as well as kayak and bike tours, jeep-led excursions, and Nordic walking. If you are looking to discover Florence and its province from a different angle and perspective, book a walking tour with **Italian Footprints**, a company led by two women: Angelica Turi (Italian) and Elizabeth Namack

(American). For those wishing to discover the wild beauty of the Maremma, in southern Tuscany, we recommend looking into one of the tours lead by **Le Orme** or by **Maremmagica**. Whether you are interested in discovering the treasures of the archaeological park in Sorano, the Etruscan paths near Pitigliano, or the natural reserves of the Maremma, they will be able to offer a suitable tour. Activities are available for all fitness levels, including tailor-made tours for handicapped people. Lastly, consult the tours and guided hikes recommended in tips 51 and 54 for more options.

Terre di Mare,
www.terredimare.org.

Italian Footprints,
www.italianfootprints.com.

Le Orme,
www.leorme.com.

Maremmagica,
www.maremma-online.it.

🏃 131 Enjoy the Panoramic View from One of Our Top Ten Favorite Spots in Tuscany

Choosing the best view in Tuscany is an impossible task. There are simply too many options. While writing this list, we couldn't stop debating—should we focus on the famous options, like the view from the dome of the Duomo in Florence? Or should we concentrate on pleasant little surprises encountered when driving along a country road—that beautiful view that reveals itself when you turn a corner and suddenly there it is, a striking vista you won't soon forget?

After intense discussion, we decided to simply make a list of our personal favorites, a mix of panoramic viewing spots and spectacular drives that left us stunned by their beauty. Some places are well-known, while others you probably won't find in any guidebooks. All ten places are special, and we dare say none will disappoint. Note that the views do change with the seasons, and some of the recommendations are specifically intended for a certain time of the year. Lastly, don't waste

your time climbing to top panoramic spots on foggy, rainy days. The vista will be very limited and disappointing.

1. **The view from the top of the tower of Palazzo Vecchio, Florence:** From here you can get a bird's-eye view of all of Florence, including the Duomo, and survey the little roofs and buildings that make up this timeless city. It also happens to be in a great location–right on Piazza della Signoria, the beating heart of Florence, with the Uffizi Gallery on one side, the Arno River and Ponte Vecchio on the other, and the Duomo just minutes away. It's best to visit in the summertime, on a clear and sunny day, to fully enjoy the view (the tower is closed to visitors on rainy days).

2. **The view from Piazzale Michelangelo, Florence:** Okay, so it's swarming with tourists, but still, what a way to see the entire city! The best time to come is at sunset, when the dying sun fills the sky with a warm pink and orange glow, but the monuments of Florence can still be easily recognized

from a distance. To say the scene is special barely does it justice.

3. **The view from the Torre Grossa, San Gimignano:** This is one view that has to be earned. After a tough climb up a fair number of stairs, you will be rewarded with the perfect viewing point for this gorgeous area. The fairytale medieval town itself is a pleasure to look down on, while the beautiful countryside, filled with vineyards and hills and dotted with little houses, is enchanting.

4. **The view along the road leading from Radda in Chianti to Volpaia:** Radda itself is surrounded by stunning scenery, but the drive from this lovely little town to the tiny borgo of Volpaia offers even better views. As you make your way along the winding road, you will enjoy a tapestry of colors, endless fields and vineyards, and hills that serenely rise and fall far off in the distance.

5. **The view surrounding the Teatro del Silenzio, Lajatico:** Visiting here in summer (when the famous yearly concert by opera singer Andrea Bocelli is held) doesn't do it justice; this sight is at its best after it has rained for a while. If you are visiting Tuscany off-season, in late autumn or early spring, you really must come here for a picnic or even as a quick stop on your way to Volterra. This little corner of Tuscany is spectacular. Even from mid-November to early-December there are still many cold, clear winter days during which you can take in the lush green landscape. The experience is peaceful, almost meditative, and the fact that it's off-season means it's very unlikely there will be other people around to distract you from the amazing scenery.

6. **The view from the Torre del Mangia in Siena:** Much has been written about Piazza del Campo in Siena (one of the most impressive town squares in all of Italy) and the beauty of the *Palazzo Pubblico* (town hall) that stands at the piazza's narrow base. If you go into the *Palazzo*

Pubblico, take the opportunity to climb the 290-foot tower, too. It not only affords a wonderful view of the architectural ingenuity of the piazza below, but you will also enjoy a bird's-eye view of the entire historical center.

7. **The view from behind the Duomo in Pienza:** This is another area that shows its true beauty off-season, either in May, just after the harvest, or on a clear day in winter, when the fields are lush, green, and wild. From here, the views of the famous Val d'Orcia are simply amazing. Combine it with a drive around the stunning Valley itself (ideally, the road from Montalcino to Pienza) for a breathtaking experience.

8. **The drive up to Pitigliano:** There is a moment as you approach Pitigliano, a splendid *borgo* in the Maremma, also known as Little Jerusalem, when the town is suddenly revealed from between the hills. The impressive town, masterfully sculpted from the tufa rock on which it stands, appears, its buildings towering impressively above the gorge below. It's impossible to resist the urge to stop the car and take a photo. Luckily, there is a small parking lot and a pizzeria on the roadside where you can stop for a quick snap of this visually imposing town.

9. **The drive from Carrara to Colonnata:** When you drive to Carrara you can already enjoy the spectacular view of the mountains where the white and blue-grey marble quarries are. However if you leave the town and head farther up north, to the tiny village of Colonnata (famous for its unique seasoned lard, see tip 124), you are in for a truly magnificent view. White veins crisscross the dark black rock of the mountains, and the brilliantly white quarries seem to cascade down the mountainside. Naturally, make sure you go on a clear day. Don't go up in bad weather or fog; it's dangerous and you won't see anything anyway. Avoid private roads, which are only meant for service cars, and if you do decide to drive all

the way up, make sure your car is up for the challenge. A tiny Smart or a Cinquecento probably won't be powerful enough. To make the best of your day, combine your drive with a tour of the quarries themselves–Cave di Marmo (cavedimarmotours.com), for example, offer three-hour tours in a 4X4 jeep, driving right into the quarries.

10. The drive from Gaiole in Chianti to Castelnuovo Berardenga: This journey offers ideal Tuscan scenery. Endless vineyards and rolling hills, small villages and lonesome farmhouses, all set under the beautiful glowing sun. On a warm summer day, this is just inspiring.

Palazzo Vecchio Tower,
Piazza della Signoria, Florence.
Tel: 055.276.8325,
www.museicivicifiorentini.comune.fi.it/
palazzovecchio.
Open April-September, Friday-Tuesday, 10:00 a.m.-9:00 p.m.; Thursday, 10:00 a.m.-2:00 p.m. Last entry one hour before closing time.

Torre Grossa,
Piazza Duomo 2, San Gimignano.
Tel: 0577.990.312. Open April 1-September 30, daily, 9:30 a.m.-7:00 p.m.; October-March 31, 11:00 a.m.-5:00 p.m.

Torre del Mangia,
Piazza del Campo 1, Siena.
Tel: 0577.292.342. Open daily year-round, 10:00 a.m.-7:00 p.m. Last entry: 6:15 p.m. (If visiting off-season, call to make sure the tower doesn't close early, at 4:00 p.m.) Note that the tower closes down in case of rain, regardless of the season.

132 Taste Delicious Craft Beer at the Best Artisanal Breweries of Tuscany

Prestigious wine is, naturally, one of the first things that come to mind when thinking of Tuscany. However, in recent years, the region has been buzzing with a new trend—the opening of micro-breweries, specializing in quality craft beer, made strictly from local ingredients. Many of these craft beers can now be found in restaurants across the region, proudly displayed on the same shelves that host bottles of Chianti, Brunello and Vermentino. But why settle for a second hand experience at a restaurant when you can go straight to the foamy source?

Of the many breweries in the region, we've chosen three that stand out for their quality and style. The first is a highly original establishment known for making their beer using unconventional methods (to say the least), and the other two are located in the beautiful Orcia valley (Val d'Orcia) and offer a welcome break from the many wine tours in the area.

Vapori di Birra is a personal favorite—their beers are excellent (we absolutely love the Sulfurea Weiss beer) and are made exclusively using geothermal energy. Edo Volpi, thr founder, grew up in this area and had always wanted to put to advantage his native land's geothermal vapor - a sustainable and renewable energy recource. After he met beer master Enrico Ciani in 2011, he knew exactly how to put his dream into action. In 2013 he opened the brewery, in which every machine works exclusively on geothermal steam power. If you come all the way here, we highly recommend you call first, and also book a guided tour, to learn more about the unique production process.

Just minutes from beautiful Montepulciano hides **Birrificio L'Olmaia,** an award-winning boutique brewery that will delight any beer fan. There are six types of beer on offer, as well as the occasional seasonal, limited-edition bottle. All of their beers are unpasteurized, unfiltered and re-fermented, both in the keg and in the bottle. Your tasting experience here will be a zero-frills affair, but still very enjoyable. The small tap room where all tastings take place is open to the public on weekdays, and it's always a good idea to call in advance and the let the owners know that you are planning a visit. Then, head to **Agriturismo la Fonte**. Perfectly located at the heart of the valley, the owners here offer every imaginable activity, from cooking lessons to vintage cars for rent (imagine touring southern Tuscany aboard a Fiat 850 spider...). Their latest adventure is their micro brewery, which so far has already managed to win a number of laudable mentions for the quality of their beer.

Vapori di Birra - Birrificio Artigianale,
Via dei Lagoni 25, Sasso Pisano (near Castelnuovo Val di Cecina).
Tel. 0588.26156, Cell. 328 2334464,
www.vaporidibirra.it.

Agriturismo "La Fonte",
Podere Fonte Bertusi di Sopra 73, Pienza.
Tel: 0578.749.142, cell: 339.869.8900,
www.lafonte.toscana.it.

Birrificio L'Olmaia,
Via delle Robinie 15, Sant'Albinio, Montepulciano.
Cell:328.665.9788 / 349.770.5852,
www.birrificioolmaia.com.
Open weekdays only, 8:30 a.m.-1:00 p.m. & 2:30 p.m.-6:30 p.m. Booking in advance is advised.

🏃 133 | Visit One of Tuscany's Fun Antique Markets

For antique enthusiasts, Tuscany offers great variety. Both casual buyers and more experienced antique hunters can find everything from mid-century silver cutlery and exquisite tea sets to 19th-century lamps, handicrafts, furniture, and even swords (though getting them through Customs might be challenging!).

Florence is a good place to get your first taste of Tuscan antique markets. As the capital of the region, Florence has a nice variety. **Piazza dei Ciompi**, for example, hosts a small daily antique market. Though it's vibrant and popular, with plenty of souvenirs to be had, we do find this place to be too touristy. For something more prestigious, head out to the **Fortezza Antiquaria market**, which is held every third weekend in the garden of Fortezza da Basso (due to renovations in the area the market may be temporarily moved to a different location nearby; consult with the tourist office before your visit). With nearly 120 stands, and sellers that come from all over Italy, the selection here is unique and varied, if a little pricey! A third option is the *Mercatino dell'Artigianato e del Piccolo Antiquariato*, a small market held once a month in Piazza Santo Spirito, where you will find a combination of antiques, knickknacks, and artists selling their handicrafts. Lastly, more serious buyers won't want to miss the world-renowned **BIAF** (Florence International Biennial Antiques fairs—www.biaf.it) held once every two years, and the stunning (though very expensive) antique shops in town, which are concentrated mostly along **Via del Moro** and **Via Maggio**.

For a more ample selection, leave Florence and head towards **Arezzo**. This off-the-beaten-track town, located just an hour southwest of Florence (see tip 61), hosts one of the biggest markets in all of Italy, and comes to life on the first weekend of every month when nearly 500 stalls spread through the historical center. The fact that Arezzo is also home to Piero della Francesca's world famous cycle of frescoes, *The Legend of the True Cross*, makes Arezzo a particularly interesting destination for art lovers.

Moving north, antique lovers and keen buyers will find satisfaction in charming **Lucca**. Though the town is quite small, it boasts a fairly large market, almost twice as large as its Florence equivalent. Lucca is worth a visit in itself, but we recommended making a special effort to come on market day. To complete your visit, explore some of the town's fantastic little antique shops and regular shops (see tips 113 and 114), where you can interact with experienced antique dealers and hunt for hidden treasures.

Lastly, Pisa and Siena also have their own markets. In **Pisa**, on the second weekend of most months, there is an interesting little market on Piazza dei Cavalieri and the surrounding streets. Buyers can pick up antiquarian books, delicate china, hats, antique furniture, jewelry, and much more. The few but interesting antique shops dotted across Pisa (see tip number 96) will fulfill the needs of more serious buyers. **Siena** also has a monthly antique market with about 50 stands in Piazza del Mercato, just behind the Palazzo Pubblico and Piazza del Campo.

Please note that dates and hours may vary, and some markets may close down in August or off season with no warning. For this reason, it is highly recommended to call the local tourist office before driving especially to any market in Tuscany.

Florence:
Mercato di Piazza Ciompi, open Monday-Saturday, 9:00 a.m.-1:30 p.m. May close down in the summer months; Fortezza Antiquaria, third weekend of the month, closed in July and August; Mercatino dell'Artigianato e del Piccolo Antiquariato, Piazza Santo Spirito, second Sunday of the month, closed in July and August.

Arezzo:
Piazza della Repubblica and the adjacent streets, the first weekend of every month, 9:00 a.m.-6:00 p.m. (may close earlier during the winter months).

Lucca:
In the area around Via del Battistero, Piazza San Martino and Piazza San Giusto, the third weekend of every month, 8:30 a.m.-7:00 p.m. The market usually closes down January through March.

Pisa:
Piazza Cavalieri, second weekend of the month, including July and August. The market may not take place off-season.

Siena:
Piazza del Mercato, third Sunday of the month, usually closed in August.

Index by subject

Hotels, Agriturismi, B&Bs, Resorts and Luxury Rentals

Wine Tastings and Tours

TOURS

ENOTECHE

CHIANTI ESTATES

BOLGHERI AND THE SUPER TUSCANS ESTATES

SAN GIMIGNANO VERNACCIA ESTATES

BRUNELLO DI MONTALCINO ESTATES

Artisanal Produce & Breweries

Cooking Classes

Aperitivo and Brunch

Attractions & Activities

Shopping

Events & Markets

Spas & Thermal Pools

P.5: stocker1970/Shutterstock.com; p.8: JeniFoto/Shutterstock.com; p.13:
Malgorzata Kistryn/Shutterstock.com; p.16: Maxim Blinkov/Shutterstock.com; p.21: Peter
Bernik/Shutterstock.com; p.23: Africa Studio/Shutterstock.com; p.27: Goodluz/Shutterstock.
com; p. 32: Ariela Bankier; p.33: Oleg Znamenskiy/Shutterstock.com; p.59: The Royal Suite
at the Four Seasons, photographer: Barbara Kraft, photo courtesy of the Four Seasons Hotel
Firenze; p.37 FelinoQ/Shutterstock.com; p.38 By Alessandro Scagliusi/Shutterstock.com; p.
39 the SESTO panoramic restaurant, photo courtesy of the Westin Excelsior Hotel; p.40 top
photo KatarinaVe/Shutterstock.com, bottom photo: TMON/Shutterstock.ocm; p.42 photo
courtesy of Florence with a View apartments; p.43: photo courtesy of St. Mark's
Opera Florence; p.44 photo courtesy of Vestri ice cream shop; p.45-46 Ariela Bankier;
p.48 Andrey GrigorievShutterstock.com; p.49 Natalia Lebedinskaia/Shutterstock.com;
p.50 photo courtesy of Enoteca Alessi; p.52 top photo:TixXio/Shutterstock.com, bottom
photoNatn/Shutterstock.com; p.54 photos courtesy of Soulspace Spa; p.55: Syda
Productions/Shutterstock.com; p.57 Shebeko/shutterstock.com; p.58-59 Ariela Bankier;
p.60 Giuliano Del Moretto/Shutterstock.com; p.61 buruhtan/Shutterstock.com; p.62 Ariela
Bankier; p.64: top photo: Thoom/Shuttertock.com, bottom photo: goodcat/Shutterstock.
com; p.66 top photo: Il Palagio restaurant, photographer: Peter Vitale. Bottom photo: The
Royal suite at the Four Seasons Hotel Firenze, photographer: Barbara Kraft. Both photos
courtesy of the Four Seasons Hotel Firenze; p.67: the Four Seasons Hotel Spa, photographer:
Peter Vitale. Photo courtesy of the Four Seasons Hotel Firenze; p.68 photos courtesy of the
Magnani Feroni Hotel; p.69 top photo courtesy of Flo Concept store, bottom photo courtesy
of Il Fiorentino Leather shop; p.71 top photo courtesy of Genten Firenze, bottom photo
courtesy of Scuola del Cuoio Firenze; p.73 Baloncici/Shutterstock.com; p. 74 photo courtesy
of Loretta Caponi; p.76 top photo Ariela Bankier, bottom photo Tphotography/Shutterstock.
com; p.78 photo courtesy of Madova gloves; p.79 top photo Minoru K/Shutterstock.com,
bottom photo Ariela Bankier; p.80 BAMO/Shutterstokc.com; p.81 karamysh/Shutterstock.
com; p.82 Villa Petraia, Malgorzata Kistryn/Shutterstock.com; p.83 Circumnavigation/
Shutterstock.com; p.85 photo courtesy of The Mall; p.87 Syda Productions / Shutterstock.
com; p.88: top photo: 4Max/Shutterstock.com, bottom photo courtesy of Castello Poppiano;
p.90 S Tatiana/Shutterstock.com; p.92 Magati/Shutterstock.com; p.94: Shaiith/Shutterstock.
com; p.95: THE LABYRINTH by Jeff Saward, photo courtesy of the Chianti Sculpture
Park; p.96: top photo: Polifoto/Shutterstock.com, bottom photo: castello di Ama and the
artwork in the estate, all rights reserved to Alessandro Moggi (www.alessandromoggi.com);
p.97: castello di Ama and the artwork in the estate, all rights reserved to Alessandro Moggi
(www.alessandromoggi.com); p.98: top photo: Africa Studio/Shutterstock.com, bottom photo
courtesy of Le Pietre vive di Montaperti; p.100: photo courtesy of Dario Cecchini-Antica
Macelleria, photographer:Tommaso Iorio; p.102-103 the Antinori Estate, photos courtesy of
Marchesi Antinori; p.104 top photo: Malgorzata Kistryn/Shutterstock.com, bottom photo:
all rights reserved to Alessandro Moggi (www.alessandromoggi.com); p.106: Julie Vader/
Shutterstock.com; p.107 Macondo/Shutterstock.com; p. 109 Litvin Leonid/Shutterstock.com;
p.110: bonzodog/Shutterstock.com; p.111: Maria Uspenskaya/Shutterstock.com; p.112: AMB/
Shutterstock.com; p.113: Blazej Lyjak/Shutterstock.com; p.114 Sean Heatley/Shutterstock.
com; p.115 photo courtesy of Lamole restaurant; p.116 Hquality/Shutterstock.com; p.117
PRESSLAB/Shutterstock.com; p.118 Belish/Shutterstock.com; p.119 Ariela Bankier; p.120:
photos courtesy of Podere Fornaci; p.121 photo courtesy of Museo Ferrari, all rights reserved;
p.122: JeniFoto/Shutterstock.com; p.124: Jaroslaw Pawlak/Shutterstock.com; p.125: photos
courtesy of Campo Regio Relais Siena; p.126-127 photos courtesy of La Taverna di San
Giuseppe; p.128: StevanZZ/Shutterstock.com; p.129: Szasz-Fabian Jozsef/Shutterstock.com;
p.130: S_Photo/Shutterstock.com; p.131: Quanthem/Shutterstock.com; p.132: StevanZZ/
Shutterstock.com; p. 133: JuneJ/Shutterstock.com; p.134 holbox/Shutterstock.com; p.135:
Ariela Bankier; p.136: Roberto Cerruti/Shutterstock.com; p.137: AJancso/Shutterstock.
com; p.138 top photo: Alessandro Colle/Shutterstock, bottom photo: Rido/Shutterstock.
com; p.140 photo courtesy of Hotel Castello delle Serre; p.141-142 photos courtesy of the
Fonteverde Tuscan Resort and Spa; p.143 photo courtesy of the Giuseppina cooking school;
p.144: photo courtesy of Il Borro resort; p.145: Maciej Czekajewski/Shutterstock.com; p.146:
Panaccione Robertino/Shutterstock.com; p.147: Ariela Bankier; p.149: photos courtesy of
Castello di Montebenichi; p.150 Alexander Chaikin/Shutterstock.com; p.151 Marco Bicci/
Shutterstock.; p.152 Piotr Krzeslak/Shutterstock.com; p.154: Dream79/Shutterstock.com;
p.156 Angelo Ferraris/Shutterstock.com; p.157 Maxdis/Shutterstock.com; p. 158 photos
courtesy of Il Borro Resort; p.160 photos courtesy of Il Pellicano Resort; p.161: photos
courtesy of Terme di Saturnia Spa & Golf Resort; p.162 Jaroslaw Pawlak/Shutterstock.com;
p.163: Oscity/Shutterstock.com; p.164: Dmitriy Yakovlev/Shutterstock.com; p.166: photo
courtesy of Il Pellicano Resort; p.167: Dmitriy Yakovlev/Shutterstock.com; p.169: jokihaka/
Shutterstock.com; p.170 dinosmichail/Shutterstock.com; p.171: StevanZZ/Shutterstock.

Made in the USA
Middletown, DE
30 October 2018